PERFORMING AMERICAN MASCULINITIES

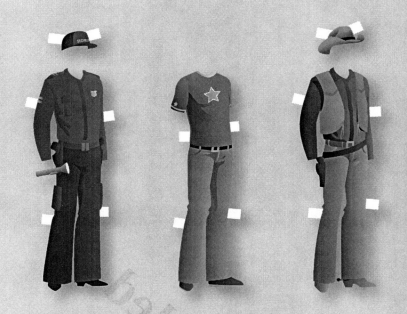

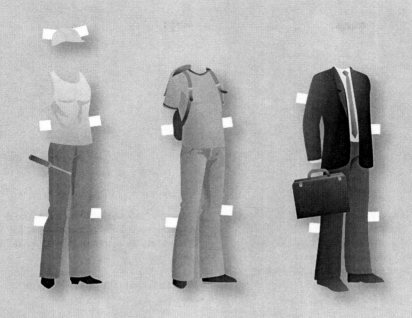

PERFORMING AMERICAN MASCULINITIES

*The 21st-Century Man
in Popular Culture*

*Edited by
Elwood Watson
& Marc E. Shaw*

INDIANA UNIVERSITY PRESS
Bloomington & Indianapolis

This book is a publication of

Indiana University Press
601 North Morton Street
Bloomington, Indiana 47404-3797 USA

iupress.indiana.edu

Telephone orders 800-842-6796
Fax orders 812-855-7931
Orders by e-mail iuporder@indiana.edu

Manufactured in the United States of
America

Library of Congress Cataloging-in-
Publication Data

Performing American masculinities : the
21st-century man in popular culture / edited by Elwood Watson and Marc E. Shaw.
    p. cm.
  Includes bibliographical references and
index.
  ISBN 978-0-253-35573-7 (cloth : alk.
paper) — ISBN 978-0-253-22270-1 (pbk. :
alk. paper) 1. Masculinity in popular
culture—United States. 2. Masculinity
—United States. I. Watson, Elwood. II.
Shaw, Marc E.
  HQ1090.3.P46 2011
  305.310973—dc22

                        2010029431

1 2 3 4 5 16 15 14 13 12 11

I dedicate this book to Annie B. Shaw and Catherine M. Cole. Both showed me the way.   M.E.S.

I dedicate this book to my siblings as well as to the cultural environment that made it possible to publish this collection of essays.   E.W.

CONTENTS

ACKNOWLEDGMENTS

I acknowledge the support of Hartwick College, especially my colleagues in the English and Theatre Arts Department.

Marc E. Shaw

I acknowledge my co-editor, Marc E. Shaw, who was nothing short of great in this process. Thank you. I also salute Jane Behnken, Chandra Mevis, Miki Bird, Brian Herrmann, and the other people at Indiana University Press who made this anthology possible.

Elwood Watson

PERFORMING AMERICAN MASCULINITIES

FROM SEINFELD TO OBAMA: MILLENNIAL MASCULINITIES IN CONTEMPORARY AMERICAN CULTURE

MARC E. SHAW AND ELWOOD WATSON

While this collection of essays focuses on a topic in one particular time and place, the subject matter allows plenty of room for play. One of the goals of this collection—which explores masculinities in American popular culture at the turn of the millennium and since—is to show how varied, open, relative, contradictory, and fluid masculinities can be.

The study of masculinities as an academic endeavor found a high point during the '90s with works by social scientists like R. W. Connell and Michael Kimmel and by other scholars in wide-ranging disciplines. What does this collection offer that extends or adds to those precursors? One answer lies in the matrix of time and place; as the world is ever changing, so are adjusted the identities within. Those adjustments are worth our concern: specifically, the exploration of masculinities in this collection focuses on the possibilities for identity formation for men in the United States since the mid-1990s. The authors mine American popular culture—theatre, film (narrative and documentary), literature, music, advertising, internet content, television, photography, politics, and current events—to posit questions about the processes of gender creation and the contestation of masculinities as constantly changing political forms. Of course, as the global community grows smaller, many of these issues reach far beyond a single national boundary, and our decision to focus this book geographically surely necessitates a call for companion volumes from beyond U.S. borders.

Masculinity is not a solid, immovable construction. An individual does not guard one definitive gender position: from moment to moment, forces redictate, replace, and reimagine its reconstructing. In *A Thousand Plateaus*, Gilles Deleuze and Félix Guattari rebuff the familiar metaphor of

Western thought as a "tree" with knowledge flowing from a unified central core to branches of subsets of knowledge.[1] In its place, they suggest a rhizo-matic structure which spreads out multidirectionally from different nodes (as opposed to a central trunk, which would constitute a plotted, fixed order). "The rhizome operates by variation, expansion, conquest, capture, offshoots. . . . [It] pertains to a map that must be produced, constructed, a map that is always detachable, connectable, reversible, modifiable, and has multiple entryways and exits and its own lines of flight."[2] The rhizome cre-ates a meshwork of ideas and possibilities, as opposed to the older binary and hierarchical way of thinking. Deleuze and Guattari continue, "In con-trast to centered . . . systems with hierarchical modes of communication and pre-established paths, the rhizome is a centered, nonhierarchical, non-signifying system without a General and without an organizing memory or central automation, defined solely by a circulation of states."[3]

What does this theoretical configuration mean for gender processes or identity in general? Besides the obvious dismissal of cemented hierar-chical and binary modes of thinking, it also suggests the repeated process of identity formation—a unique progression to each individual, a forever changeable and always-changing meshwork. Opposed to a limited, sin-gular gender construction or solid identity, the rhizome model suggests a plural and fluid process. Deleuze and Guattari contrast the old and new ways of thinking: "The tree imposes the verb 'to be,' but the fabric of the rhizome is the conjunction, 'and . . . and . . . and . . . ' This conjunction car-ries enough force to shake and uproot the verb 'to be.'"[4] Following this model, Linstead and Pullen describe "gender identity then [as a] constant becoming—rhizomatic, nomadic, a constant journey with no final des-tination . . . never still, always relational, always to come, always to con-nect."[5] Masculinities, then, are ever changing according to time, place, and relation to others—a whole host of possibilities.

With this poststructural freedom, we move to the present moment and our contemporary "becoming." Take, for example, the two most noteworthy national events since 2008: the troubled economy (or "great recession") and the election of President Barack Obama. These two major events, immensely important in both real and symbolic terms, led us to ask how they might dictate or influence individual identity. To take the former event first, masculinities are closely tied to the economic circumstances in which they are formed and re-formed. With unemployment and foreclosures climbing higher and higher, what strain is placed on men and women as workers, consumers, breadwinners, spouses, parents, and citizens? How does gender adjust to economic influences or financial troubles? And more generally, how does the workplace reconfigure gender identity? How does late capitalism regulate sexuality or market specific gender possibilities?

These questions fit into this volume's first part—"Masculinities and the Market: Late Capitalism and Corporate Influence on Gender Processes"—which includes essays that explore masculinities within the economic realm of corporatism and late capitalism. Michael Kimmel, Jeff Hearn, and R. W. Connell underscore the importance of this line of inquiry while writing about the "future of the field" of masculinities (2004). To them, the "most obviously important" issue "growing in significance" is the "relation of masculinities to those emerging dominant powers in the global capitalist economy, the transnational corporations."[6] Part 1 of our collection begins that work here in the United States, the origin of many of the ever-expanding numbers of corporations. Kimmel, Hearn, and Connell call for "new or underdeveloped perspectives that may give new insight even into well-researched issues"; and each contributor in the first half of this book offers various points of convergence among gender processes, sexuality, and the influences of late capitalism.[7]

The first chapter of our collection, C. Wesley Buerkle's "Masters of Their Domain: *Seinfeld* and the Discipline of Mediated Men's Sexual Economy," shows one influence that capitalistic discourse has on sexuality and gender. Turning his focus to television, Buerkle uses a *Seinfeld* episode and *Queer Eye for the Straight Guy* to explore "the tensions at the close of the twentieth century between an industrialized model of masculine sexuality" and "an emerging consumerist [neoliberal] model." Buerkle contrasts a modernist ideal of sexuality and its pejorative view of self-pleasure with neoliberalism's more open stance. Brenda Boudreau's chapter, "Sexually Suspect: Masculine Anxiety in the Films of Neil LaBute," analyzes a range of LaBute's male characters who are pressured by class expectations and a desire to perform in their daily corporate lives and in bed. Their anxieties stem from the expectations of the workplace and the consumer marketplace and reveal the grey areas among homosociality, homoeroticism, and hyper-heterosexuality.

While Boudreau's analysis of LaBute shows how certain masculinities can be bought and sold, the chapter by Margaret C. Ervin, "The Might of the Metrosexual: How a Mere Marketing Tool Challenges Hegemonic Masculinity," argues that metrosexuality was more than just a passing fancy. What started as a marketing ploy by corporations looking to sell new products later turned into a strangely subversive power that might have made a lasting change in the way we view masculine identity. Ervin finds that even an anti-metrosexual backlash has "furthered the acceptance of plural male identities as opposed to hegemonic masculinity."

Latham Hunter's "Fathers, Sons, and Business in the Hollywood 'Office Movie'" focuses on a group of '90s films in which the male protagonists are all "disempowered late capitalist office worker[s]" in "globalized management culture" whose successes and failures in the corporate realm are "closely linked" to the protagonists' competence as fathers. Hunter updates the "traditional breadwinner ethic by connecting [it] to contemporary experiences of middle- and upper-class work" but also asks a poignant question about mainstream films: "What is it about America's political economy that necessitates the circulation and then containment of messages about masculine crisis that divert attention from other more oppressively marginalized masculinities?"

While this collection asks questions of masculinity, it also questions the academic positioning of a book on masculinities. If identity is a rhizomatic mapping, can gender exist alone on that constant journey of self? If we ask "and . . . and . . . and . . . ," then what is the "and . . ." of gender? What are the other dimensions to a multidimensional model of identity?

The second part of this book, "Beyond Gender Alone: Defining Multidimensional Masculinities," focuses more closely on identities when masculinities intersect and mesh with various other nodes, including race, religion, (dis)ability, and sexuality. John Kille's "Popular Memory, Racial Construction, and the Visual Illusion of Freedom: The Re-mediation of O.J. and Cinque" draws striking comparisons between the public spectacle of O.J. Simpson's murder trial and the trial scenes in Spielberg's *Amistad,* arguing that some of the tropes and racial tensions of the narrativized black masculinities on trial were eerily similar.

Earlier, in placing this volume in our present moment, we mentioned two contemporary events as most impactful. President Obama's election clearly holds historic importance. His particular identity and its questionings of race, power, and gender are often the subject of impassioned debate. "Obama's Masculinities: A Landscape of Essential Contradictions" by Marc E. Shaw and Elwood Watson frames the contradictory nature of President Obama's masculinities, showing how Obama's identity is always in motion depending on who is observing and to what other identities he is in relation at any given moment. The chapter shows the difficulty in both capturing Obama's gender and attempting to move past the limiting binary of black and white.

Johnson Cheu and Carolyn Tyjewski analyze an interesting contemporary filmic trope in "The Male Rapunzel in Film: The Intersections of Disability, Gender, Race, and Sexuality" and show that the notion of fixed nodes of identity, an unmoving positionality, is an illusion. Jimmie Manning looks at the intersection of various nodes of identity in his analysis of television reality shows, "Masculinities in Dating Relationships: Reality and Representation at the Intersection of Race, Class, and Sexual Orientation." And in a much-needed queering of the entire subject of masculinities, Michel J. Boucher reframes the textual body of this collection with "'Do You Have What It Takes to Be a Real Man?': Female-to-Male Transgender Embodiment and the Politics of the 'Real' in *A Boy Named Sue* and *Body Alchemy*." Boucher's contribution is a fitting ending to this volume: he again reminds us of the possibilities that result from posing questions of identity and gender.

NOTES

1. Deleuze and Guattari, *A Thousand Plateaus,* 7.
2. Ibid., 23.
3. Ibid.
4. Ibid., 27.
5. Linstead and Pullen, "Gender as Multiplicity," 1292.
6. Kimmel, Hearn, and Connell, "Introduction," 9.
7. Ibid., 9–10.

BIBLIOGRAPHY

Deleuze, Gilles, and Félix Guattari. *A Thousand Plateaus.* Trans. Brian Massumi. Minneapolis: University of Minnesota Press, 1987.
Kimmel, Michael, Jeff Hearn, and Raewyn Connell. "Introduction." In *Handbook of Studies on Men and Masculinities,* ed. Kimmel, Hearn, and Connell. Thousand Oaks, Calif.: Sage, 2004.
Linstead, Stephen, and Alison Pullen. "Gender as Multiplicity: Desire, Displacement, Difference and Dispersion." *Human Relations* 59, no. 9 (2006): 1287–1310.

PART ONE

MASCULINITIES AND THE MARKET: LATE CAPITALISM AND CORPORATE INFLUENCE ON GENDER PROCESSES

MASTERS OF THEIR DOMAIN: *SEINFELD* AND THE DISCIPLINE OF MEDIATED MEN'S SEXUAL ECONOMY

C. WESLEY BUERKLE

> I must confess that I am much more interested in problems about
> technologies of the self and things like that rather than sex.... Sex is boring.
>
> MICHEL FOUCAULT

Masculine representation has noticeably shifted since the 1980s with the changing tides of capitalism. Industrial definitions and images of masculinity, emphasizing the importance of personal restraint and the investing of resources into productive ends, dominated popular discourses through much of the twentieth century. A neoliberal orientation, which has become increasingly pronounced since the 1990s, has produced images of masculinity that emphasize consumption and gratification as their own rewards. The pull and play between these competing capitalistic modes has manifested in shifting cultural understandings of masculine sexuality as exhibited in men's mediated representations. Looking at the NBC situation comedy *Seinfeld*, which enjoyed a nine-year run (1989–1998) in primetime before beginning a robust life in syndication, we see emerging cultural changes in ideals of masculine sexuality playing themselves out. *Seinfeld*'s effect on popular culture has manifested most clearly in white, middle-class vernacular, including sexual euphemisms such as "shrinkage," "yada, yada, yada," and "master of your domain."[1] More than adding to the cultural lexicon, *Seinfeld* has demonstrated the ever-changing discourses of gender and sexuality in the United States as we have shifted from a gender ideology grounded in modern/industrial ideals to one directed toward neoliberal/consumerist ends.

In his most-cited works, *Discipline and Punish* and *The History of Sexuality*, Michel Foucault demonstrates less interest in understanding prisons or sexuality in Western culture than in the social organizations—the history, politics, economies, and ethics—that both create and sustain cultural notions of correction and sexual expression.[2] Moving beyond the objects of analysis, Foucault dwells on what social practices reveal about the culture that produces them: "the will that sustains them and the strategic intention that supports them."[3] Examining representations of masculine sexuality, then, is to analyze the changes occurring within a culture, here, the dominant U.S. culture at the close of the twentieth century. Foucault dismisses the common habit of thinking of power as a force held by individuals and used to oppress others. Instead, he argues for conceptualizing power as a productive force, one which constructs bodies and knowledge fashioned in particular ways. Therefore, it is society that "fabricates" individuals into subjects within a particular discourse.[4] Rather than speaking of power as repressing or restricting bodies and knowledge based on some true ideal existing a priori, this approach recognizes that individuals are produced in accordance with one model, admittedly to the exclusion of others.[5]

Gender performance, for both men and women, provides an especially useful instance to study the production of bodies to meet cultural expectations. Despite the diversity of personal preferences, a recognizable system of signs and performances has emerged for what is deemed respectively appropriate for men and women as an attempt to stabilize gender for the individual and for society as a whole.[6] Whether it be fashions that idealize women as physically appealing but restricted through the use of corsets and high-heeled shoes or an insistence that men be physically aggressive and professionally/financially successful, both sexes receive training over the course of their lives to comply with cultural ideals that maintain strict, dichotomous distinctions between men and women.[7]

Sexuality, too, is produced through cultural discourses. In *The History of Sexuality*, Foucault focuses not on describing the sexual predilections, prohibitions, and peccadilloes of Western culture but instead on the discursive practices that produce understandings of sexuality in the West and the ways those discourses are transgressed and maintained, often concurrently.[8] Recognizing sexual categories and definitions as discursive productions rather than natural facts places sexuality in the "realm for the operation of power (in the sense of social control)."[9] Foucault cautions us against thinking of power as controlling sexuality through oppression, what he calls the "repressive hypothesis," and urges us to recognize the myriad discourses of sexuality in culture that dwell on (im)proper sexual conduct and compel individuals to confess their sexual transgressions.[10] Amid the very mandates of sexual prohibition resides a discussion about sex in terms of its proper uses and functions. The enforcement of these mandates prompts further talk of sex in the form of confession, whether to a priest, therapist, parent, or friend.[11] To say, then, that restrictions on sexual behaviors and displays silence us is to be blind to the extent to which those rules and their effects bring sexuality into discourse.

Concentrating on performances and representations of gender and sexuality allows us to understand the operations and goals of specific ideologies for, as Klaus Krippendorf notes, "Power is most profitably seen as *embodied* in the lives of people with very real bodies saying things to each other, in their actual languaging, which includes uttering explanations, commands, dismissals, threats, and promises—as well as giving indications of acceptance, obeyance [*sic*], compliance, submission or agreement."[12] These productions of bodies and knowledge—gender or sexuality—occur through dispersed discourses that often act inconspicuously to perpetuate an ideology. Consequently, "[t]he analysis of the discourse of power thus must begin with the assumption that any articulatory practice may emerge as relevant or consequential—nothing can be 'taken-for-granted' with respect to the impact of any particular discursive practice."[13] For that reason, this chapter focuses on the "taken-for-granted" discourses of a television comedy that prides itself on being "about nothing" when in fact it says a great deal about idealized masculine sexuality in the United States. As a case in point, *Seinfeld's* "The Contest" demonstrates the tensions at the close of the twentieth century between an industrialized model of masculine sexuality and an emerging consumerist model.

Using "The Contest" as a case study, this chapter focuses on the tensions and ambiguity experienced amid the social transformation from industrial modernism to consumerist neoliberalism as they manifest in discourses of masculine sexuality. Drawing chiefly from Foucault's project on sexuality and power in society, this chapter maps the ways in which

Seinfeld represents the conflict between early and late capitalism in its discussion of masturbation and abstinence. To begin, we will look at the competing sensibilities of modern and neoliberal capitalisms and their effects upon masculine sexuality as presented in discourses surrounding masturbation. Having established an understanding of masculine sexuality in U.S. culture, we will then turn to *Seinfeld*'s "The Contest" as a way to understand the tensions inherent in the transition between early and late capitalist models. In conclusion, we will consider the example of *Queer Eye for the Straight Guy* as representing a masculinity ensconced in neoliberalism/consumerism yet retaining vestiges of a modern/industrialist masculinity.

CAPITALIST SEXUALITY

As a fiercely capitalistic society, the United States has succumbed to what Kenneth Burke terms an "occupational psychosis," which is to say we organize and understand all aspects of life in terms of our economic system.[14] As Emily Martin notes of scientific discussions concerning menstruation and menopause, human reproductive functions have long been described in terms of capital production and ability.[15] Sexuality, as well, has long been subject to its role in capitalism. In the following section, I will focus attention on understanding sexuality as it is produced by capitalist discourses. Here, I differentiate the ethics that result from competing modes of capitalism, specifically industrialism and consumerism. I will then highlight a brief history of discourses on masturbation in the West as a way of demonstrating industrial capitalism's pervasiveness in producing sexuality in a manner consistent with economic concerns.

From the two basic operations of the market system, production and consumption, two distinct modes of behavior emerge. On the one hand, a period of elevated market regulation and concern for national interests characterizes modernism, emphasizing the production of capital. On the other, a period of increased deregulation of the market that emphasizes personal interests typifies (neo)liberalism, wherein we see concern directed toward consumption.[16] Modernism, with economic behavior often described as industrialist or Fordist, sought "progress" by taming nature and human desire alike for the purpose of increasing production.[17] The modernist sensibility thinks more communally than does liberalism, asking its citizens to consider the implications of their own actions on the collective's goals for increased capital. In contrast, neoliberalism, the reemergence of nineteenth-century liberalism, eschews government intervention and market regulation for privatizing interests.[18] This post-Fordist, consumerist approach bases capital's value on its use and service to individual needs and pleasures.[19]

The capitalistic occupational psychosis during the modernist period, a time that focused upon building industrial strength, placed the greatest emphasis and concern upon production and, when speaking of sexuality, reproduction. Michael Kimmel discusses the history of masculinity in the United States, noting the emergence of a "marketplace masculinity" during the time of the industrial revolution, when accumulated wealth represented masculine accomplishment.[20] Popular Christian discourses in the late nineteenth century likewise imagined Jesus as a muscular, tough, working man—he was a carpenter, after all, who made things with his hands for a living—who emboldened men to similarly develop their own bodies as testaments to their moral/industrial character.[21] The well-developed male body as a moral undertaking demonstrates to a modernist mindset a body perfected for increased production. In the mid-twentieth century, Jack LaLanne, in the footsteps of Charles Atlas, advocated exercise as the alternative to an early death from "pooped-out-itis," a body collapsing from complete disrepair.[22]

Within such a framework, men's relation to sexuality grows out of the demand to mediate between investing physical energy in material production and applying only the most necessary amount toward reproduction. In all this, the family serves as the central "deployment of sexuality," the place where children learn the role and function of sexuality as an expression of love put toward producing offspring and maintaining familial solidarity, both of which translate into financial stability.[23] Thus, the expenditure of time and energy in (hetero)sexual intercourse—and not in other, fruitless sexual activities—only temporarily diverts resources away from market production with the hope of profiting by the "fabrication of children," which ultimately makes a return into the coffers of the labor force.[24] This view, however, restricts married couples from indulging in sexual intercourse for its own sake. J. H. Kellogg, in an advice manual from 1891, details the health consequences—including the onset of tuberculosis—suffered primarily by men (as the ones who must emit their life force through ejaculation) from having overexerted themselves by too frequently engaging in sexual intercourse with their wives.[25] Arguments made against sexual misconduct sought to maintain the "marital bed . . . as the only acceptable venue for sexual expression."[26] Such "expression" has the potential for labor force reproduction, thereby serving capitalist needs.[27]

Worse than men who needlessly spend their energies on sex are the men who waste their potential resources for laboring by sexually gratifying themselves. In modernism, when industrialist capitalism flourishes, sex serves the purpose of (re)production, and masturbation, therefore, contradicts the "proper" use of sex. Other than the twentieth century's medicalized use of male masturbation for the purpose of in vitro fertilization, masturbation's end is futile. The now-dismissed descriptions of masturbation's effects on men's bodies consistently related men's wasting their resources for fruitless ends with the corrosion of their overall potential for material productivity. The ancient Greek physician Aretaeus, writing in the first century of the Common Era, provides an early and strikingly clear example of such an equation, predicting that men who engage in regular masturbation risk becoming "dull, languid, dispirited, sluggish, stupidly silent, weak, wrinkled, incapable of any exertion, sallow, wan, effeminate . . . with many the disease goes on to palsy. For how could it be otherwise, that the power of the nerves should suffer when the generative principle is chilled?"[28] Such a calculus dooms the masturbating worker to becoming as useless as his spilled seed. Nearly two thousand years later, Kellogg describes the myriad health-wrecking consequences seen in masturbators, including heart palpitations, seizures, bed wetting, and a stiffened, shuffling gait.[29] An 1875 tract by Emery Abbey goes so far as to illustrate the male masturbator vis-à-vis the male abstainer, showing the self-gratifying man visibly weakened, stumbling, and seemingly suffering from facial paralysis.[30]

The link between men's ejaculation and their industrial potential manifested most clearly in the late nineteenth century's discussion of a "spermatic economy."[31] In the nineteenth century, any sexual act without the potential of procreation (coitus interruptus, homosexuality, masturbation, etc.) went under the heading of onanism, which later would only apply to masturbation.[32] Invoking the term *onanism* for its biblical reference to Onan, who intentionally performed coitus interruptus, links any "fruitless" use of energy in sexual exploits with a man punished by God for not procreating when so instructed, thus further bonding industrial interests with Judeo-Christian morality.[33] Dr. Elizabeth Blackwell notes that women who practice birth control and those who masturbate have equally damaged reproductive organs, caused by a lack of love in sexual acts.[34]

Capitalism's focus on production developed into Victorian attitudes that held abstaining from masturbation as essential to maintaining a disciplined body. As Kimmel puts it, "Willful sexual control of a body was the ultimate test of mind over matter."[35] Kellogg so fervently supported men's mastery of their bodies and controlling their desire for sexual release through masturbation that he not only developed cornflakes as an anaphrodisiac (suppressing sexual desire), but suggested such extreme measures as sewing silver sutures over a man's foreskin to prevent erections.[36] The euphemism "self-abuse" for masturbation frames sexual release as destructive and casts refraining from self-gratification as demonstrating "a self-respect that is exercised by depriving oneself of pleasure."[37] Masturbation assaults such modernist thinking by encouraging a narcissistic behavior, one that concentrates solely on the pleasurable manipulation of one's own genitals.[38] The virile, self-denying modernist exhibits the necessary traits for capital production and for reproduction.

By contrast, the neoliberal, who concentrates more on consumption than production, measures the quality of an act by its potential for pleasure rather than strength and wealth. Where modernism focuses on building up a larger and stronger workforce, neoliberalism concerns itself with creating more and greater opportunities for pleasure. Such a mode of capitalism seemingly necessitates masturbation to meet the constant hunger for pleasure and satisfaction. Industrial and consumerist goals do not exist in the absence of one another, for consumption itself necessitates further production for the sake of continued pleasure.[39] Nevertheless, the emphasis of this later capitalism values production only so far as it continues and increases gratification. Despite neoliberalism's drive for individuality, it does not seek detachment but rather the negotiation of civic relations, which allows for individualized interests and needs.[40] If we use *Seinfeld* as an example, some observers challenge the broad criticisms of the show's characters as utterly narcissistic, noting that, for all their individualism, they still respect and yearn for some level of commitment and do indeed care about and for each other.[41] Put in terms of sexuality, neoliberalism does not regard solo masturbation as the supreme sexual expression for its singular/solitary and relationally uncomplicated pleasures but instead accepts self-pleasuring as but one means of gratification—presumably not excluding other, interactive sexual possibilities.

The source of regulation—for no system operates completely outside the bounds of such concerns—takes an ironic shift from modernism to neoliberalism. Where industrialists look to the state to provide controls, consumerists take the responsibility of regulation upon themselves.[42] Rather than a case of the fox guarding the henhouse, neoliberalism's control in the hands of individuals forms each person as a subject for his/her control, which actually increases the level of surveillance possible as every subject becomes an object of his/her own control.[43] Consequently, neoliberalism depends upon confession to make each person responsible for bringing forth the truth of his/her sexuality, whether in terms of identity, desires, or acts. The confessor cements his/her own self in the restrictive discourse by feeling compelled to disclose to another acts that bear the brand of immorality. Through confession, the self grants to another power and authority by acknowledging that violations have occurred, a breach of absolute individualism that maintains the community. Thus, confession brings transgressive moments under the control of the overriding power structures by stigmatizing the act that violates a cultural norm.[44] What one must confess and how that confession occurs speaks to the sustaining practices within the collective.[45] The very existence of a national Coming Out Day (October 11, annually) represents the increase in sexual discourses in general and the simultaneous need for persons to make public what is otherwise known in private.

The changes in economic ethics discussed here, those from industrial to consumerist concerns, though moving from production to consumption, perpetuate concern with capital itself. Likewise, the concern about behaviors manifests through self-monitoring and confession as opposed to external condemnation. We feel these transformations in our cultural norms and can appreciate them in alterations to our gender and sexual ideologies. Jim McGuigan states plainly, "We live in an age of neo-liberal globalisation—by which I mean the revival of free-market economic policy and its rapid diffusion around the world with enormous social-structural consequences."[46] This chapter seeks to understand the "social-structural consequences" of the shift from modernism to neoliberalism on discourses of sexuality in general and on representations of masculine sexuality in particular. As Foucault asks:

> Why has sexuality been so widely discussed and what has been said about it? What were the effects of power generated by what was said? What are the links between these discourses, these effects of power, and the pleasures that were invested by them? . . . The object, in short, is to define the regime of power-knowledge-pleasure that sustains the discourse of human sexuality in our part of the world.[47]

The analysis that follows endeavors to grasp the effects of changing economic ethics upon masculine sexuality, as seen through mediated representation, with special regard to the function of sexual pleasure enjoyed for its own sake. My reading of *Seinfeld*'s "The Contest" considers the tensions and ambiguities that arise from the transition from modernism to neoliberalism by examining the discourses that surround the topic of masturbation, which represents an abomination to the ideals of modernism and a necessity to neoliberalism. We will look at a moment in the continual ebb and flow of competing discourses that never fully replace one another.

TAKING MATTERS INTO THEIR OWN HANDS

Paul Wells finds that audiences of situation comedies, like *Seinfeld,* have historically "empathized with characters and situations, and were offered scenarios which rehearsed their own anxieties and concerns, but in a way which afforded them the relief of humor."[48] Likewise, Shane Gunster suggests that television comedy shares with Brechtian theatre the possibility of political critique if not change.[49] While *Seinfeld* demurred from overtly offering change, it did reflect the social changes occurring in the dominant U.S. culture, displaying the conflicts and pulls people endure during ideological shifts while providing comic relief from and reminders of ethics during the transition. We will look at the display and critique of the economic transformation that occurred at the twentieth century's close. Watching *Seinfeld*'s characters (re)negotiate sexuality, especially masturbation, within changing capitalist modes, we see four friends who retain the vestiges of industrial concerns as they attempt to embrace a neoliberal style. The ways in which the characters discuss masturbation, manage it as part of their lives and interactions, and relate their sexual experiences—both acts and desires—provide an especially telling instance of cultural norms in transition.

Seinfeld focuses on the interactions and often-mundane lives of four principal characters: Jerry (Jerry Seinfeld), George (Jason Alexander), Elaine (Julia Louis-Dreyfus), and Kramer (Michael Richards). One of the show's best-known episodes, "The Contest," focuses on the characters competing to see who can abstain the longest from masturbating. This episode, like many others, demonstrates David Pierson's thesis that Seinfeld is a modern comedy of manners. As Pierson argues, much like comedies of manners, Seinfeld focuses on the human body and its functions.[50] "The Contest" provides an especially clear example by "[elevating] sexual functions of the lower body stratum to a higher discursive level."[51] Neither modernism nor neoliberalism has a monopoly on the concern for how individuals use their bodies. Both systems involve themselves with the body, but the ultimate focus of each differs significantly. As we have already seen in the discussion of the literature on masturbation, modernists concentrate on the proper application of the body to increasing productivity. Neoliberals maintain a concern for socially acceptable behavior but put considerable attention on using the body to maximize pleasure.

"The Contest" opens on the benign setting of Jerry, Elaine, and Kramer in their favorite neighborhood diner in New York City. When George joins the table, he confesses without any provocation that his mother walked in on him masturbating. Already, we see the power of internalized control working on the characters as George freely confesses his guilt. Although he admits to masturbating, neither he nor any other character will actually say the word masturbation. Instead, they allude to the activity with such phrases as "You know. I was alone." The hypocrisy of the repressive hypothesis makes itself apparent as individuals feel compelled to discuss that which they simultaneously feel they cannot actually name. Arguably, the absence of the word masturbation only heightens the emphasis on it, inviting more attention and energy from Seinfeld's characters and audience alike. In confessing the details of his act, George reveals that he felt inspired to masturbate while leafing through a copy of Glamour. The choice of text for stimulation seems rich with irony as Glamour, used as a pseudo-pornographic text in this instance, encourages economic consumption broadly as well as the visual consumption of the women within its pages, the latter of which George acted on.[52] George's explanation for choosing to masturbate makes salient the link between a consumer-pleasure-filled text and masturbation: "I started leafing through it.... One thing led to another." As he recounts it, his mother implored, "Why, George, why?" to which George responded, "Because it's there." It is not exactly clear which "it" explains his reason to masturbate: his penis or the gazed-upon copy of *Glamour*. Either option justifies George's masturbation as a matter of course for a consumerist: his penis represents a supposed natural impulse to exploit all opportunities for pleasure, while *Glamour* speaks to the display of women's bodies as both inciting and gratifying sexual desire.

While George's compulsion to confess and the talk of the pleasure of consumption as natural ("Because it's there") illustrate neoliberal tendencies, some modernist concerns remain. Burdened by the shame of his mother catching him in flagrante delicto, George proclaims, "I am never doing *that* again," which sets into motion an inevitable competition of sexual discipline. Challenged by George, Jerry replies, "I know I could hold out longer than you," and wagers $100 in a rivalry of sexual restraint. After Kramer joins the competition, Elaine upsets the men by asking to participate. As Jerry explains, the men see Elaine as advantaged over them: "It's easier for a woman not to do it than a man. We have to do it; it's part of our lifestyle." Forcing Elaine to take odds of 1½:1 over the three men makes plain the cultural discourse that assumes sex "belongs, *par excellence,* to men, and hence is lacking in women."[53] In general, the appropriation of athletic metaphors provides further proof of the capitalist psychosis of laissez-faire, which has an "intensely competitive emphasis."[54] It also makes stronger the links among sex, athleticism, and men by constructing men as athletes so suited to competition (and sex) that they require no allowances, whereas female competitors do.

The wager adds another point of tension between modernism and neoliberalism. At once, the money rewards a test of personal discipline while it enhances the capitalistic tone of industrial strength and weaves into it the thrill of gambling. As Walter Benjamin notes, gambling shares certain attributes with the illicit pleasures of prostitution: "For in gambling hall and bordello, it is the same supremely sinful delight: to challenge fate in pleasure. ... Thus in the gambler and the prostitute [one finds] that superstition which arranges the figures of fate and fills all wanton behavior with fateful forwardness, fateful concupiscence, bringing even pleasure to kneel before its throne."[55] The merging of sexual pleasure and gambling in "The Contest" demonstrates the ambiguities experienced between modernism and neoliberalism. It also provides the means by which *Seinfeld* can openly (i.e., on network television) take pleasure in friends discussing their masturbatory habits.

The means for monitoring furthers the tensions within the contest's design between modernist and neoliberal conduct. With the roster for the competition set, the persistent need for regulation rises again. Neoliberalism's dismissal of external regulation and control accepts a privatized governmentality. Accordingly, Jerry, George, Kramer, and Elaine agree to self-policing through the time-honored tradition of confession; says Jerry, "We all know each other very well. I'm sure we'll all feel comfortable within the confines of *the honor system*." As Jerry says "the honor system," he points his finger at his three peers, laying the responsibility of self-monitoring and accounting heavily before them. Against modernity's reliance upon governmental oversight, neoliberalism desires privatized regulation. George (unsuccessfully) hides his masturbation from his mother, who is an externalized agent who can castigate him for his behavior. Now, the responsibility for monitoring falls into the hands of the competitors. Relying upon confession as internalized monitoring allows the system "to discipline individuals with the least exertion of overt force by operating on their souls."[56] The detachment of power from a central governing figure, which simultaneously increases the level of surveillance, models the inability of neoliberalism to abandon altogether modernist practices, here the need for regulation.

The next day at Jerry's apartment, George and Jerry are discussing Jerry's current girlfriend, "Marla the virgin," when Kramer bursts into the room announcing, "There's a naked woman across the street."[57] The three men pile against the window to view the nude woman in her apartment (she does not close her curtains). After a few moments, Kramer quietly excuses himself and goes back to his apartment across the hall. When Elaine enters and sees that George and Jerry cannot take themselves away from the view of the naked woman across the street, she quickly assesses, "This is going to be the easiest money I've ever made in my life." Her confidence in the men's propensity to sate their desires rather than win the wager has some merit as Kramer soon returns (not more than a minute after he left) and slams a handful of money onto the kitchen counter declaring, "I'm out!" Providing the reason for his behavior, Kramer confesses, "It was that woman across the street." In so doing, Kramer demonstrates his preference for experiential pleasures over capital, which is consistent with his status as the "most sexualized" character of the group.[58] Furthermore, Kramer proves the effectiveness of relying upon confession for policing private behaviors within neoliberalism.

Later that day, George goes to visit his mother, Estelle (Estelle Harris), who is in traction at the hospital after injuring her back when she fell to the floor upon seeing George masturbating. George must endure from his mother the reprimands of industrialism for engaging in pleasures that serve only to gratify the self. Estelle blatantly links the time and energy spent in nonproductive sexual pursuits to capital loss: "You have nothing better to do at three o'clock in the afternoon? . . . Too bad you can't do *that* for a living. You'd be very successful at it." Estelle continues to berate George's behavior, clearly striking at neoliberalism's sanction of the pursuit of pleasure: "I come home and find my son treating his body like it was an amusement park." She goes so far as to pathologize his industrially delinquent pursuits by demanding that he see a psychiatrist. George refuses to visit a psychiatrist and in so doing demonstrates the struggle between modernism and neoliberalism. The pull of modernism comes from George's mother, who has literally policed his behavior and wishes to intervene by retraining his body through a medical apparatus, while George attempts to claim/maintain a neoliberal position that allows him to seek pleasure for its own sake and to decide its appropriate application. Barbra Morris finds that George's comic relief is just that, a bit of laughter from a trickster figure who battles, upsets, and subverts faulty social systems—whether work, family, or romance—rather than simply acquiescing.[59] Even so, when George's cousin comes to visit Estelle and asks how the injury occurred, George defensively yells, "Is that important?" His refusal to name the practice he defends his right to enjoy speaks to an ambivalence between the positions of modernism and neoliberalism much like *Seinfeld* itself, which claims a right to discuss masturbation but only under the guise of gambling.

While at the hospital, George experiences what all four competitors must confront—temptation. For each contestant, a personal temptation sets a standard for measuring personal restraint. In the tradition of body-building and endurance tests so familiar to industrialist proclivities, these feats of strength test individuals' mettle. Such industrialist tests resemble epicurean stoicism, which finds delight in refusing anything considered unnecessary.[60] For George, temptation comes in the form of an erotic shadow show. As George speaks to his mother and cousin, a female nurse enters the room and goes behind the curtain of Estelle's roommate to give the other patient, a woman, a sponge bath. From behind the curtain comes a homoerotic coded play of shadows and words as one woman un-dresses the other and sponges her body, providing a somewhat common hetero male fantasy. Later, George will describe to Jerry the veiled scene's erotic power: "The nurse was gorgeous. Then I got a look at the patient [chortle]. I was going nuts." For all the condemnations and embarrass-ment, George continues to openly consume as much sexual delight as possible without losing his bet. Estelle's presence when George witnesses the homoerotic shadow play mimics the industrial ethics that continue to nag him even as he revels in the pleasure of watching. Jerry's test comes from his girlfriend, Marla the virgin, who, as her nickname implies, stops physical activity with Jerry short of reaching orgasm. Elaine confronts temptation at her gym when she works out behind John F. Kennedy Jr., admiring his backside and then later flirting with him as they leave the health club. Kramer's temptation and competitive undoing came in the form of the nude woman in the apartment across the street from Jerry's. Initially, Kramer alone partakes of the opportunities for pleasure pre-sented to him.

The next morning, Kramer acts in a rather biblical fashion, forming himself as his brother's keeper by monitoring Jerry's competitive abilities: "Did you make it through the night?" When Jerry affirmatively replies, Kramer pronounces Jerry the "master of your domain." The title "master of your domain" represents the hallmark of neoliberal self-governance by making explicit the body as a domain needing control as in the ancient Greek tradition in which "one was expected to govern oneself in the same manner as one governed one's household."[61] Consequently, the moniker "master of your domain" implies both the athletic discipline required and the activity denied. When Jerry later meets with George at the neighbor-hood coffee shop, Jerry inquires about George's discipline:

Jerry: Are you "master of your domain"?
George: I am "king of the county." You?
Jerry: "Lord of the manor."

Entering the conversation, Elaine responds to the same question by declaring herself "queen of the castle." Once more, we see the importance of confession to maintaining order. For all three, resisting the temptation to masturbate represents a form of discipline over their body as though it were a municipality, or an independent subject, just as Epictetus advised that "one [should] adopt, vis-à-vis oneself, the role and posture of 'night watchman.'"[62] Consequently, when Elaine must confess to her masturbation the next day, George exclaims, "You caved?" and Jerry proclaims, "The queen is dead."[63] Both men reiterate the emphasis upon discipline: George refers to masturbating as "caving"—giving in to desire—and Jerry declares Elaine's rule over her own body "dead."

As the episode nears its end, "The Contest" provides punishment to the characters who maintained the fiction of necessary restraint the longest. By this point, Kramer has long lost the contest, Elaine has succumbed only after struggling to maintain her position, and Jerry and George still persevere. On his couch with Marla the virgin, Jerry shares with Marla the contest he and his friends have invented. Before we can hear Jerry describe the matter, the camera cuts to Elaine standing outside Jerry's building for a meeting with JFK Jr. The camera returns to the scene of the apartment after Jerry has explained the contest, thus avoiding too blatant a discussion of masturbation and spoiling the hoax that "The Contest" focuses on gambling rather than sexual pleasure. Before Marla storms out of Jerry's apartment, she cries out, "Contest! Contest! This is what you do with your friends?" Marla's shock stems from the point that the four were in a contest—that they participated in this strange wager—rather than the roundabout admission to masturbating. Later that evening, Elaine and George join Jerry in his apartment, and George says that he has just seen Kennedy with Marla. Jerry's and Elaine's anger, and the humor, come from the unification of their objects of sexual desire turning to one another and denying their pursuers. The pairing of Marla and JFK Jr. mocks Jerry and Elaine for their emphasis on denying personal pleasure rather than seeking it. The anger in the scene breaks when Jerry sees that Kramer (presumably nude) has joined the naked woman across the street. During the closing credits, "The Contest" shows each character in bed: Kramer with (we can presume) the nude woman; George, Jerry, and Elaine each alone; and Marla with JFK Jr. And the three who withheld from masturbation the longest—George, Jerry, and Elaine—have only masturbation for sexual release rather than an interactive sexual outlet.

Foucault notes Plato's concern regarding "the danger of what might be called 'athletic' excess; this was due to repeated workouts that over-developed the body and ended by making the soul sluggish, enveloped as it was within a too-powerful musculature."[64] In "The Contest," as the episode title affirms, the competitors give themselves over to the risks of athletic excess for the sake of earning the respect as the most athletically disciplined. Ancient sexual morality did see sexual release for pleasure's sake as inferior to procreative purposes, but it understood sexual pleasure along a continuum between proper and improper use, moderation and excess.[65] George's mother, Estelle, who rants that he treats his body "like it was an amusement park," assaults the consumerist ideology that respects the need for frequent/immediate gratification without any allowance for pleasure and release as both desirable and necessary.

"The Contest" mocks modernism's demand for athletic excess by contrasting those who have found pleasure and those who have not. Over the course of the episode, sleeping soundly is used as a metonym for sati-ated desire. When Kramer has masturbated and Jerry, George, and Elaine have continued to abstain, we see the latter three in their own beds frus-trated and unable to sleep while Kramer rests soundly. Later, Elaine and Kramer both enjoy deep sleep, while Jerry and George toss tormented in their beds, starving themselves of sexual pleasure. George and Jerry both admit to increasing peevishness because of their sexual withholding; as Jerry says, "I haven't been myself lately." Like the classic stoic, Jerry, Elaine, and George rely upon a test "to mark the threshold where priva-tion could start to make one suffer."[66] The choice to embrace suffering speaks to an industrialist mindset that prefers winning money to enjoy-ing life. As others have noted, most of the characters—Jerry and George especially, but also Elaine—care more about winning the monetary prize and getting credit for self-discipline than about embracing pleasure.[67] Their flight toward industrial practices only holds out until the episode's conclusion, however, when all have experienced sexual release. Jennifer Simmons suggests that the true masters of their domains "are those who allow themselves the pleasures and selfhood of masturbation."[68] Therefore, those, like Kramer, who embrace pleasure as a worthwhile part of life not only sleep better at night but also find the satisfaction of sexual partners. "The Contest" provides no final pronouncement about industrialism or consumerism, per se. It does, however, demonstrate the tension within sexual discourses as dominant U.S. culture moves from modernism to neoliberalism, trying to find the balance between building resources and regulating social behavior (modernism) and embracing the pleasures of life without slipping into complete narcissism (neoliberalism).

COMING TO A HEAD: TRADING KELLOGG FOR THE FAB FIVE

"The Contest" represents a vacillation amid the shift from an industrialist modernism to a consumerist neoliberalism among the baby boomers who have experienced those cultural changes in more diverse ways.[69] Where *Seinfeld* presents the conflict between modernism and neoliberalism occurring through the 1990s, *Queer Eye for the Straight Guy* heralds consumerism's prominence in the new millennium. By comparing the characters' experiences in "The Contest" with the themes developed in *Queer Eye,* we can contrast a masculine sexuality in transition between capitalistic modes, as seen in *Seinfeld,* with a gendered performance of sexuality comfortably ensconced in self-benefiting practices. Though we readily characterize modern industrialism as being built upon regimens of behavior (e.g., disciplining one's body) and suggest that consumerism frees individuals to a life without external demands, a show like *Queer Eye* demonstrates that neoliberalism merely replaces one set of personal regimens with another. Where ardent industrialists, like J. H. Kellogg, call for men to build up their bodies as instruments for hard work—largely through denying themselves pleasures (especially sexual pleasures) that sap their bodies of strength and energy—passionate consumerists, like the experts of *Queer Eye,* instruct men in the precise means of perfecting their bodies and behaviors to meet aesthetic standards.[70]

Both perspectives focus on forming the male body to meet cultural dictates of masculine sexuality. In coining the term *metrosexual,* Mark Simpson notes the replacement of a hard-working masculinity with a good-looking masculinity:

For some time now, old-fashioned (re)productive, repressed, unmoisturized heterosexuality has been given the pink slip by consumer capitalism. The stoic, self-denying, modest straight male didn't shop enough (his role was to earn money for his wife to spend), and so he had to be replaced by a new kind of man, one less certain of his identity and much more interested in his image—that's to say, one who was much more interested in being looked at. . . . A man, in other words, who is an advertiser's walking wet dream.[71]

Enter *Queer Eye for the Straight Guy.*

Queer Eye provides a vivid example of a neoliberal orientation enveloped in consumerism that purges modernist industrialism and fills the void with a new set of bodily disciplines. First airing in 2003 (its run ended in 2007), *Queer Eye*'s catchphrase describes the show best: "Five gay men out to make over the world—one straight guy at a time." As the tagline suggests, the show participates in cultural change through aesthetically making over men, operating at the level of the individual. The Fab Five are witty gay men with expertise in grooming, food and wine, interior design, fashion, and culture, who teach a single straight man (though occasionally two or a few at once) how to style his hair and preserve/improve his skin, prepare a somewhat epicurean meal, live in a stylish home, select a fashionable wardrobe, and demonstrate cultural sophistication. The basic format for the show begins with the Fab Five invading the straight man's home and mocking his personal tastes and behaviors, ranging from his choice of clothes and furnishings to his generic shampoo-conditioner combination and the food he keeps in his refrigerator. After a series of one-on-one sessions between the queer experts and the straight student, the show releases the transformed man back into his own environment to show off the new style he has inherited. The process creates a man reborn, washed in the joy of displaying his newfound style: "This call to personal redemption through product consumption, reflected in *Queer Eye*'s metrosexual aesthetic, is driven by contemporary culture's moral imperative that we always look our best."[72] The remade man in *Queer Eye* ends the show with the confidence of a man now well suited to engage with a restyled capitalistic ethic.

The new body ethic established by metrosexuality and reinforced by *Queer Eye* perpetuates capitalism and masculinity as dominant forces but does so by giving both a more attractive appearance. Scholars studying the industrialist tradition define *hegemonic masculinity* as emphasizing physical force, occupational achievement, familial patriarchy, frontiersman-ship, and heterosexuality.[73] Neoliberalism's emergence hardly challenges the privilege of men in society, for the real transformation within *Queer Eye* occurs by giving hegemonic masculinity a fashionable makeover, transforming brute force into physical perfection, occupational achieve-ment into cultural literacy, and frontiersmanship into urban sophistica-tion.[74] Through developing heterosexual men's sexual prowess—training them as more desirable relational partners—and class performance, the Fab Five "safeguard the reproductive logics of capitalism."[75] The consum-erist paradigm co-opts any challenges by way of diversity by producing varied masculinities but only to the extent that each demographic market segment has the best tailored pitch.[76] The subsequent model of dominant masculinity remains a white heterosexuality—only now with a refigured class performance.[77] The means of expressing capital success, not the need for it, constitutes the ultimate change from *Seinfeld*'s masculinity to *Queer Eye*'s.

A sample episode from *Queer Eye* demonstrates a new discipline of bodily maintenance replacing modernist demands for productivity. In season 3, the Fab Five chose to make over Jim B., a nudist.[78] The Fab Five's experience with Jim demonstrates the compulsion to apply appropriate material prescriptions to the body, even when the individual enjoys shed-ding the material. As they discuss clothing-free socializing, Carson, the fashion expert, notes nudism's democratic potential:

> Carson: Very egalitarian, this nudism.
> Jim: Everybody's equal, right. Because you do have your doctors, your law-yers, your businesspeople, and when you're nude—and everybody's nude—you're on the same level.

Jim, who works as a mechanic and lives with his mother, seems to enjoy opportunities where class and capital distinctions lie in a heap in the corner. Despite Carson's admiration for egalitarianism, the Fab Five's time with Jim focuses on "elevating" him, which partly involves inscribing class acuity whenever possible. When Carson tries nudism for himself on the show, Kyan (the grooming expert) compares Jim's and Carson's nudism to note Jim's poor performance:

> Kyan: Carson's nude, and you are nude. But Carson has a refined sort of nu-dity to him. His hair is done. He's got an accessory [a necklace with a small

trinket hanging from it]. I think that even though you are a nudist there is still a way to sort of *elevate* your experience, your look [emphasis added].

Ted [food and wine expert]: You can be a more sophisticated kind ofnaked.

Throughout the episode, the Fab Five attempt to elevate nudism, which they elsewhere recognize as equalizing and liberating. When the culture expert, Jai, takes Jim to a life-drawing class, he tells Jim, "You get a lot of slack for being a nudist, but I wanted to find a way to *elevate* that" (emphasis added). In teaching Jim about the nude form in art and how to draw it himself, Jai seeks to add a consumerist validation to nudism by recognizing nudity as part of a sophisticated tradition and craft.

Other comments directed toward Jim's clothing, appearance, and home emphasize the need to create a capitalistically savvy performance, even if one is enjoying literally shedding material. The comments made about clothing reveal the inability of consumerism to quietly let go of those who prefer clothing-free opportunities. While explaining the need for Jim to have a Brooks Brothers tuxedo, Carson says, "If you're going to wear clothes, you might as well wear beautiful ones just for a night." Kyan quickly chimes in, noting the need to display one's capital until the last moment possible, "And even if you're going to take them off, take off beautiful clothes." Comments about Jim's existing wardrobe mock his clothing and imply that nudism seems appropriate for those with poor capitalistic taste. Looking in Jim's closet, Kyan remarks, "Maybe it *is* good that he's a nudist" (emphasis in original). When Jim puts clothes on, Carson jabs at Jim's attire, saying, "I think I liked you better nude." Though he may want to go clothing-free, the Fab Five make sure that Jim finds plenty of other ways to display and consume capital.

Early on, Kyan asks Jim, "What is this [nudity] about for you?" Jim replies, "Being comfortable with yourself; being comfortable with your surroundings and around other people." Despite Jim's desire to find comfort with himself and his surroundings, the Fab Five identify his deficiencies. After redecorating a den for Jim's use, Thom, the interior design expert, notes that the frosted-glass door he installed provides privacy and protects the aesthetics of the new space from Jim's mother's decorating: "Not only does this door allow you to be nude in the house but—with all due respect—it kind of keeps out the ugliness." Near the end of the transformation, Kyan says flatly, "My whole vision for you was to get you looking your best naked." To that end, he hands Jim a tooth-bleaching kit (to be used twice a day for thirty minutes for ten days) and moisturizing gloves and socks (to be worn twenty minutes a day in conjunction with moisturizing creams). Kyan's cosmetic disciplines substitute nicely for the bodybuilding regimens of old.

At the show's conclusion, alone in their stylish loft, the Fab Five toast Jim—without any sense of irony or self-awareness—and celebrate his liberation to be himself:

> Ted: Let your freak flag fly, Jimmy; that's all I say.
> Carson: Here's to letting it all hang out and being yourself.
> Ted: To letting it all hang out.
> Kyan: To each his own.

Despite using their talents to show Jim how to dress nicely when he does wear clothes, select expensive eyewear, improve his teeth coloring and skin texture, choose stylish furnishings, mix special cocktails, and express nudism through accepted artistic practice, the Fab Five celebrate "letting it all hang out and being yourself." Their celebration of personal liberation amid the commands to conform to consumerist ideals embodies the inherent irony of neoliberalism, which purports to shun governance as it recreates it in a myriad of ways.

The conflict between the two strands of capitalistic, occupational psychoses, one driven by production, the other by pleasure, is the strife that *Seinfeld* attempts to reconcile. The absence of such tension in *Queer Eye* speaks to a possible completion of our cultural shift. *Seinfeld* is able to discuss masturbation on network television by transferring the subject of sexual gratification to the related topic of gambling. Gambling represents the ambiguity between modernism and neoliberalism: the competition itself has a clear modernist orientation (emphasizing discipline toward sex as a reproductive technology), yet as a contest with wagers it carries the erotic pleasures of gambling and the necessity for individualized regulation in the form of intimate confession. Unburdened by such tensions, the straight men of *Queer Eye* go through a public makeover of their intimate lives, shamelessly immersing themselves in capitalist pleasures. This is true even of those like Jim, who prefer to find comfort within themselves and egalitarianism by freeing themselves from material concerns.

This charting of "The Contest" and its comparison with *Queer Eye* demonstrate the ambivalence that occurs when discussing the topic of masturbation as exemplary of the tension-filled transition between modernism and neoliberalism. "The Contest" transgresses the shame of (discussing) masturbation by bringing to the forefront the idea that masturbation occurs as a regular part of (at least some) people's sexual lives.[79] *Seinfeld* frames the willful refraining from masturbation as unnatural as compared to performing the act itself, for when George, Jerry, and Elaine impose austere notions of sexuality upon themselves, they are beset with anguish and lose the opportunity for (possible) sexual fulfillment with another. The "perversion" of "The Contest" lies in treating masturbation as an athletic event as opposed to a more natural part of sexual life. Torn between modernism and neoliberalism, we see the taboo concurrently maintained by the protected discussion of masturbation that never uses the actual word *masturbation,* thus preserving its forbidden nature. The text again represents the tensions and contradictions of the repressive hypothesis by bringing the topic of masturbation into the field of play but then demanding that the discussion occur in a clandestine manner. *Queer Eye,* by contrast, openly discusses both material and sexual pleasures, often sexualizing the Fab Five's talk of the material.[80] When showing Jim his new hot tub, Thom notes, "Look, there's a *blower.* Everybody loves a blower" (emphasis in original). The comment helps to mark the hot tub as a display of both consumerist ability and bodily/sexual pleasure.

For all this discussion of the effect on masculine sexuality brought about by changing and competing tides in capitalism, we must still consider the related yet distinct experience that women have when managing the cultural shift from modernism to neoliberalism. For instance, "The Contest" shows women as both sexually restrained and sexually desirous. Elaine mocks the men's lascivious reaction to the naked woman, and Marla the virgin, by her name alone, represents the stereotype of women's sexual restraint. Both women, however, succumb to sexual desire, Elaine even before two of her three male competitors. Further exploration of the cultural tensions present in discussing women's sexuality will likely find differences as masculine and feminine gender performances play different roles in all social discourses. The depiction of women as shopaholics who spend their husbands' money, for example, creates a subject position distinct from men's in discussing market relations, just as women's established presence in beauty culture will certainly inform a different analysis of capital tensions from that implied by men's late entry into that culture.

As *Seinfeld* lives on in the world of DVD boxed sets and syndicated reruns, it will remain a reminder that the 1990s were neither a hell nor a paradise. The comedy that prided itself on being "a show about nothing" proves to be fertile ground for analysis as the critical studies of its impacts and meanings continue with this chapter and most assuredly beyond. In this study, we have seen that media texts for entertainment purposes speak to us about cultural trends operating below the surface but manifesting in diverse ways. Also, we observe that, for all the complaints about modernism's industrial preferences and the resultant pressures to make our bodies conform accordingly, neoliberalism's consumer predilections incite just as much worry and concern about bodily disciplines and the proper performances of gender and sexuality.

Let us revisit one last time George in his mother's hospital room gazing at what he perceives to be an erotic shadow show put on by two attractive women. As George recounts the tale to Jerry, to his left neoliberalism held out the opportunity for him to sate his desires and enjoy visual and sexual consumption, while to his right his mother's voice, the voice of modernism, beckoned him to remember his social responsibilities. In his effort to mediate the tensions between competing dictates, George is not alone.

NOTES

The epigraph is quoted in Dreyfus and Rabinow, *Michel Foucault*, 229.

1. In "The Hamptons," much masculine panic ensues when a woman sees George nude as he changes out of his swimsuit following a swim for, as George explains, the cold water caused "shrinkage" of his penis, leading others to assume he is less well-endowed than he protests he is. "The Yada Yada," in part, gets its title from characters using the expression "yada, yada, yada" to dismissively mention having sexual intercourse, sometimes in cases that were less than noteworthy. The expression "master of your domain" from "The Contest" receives considerable attention later in this chapter.

2. Foucault, *Discipline and Punish*; Foucault, *History of Sexuality*.

3. Foucault, *History of Sexuality*, 8.

4. Foucault, *Discipline and Punish*, 194.

5. Butler, *Bodies That Matter*, 8.

6. Butler, *Gender Trouble*, 135–136.
7. Bartky, "Foucault, Femininity, and the Modernization of Patriarchal Power"; Murphy, "Hidden Transcripts of Flight Attendant Resistance"; Brannon, "The Male Sex Role"; Trujillo, "Hegemonic Masculinity."
8. Foucault, *History of Sexuality*, 11.
9. Connell and Dowsett, "'The Unclean Motion of the Generative Parts,'" 60.
10. Foucault, *History of Sexuality*, 18.
11. Ibid., 19–20.
12. Krippendorf, "Undoing Power," 107.
13. McKerrow, "Critical Rhetoric," 96.
14. Burke, *Permanence and Change*, 38–41.
15. Martin, *The Woman in the Body*, 27–53.
16. McGuigan, "Neo-Liberalism, Culture and Policy."
17. Clarke, *Consumer Society*, 106–108.
18. McGuigan, "Neo-Liberalism, Culture and Policy," 230; Scholte, *Sources of Neoliberal Globalization*, 7–9.
19. Clarke, *Consumer Society*, 66–67.
20. Kimmel, "Masculinity as Homophobia," 123–124.
21. Michael S. Kimmel, *Manhood in America: A Cultural History* (New York: Free Press, 1996), 177–181.
22. Ibid., 251.
23. Foucault, *History of Sexuality*, 108–109.
24. Ibid., 114.
25. Kellogg, *Plain Facts for Old and Young*, 465–469.
26. Morris, *The Male Heterosexual*, 81.
27. Foucault, *History of Sexuality*, 140–141.
28. Qtd. in Foucault, *The Use of Pleasure*, 15.
29. Kellogg, *Plain Facts for Old and Young*, 249–259.
30. See Laqueur, *Solitary Sex*, 65.
31. Barker-Benfield, "The Spermatic Economy."
32. Bullough and Voght, "Homosexuality," 83–84.
33. In Genesis 38:8–10, Onan refuses to bear a child with his late brother's wife, as mandated by the custom of levirate marriage, and dies for his transgression. Though Onan's case deals with an instance of coitus interruptus, *onanism* became a term used euphemistically for masturbation.
34. Laqueur, *Solitary Sex*, 49.
35. Kimmel, *Manhood*, 45.
36. Kellogg, *Plain Facts for Old and Young*, 290–327, esp. 296. Regarding the development of cornflakes, see Kimmel, *Manhood*, 129.
37. Foucault, *Care of the Self*, 41.
38. For a similar discussion, see Gantz, "'Not That There's Anything Wrong with That,'" 182.
39. Clarke, *Consumer Society*, 24.
40. Olbrys, "*Seinfeld*'s Democratic Vistas," 405.
41. Skovmand, "Culture of Post-narcissism," 207; Morris, "Why Is George So Funny?" 50.
42. Sender, "Queens for a Day," 135–136.

43. Foucault, *The Use of Pleasure*, 28; Foucault, *Discipline and Punish*, 206.

44. Foucault, *History of Sexuality*, 62–63.

45. Dow, "*Ellen*, Television, and the Politics of Gay and Lesbian Visibility," 136.

46. McGuigan, "Neo-Liberalism, Culture and Policy," 229.

47. Foucault, *History of Sexuality*, 11.

48. Wells, "'Where Everybody Knows Your Name,'" 184.

49. Gunster, "'All about Nothing,'" 219.

50. Pierson, "A Show about Nothing," 60–61.

51. Ibid., 61.

52. For a brief discussion of pornography as "preparatory to or as inciting the act of masturbation," see Buchbinder, *Performance Anxieties*, 104.

53. Foucault, *History of Sexuality*, 153.

54. Burke, *Permanence and Change*, 41.

55. Benjamin, *Arcades Project*, 489–490.

56. Dreyfus and Rabinow, *Michel Foucault*, 192.

57. The previous episode of *Seinfeld* introduced the character Marla (Jane Leeves), who—as the name implies—is a virgin, thus the characters' private nickname for her.

58. Simmons, "Visions of Feminist (Pom(O)Nanism)," 25.

59. Morris, "Why Is George So Funny?" 48, 51–52.

60. Foucault, *Care of the Self*, 59.

61. Foucault, *The Use of Pleasure*, 75.

62. Ibid., 63.

63. As an ironic note, "little death" is a French euphemism for orgasm.

64. Foucault, *The Use of Pleasure*, 104.

65. Ibid., 48–49.

66. Foucault, *Care of the Self*, 59.

67. Gantz, "'Not That There's Anything Wrong with That,'" 184; Simmons, "Visions of Feminist (Pom(O)Nanism)," 25–26.

68. Simmons, "Visions of Feminist (Pom(O)Nanism)," 27.

69. Skovmand, "Culture of Post-narcissism," 207.

70. Clarkson, "Contesting Masculinity's Makeover," 239.

71. Simpson, "Meet the Metrosexual."

72. Westerfelhaus and Lacroix, "Seeing 'Straight' through *Queer Eye*," 429.

73. Trujillo, "Hegemonic Masculinity," 291–292.

74. Clarkson, "Contesting Masculinity's Makeover," 239–240.

75. Allatson, "*Queer Eye*'s Primping," 210.

76. Alexander, "Stylish Hard Bodies," 552.

77. Clarkson, "Contesting Masculinity's Makeover," 252.

78. "A Nude Scary Garcia: Jim B."

79. Skovmand, "Culture of Post-narcissism," 211.

80. Weiss, "Constructing the Queer 'I.'"

BIBLIOGRAPHY

Alexander, Susan M. "Stylish Hard Bodies: Branded Masculinity in Men's Health Magazines." *Sociological Perspectives* 46 (2003): 535–554.

Allatson, Paul. "*Queer Eye's* Primping and Pimping for Empire et al." *Feminist Media Studies* 4 (2004): 208–211.

Barker-Benfield, G. J. "The Spermatic Economy: A Nineteenth-Century View of Sexuality." In *The American Family in Social-Historical Perspective,* 2nd ed. Edited by Michael Gordon, 374–402. New York: St. Martin's, 1978.

Bartky, Sandra. "Foucault, Femininity, and the Modernization of Patriarchal Power." In *Free Spirits: Feminist Philosophers on Culture,* ed. Kate Mehuron and Gary Percesepe, 240–256. Englewood Cliffs, N.J.: Prentice Hall, 1995.

Benjamin, Walter. *The Arcades Project.* Trans. Howard Eiland and Kevin McLaughlin. Cambridge: Belknap, 1999.

Brannon, Robert. "The Male Sex Role: Our Culture's Blueprint of Manhood and What It's Done for Us Lately." In *The Forty-nine Percent Majority: The Male Sex Role,* ed. Deborah David and Robert Brannon, 1–14. Reading, Mass.: Addison-Wesley, 1976.

Buchbinder, David. *Performance Anxieties: Re-producing Masculinity.* Sydney, Australia: Allen and Unwin, 1998.

Bullough, Vern L., and Martha Voght. "Homosexuality and Its Confusion with the 'Secret Sin' in Pre-Freudian America." In *The Other Americans: Sexual Variance in the National Past,* ed. Charles O. Jackson, 82–92. Westport, Conn.: Praeger, 1996.

Burke, Kenneth. *Permanence and Change,* 3rd ed. Berkeley: University of California Press, 1984.

Butler, Judith. *Bodies That Matter: On the Discursive Limits of "Sex."* New York: Routledge, 1993.

———. *Gender Trouble: Feminism and the Subversion of Identity.* New York: Routledge, 1990.

Clarke, David B. *The Consumer Society and the Postmodern City.* New York: Routledge, 2003.

Clarkson, Jay. "Contesting Masculinity's Makeover: *Queer Eye,* Consumer Masculinity, and 'Straight-Acting' Gays." *Journal of Communication Inquiry* 29 (2005): 235–255.

Connell, R. W., and G. W. Dowsett. "'The Unclean Motion of the Generative Parts': Frameworks in Western Thought on Sexuality." In *Rethinking Sex: Social Theory and Sexuality Research,* ed. R. W. Connell and G. W. Dowsett, 49–75. Philadelphia: Temple University Press, 1992.

"The Contest." *Seinfeld.* NBC, November 18, 1992.

Dow, Bonnie J. "*Ellen,* Television, and the Politics of Gay and Lesbian Visibility." *Critical Studies in Media Communication* 18 (2001): 123–140.

Dreyfus, Hubert L., and Paul Rabinow. *Michel Foucault: Beyond Structuralism and Hermeneutics,* 2nd ed. Chicago: University of Chicago Press, 1983.

Foucault, Michel. *The Care of the Self.* Trans. Robert Hurley. Vol. 3 of *The History of Sexuality.* New York: Vintage, 1986.

———. *Discipline and Punish: The Birth of the Prison.* Trans. Alan Sheridan. New York: Vintage, 1995.

———. *The History of Sexuality: An Introduction,* vol. 1. Trans. Robert Hurley. New York: Vintage, 1990.

———. *The Use of Pleasure.* Trans. Robert Hurley. Vol. 2 of *The History of Sexuality.* New York: Vintage, 1990.

Gantz, Katherine. "'Not That There's Anything Wrong with That': Reading the Queer in *Seinfeld*." In *Straight with a Twist: Queer Theory and the Subject of Heterosexuality*, ed. Calvin Thomas, 165–190. Champaign: University of Illinois Press, 2000.

Gunster, Shane. "'All about Nothing': Difference, Affect, and *Seinfeld*." *Television and News Media* 6 (2005): 200–223.

"The Hamptons." *Seinfeld*. NBC, May 12, 1995.

Kellogg, J. H. *Plain Facts for Old and Young: Embracing the Natural History and Hygiene of Organic Life*. Burlington, Iowa: Senger, 1891. Electronic Text Center, University of Virginia Library, http://etext.lib.virginia.edu/toc/modeng/public/KelPlai.html (accessed May 28, 2007).

Kimmel, Michael S. *Manhood in America: A Cultural History*. New York: Free Press, 1996.

———. "Masculinity as Homophobia: Fear, Shame, and Silence in the Construction of Gender Identity." In *Theorizing Masculinities*, ed. Harry Brod and Michael Kaufman, 119–41. Thousand Oaks, Calif.: Sage, 1994.

Krippendorf, Klaus. "Undoing Power." *Critical Studies in Mass Communication* 12 (1995): 101–132.

Laqueur, Thomas W. *Solitary Sex: A Cultural History of Masturbation*. Zone: New York, 2003.

Martin, Emily. *The Woman in the Body: A Cultural Analysis of Reproduction*. Boston: Beacon, 2001.

McGuigan, Jim. "Neo-Liberalism, Culture and Policy." *International Journal of Cultural Policy* 11 (2005): 229–241.

McKerrow, Raymie E. "Critical Rhetoric: Theory and Praxis." *Communication Monographs* 56 (1989): 91–111.

Morris, Barbra S. "Why Is George So Funny? Television Comedy, Trickster Heroism, and Cultural Studies." *English Journal* 88, no. 4 (1999): 47–52.

Morris, Larry A. *The Male Heterosexual: Lust in His Loins, Sin in His Soul?* Thousand Oaks, Calif.: Sage, 1997.

Murphy, Alexandra G. "Hidden Transcripts of Flight Attendant Resistance." *Management Communication Quarterly* 11 (1998): 499–535.

"A Nude Scary Garcia: Jim B." *Queer Eye for the Straight Guy*. Bravo, July 12, 2005.

Olbrys, Stephen Gencarella. "*Seinfeld*'s Democratic Vistas." *Critical Studies in Media Communication* 22 (2005): 390–408.

Pierson, David P. "A Show about Nothing: *Seinfeld* and the Modern Comedy of Manners." *Journal of Popular Culture* 34 (2000): 49–64.

Scholte, Jan Aart. *The Sources of Neoliberal Globalization*. Geneva, Switzerland: United Nations Research Institute for Social Development, October 10, 2005.

Sender, Katherine. "Queens for a Day: *Queer Eye for the Straight Guy* and the Neoliberal Project." *Critical Studies in Media Communication* 23 (2006): 131–151.

Simmons, Jennifer Beth. "Visions of Feminist (Pom(O)Nanism): Masturbating Female Postmodern Subjectivity in American Television and Film." Master's thesis, University of Florida, 2004.

Simpson, Mark. "Meet the Metrosexual." *Salon*, July 22, 2002. http://dir.salon.com /story/ent/feature/2002/07/22/metrosexual/index.html (accessed March 1, 2007).

Skovmand, Michael. "The Culture of Post-narcissism: Post-teenage, Pre-midlife Singles Culture in *Seinfeld, Friends,* and *Ally—Seinfeld* in Particular." *Nordicom Review* 1–2 (2002): 205–213. http://www.nordicom.gu.se/common/publ_pdf/42_205-214.pdf (accessed May 10, 2007).

Trujillo, Nick. "Hegemonic Masculinity on the Mound: Media Representations of Nolan Ryan and American Sports Culture." *Critical Studies in Mass Communication* 8 (1991): 290–308.

Weiss, David. "Constructing the Queer 'I': Performativiy, Citationality, and Desire in *Queer Eye for the Straight Guy.*" *Popular Communication* 3 (2005): 73–95.

Wells, Paul. "'Where Everybody Knows Your Name': Open Convictions and Closed Contexts in the American Situation Comedy." In *Because I Tell a Joke or Two: Comedy, Politics, and Social Difference,* ed. Stephen Wagg, 180–201. New York: Routledge, 1998.

Westerfelhaus, Robert, and Celeste Lacroix. "Seeing 'Straight' through *Queer Eye:* Exposing the Strategic Rhetoric of Heteronormativity in a Mediated Ritual of Gay Rebellion." *Critical Studies in Media Communication* 23 (2006): 426–444.

"The Yada Yada." *Seinfeld.* NBC, April 24, 1997.

TWO

SEXUALLY SUSPECT: MASCULINE ANXIETY IN THE FILMS OF NEIL LABUTE

BRENDA BOUDREAU

As several books and articles have suggested, men, particularly white men, are facing a crisis in the late twentieth and early twenty-first century. At least partial blame for this crisis is being laid on changing patterns of consumption and the displacement of the white male in the corporate arena—the displacement of what Michael Kimmel calls "Marketplace Man" who "derived his identity entirely from his success in the capitalist marketplace, as he accumulated wealth, power, status" (34). As Susan Faludi's *Stiffed: The Betrayal of the American Man* and Susan Bordo's *The Male Body: A New Look at Men in Public and Private* suggest, men have been facing a crisis since the mid-1980s because society no longer offers them a clear sense of what manhood means. Instead of participating in society in a useful and meaningful way, men are "surrounded by a culture that encourages people to play almost no functional public roles, only decorative or consumer ones" (Faludi 35). Both authors note that the crisis is, significantly, similar to the crisis women faced at the beginning of the feminist movement: "The fifties housewife, stripped of her connections to the wider world and invited to fill the void with shopping and the ornamental display of her ultra-femininity, could be said to have morphed into the nineties man, stripped of his connections to a wider world and invited to fill the void with consumption and a gym-bred display of his ultra-masculinity" (ibid., 40). Men, then, are being taught that "masculinity is something to drape over the body, not draw from inner resources" and that manhood is "displayed, not demonstrated" (ibid., 35). Significantly, masculinity is something that can be bought and paid for, if one only has the resources, as films such as *Fight Club* (1999) and *American Psycho* (2000) demonstrated.[1] Consumer capitalism courts these men relentlessly, convincing them that their very masculinity is threatened without an expensive, flashy car, designer clothes, perfect hair and skin, and a lavishly furnished apartment. If masculinity is a display, however, it is also vulnerable to being revealed as false; if it can be worn, it can also be stripped away, demonstrating the tenuousness of masculinity.

This is a danger that Neil LaBute frequently engages in his plays and film scripts through nasty, misogynistic characters who enact exaggerated performances of masculine virility counterbalanced by a barely subdued rage against women. These are men "striving to live up to impossible ideals of success leading to chronic terrors of emasculation, emotional emptiness, and a gendered rage that leave a wide swath of destruction in [their] wake" (Kimmel 134). In *In the Company of Men* (1997), *Your Friends and Neighbors* (1998), and *The Shape of Things* (2003), we have three films that literalize how the male body has become the focal point of cultural anxieties over the loss of masculine power. Thus, while their class position gives these men the time and freedom to worry obsessively about appearances, it has paradoxically emasculated them, revealing the performativity of masculinity (and, hence, its vulnerability). LaBute's films are both a response to cultural standards and expectations of masculinity and a critique of the way men (and women) respond to these often stereotypic expectations. The men in all three of these films are what Susan Bordo calls "sexually suspect."[2] This is, in part, because of their over-investment in how they look, but in LaBute, masculinity is also suspect when the ability to perform sexually is seriously questioned. Even more significant, homosexuality is the unnamed threat that seems to be coupled with this emasculation, suggested by a deliberate homoeroticism in the subtexts of all three films. The same thing Susan Bordo noted of many 1950s films seems to be true here: "the homosexual is invisible yet powerfully present—as the shadow of the straight man's sexuality, a constant unseen specter, alluded to through jokes and imitations, the figure against which the heroes must establish their difference" (155). In LaBute, this specter comes into clearer focus, however, and thus, the most "suspect" characters are often the ones who are the most successful sexually, while they are simultaneously virulently misogynistic. Women become the enemy to male bonding, one of the few arenas (even if it proves to be false) that men can collectively define what it means to be male. The men in these films demonstrate, I would argue, what Kimmel sees as the real threat to American masculinity, namely, the fear of other men, which is directly linked to homophobia: "Homophobia is the fear that the other men will unmask us, emasculate us, reveal to us and the world that we do not measure up, that we are not real men" (140). All three of these LaBute films show men whose deep fear of emasculation leads to sexism, homophobia, and violence.

In the Company of Men, the first film that LaBute wrote and directed, generated significant controversy when it was first released. Howard (Matt Malloy) and Chad (Aaron Eckhart) are businessmen who went to college together and who are feeling a sense of anxiety about their jobs and their relationships with women. Howard has recently been dumped by his fiancée, and (supposedly) Chad's girlfriend has also just left him. In the opening scene of the film, we see Howard in an airport bathroom looking into a mirror at a small cut on his ear, given, we later find out, when a woman hit him when he asked her the time. Chad is outraged by the "unprovoked assault," seeing it as evidence of a cultural assault on men in general: "We're doomed . . . as a race . . . men like us who care about the workplace, their women. We are doomed if this is how they are going to treat us." But this is a world, as Faludi points out, that no longer exists, and this is part of the problem for both men: manhood is a "performance game to be won in the marketplace, not the workplace" (37), and the women's movement has catapulted women into a position that does not require men to take care of them. More important, masculinity only has meaning as anti-femininity: "Masculine identity is born in the renunciation of the feminine, not in the direct affirmation of the masculine, which leaves masculine gender identity tenuous and fragile" (Kimmel 137). For Chad and Howard, then, the only way to assert their masculinity—their power—is an act of psychological violence.

Chad hatches a plan to restore their "dignity," one he imagines they will be able to laugh about for the rest of their lives. He and Howard have been sent to a company as consultants for six weeks, and Chad decides that they should both choose the same woman to seduce—someone who is "vulnerable as hell." They will wine and dine her and then, when she falls for them, they will hurt her by revealing the contest and the joke, destroying her. For Chad, women really are the threat to the "company of men" that he and Howard inhabit. He sees their game as a chance to take *action* together, rather than sitting in an airport "completely at the whim of those bastards upstairs," or waiting for younger men to try and take their jobs. As he asks Howard, "Life is for the taking, is it not?" Chad wants to control his environment, representing the "prevailing American image of masculinity": "A man is expected to prove himself not by being part of society but by being untouched by it, soaring above it. He is to travel unfettered, beyond society's clutches alone—making or breaking whatever or whoever crosses his path" (Faludi 10). Chad's control, however, is over those who are weaker and more vulnerable than he is. The very fact that he seems to need this game in the first place suggests that his masculinity is tenuous. Chad, then, is like the playground bully who must prove his masculinity by choosing an opponent he knows he can beat.

In each of the LaBute films discussed here, there is a character who is almost a parody of a misogynistic male. They usually do very well with women because of their good looks and fake charm, and yet their virility is quickly shown to be tenuous. These characters' reactions to females do not seem justified by their interactions with women. The womanizing becomes a screen for some kind of homosexual tendencies. At the very least, these men claim to be speaking out for and defending other men who have been mistreated by women. It is for these characters that homosocial bonding is most important. Male bonding, as Katherine Hyunmi Lee notes, "facilitate[s] identification and assuages anxieties by reifying and authenticating unstable and unreal heterosexist masculine ideals" (n.p.). Thus, men come together in groups to reassure each other that their version of masculinity is real.[3] In this film, Chad is constantly shown making sexist jokes and misogynistic comments to other men (usually at work), or trying to bond with his co-workers. Thus, he can joke with a co-worker about how much he hates a particular sales rep and then, when the co-worker leaves, immediately tell the others in the room that he thinks the man is a "prissy little cocksucker." For Chad, masculinity is a *homosocial* enactment, which, as Kimmel notes, is all about taking risks and performing feats so that other men will validate one's own masculinity (139). By calling his co-worker "prissy" and a "cocksucker," Chad is identifying himself in opposition to femininity and homosexuality.

Chad originally lies to Howard about the fact that his girlfriend, Suzanne, has left him, leaving him with a futon and his *American Gigolo* poster (minus the frame). The fact that Chad's prized possession is a poster of a 1980 film that focuses on Julian Kay (played by Richard Gere), a highly successful "escort" of older women, is not insignificant. In *American Gigolo*, Julian's job supports his expensive taste in cars and clothes and electronics. Like Julian, Chad turns out to be a hustler: he has no trouble convincing Christine (Stacy Edwards), the target of their game, that he is genuinely interested in her. Chad sees himself as being smarter than Julian, however, who is framed for a murder in the film. Chad himself becomes the "framer" by lying to Howard to get him to participate in the game, and later he betrays Howard by deliberately blowing a presentation to their boss. The other significant point about *American Gigolo* is that it was the first time that a Hollywood actor was shown fully frontally nude. Gere's body was an erotic, commodified spectacle in *American Gigolo*, and LaBute's film questions what Chad's real interest in the film might be, particularly given his voyeuristic proclivities.[4]

Later in the film, there is an even stronger suggestion that Chad has homoerotic feelings when he calls to his office one of the interns, a young African American male, on the pretext of disciplining him for his immature behavior with the other interns in the breakroom. He tells the intern, "You boys are sitting in the driver's seat. You're *in* with this company, but you're screwing around." Chad is referring to the corporation for which they work, but he is also referring to the broader meaning of the "company of men" in corporate America—a class-based homosocial bonding that Chad feels should be respected. Chad closes the blinds and then asks the man if he has balls: "You want a job like mine, you need the big brass ones for this task. You say that you've got them. Fine, let's see 'em then." The intern seems horrified, and Chad reassures him by saying, "I'm not a homo. I'm not going to leap across the table at you," and then, "That's what business is all about—who's carrying the nastiest sack of venom and who's willing to use it." When Chad reminds him that he is going to be making a recommendation for a manager-in-training program, the intern drops his pants and his boxer shorts. Chad stares for a few seconds at the man's crotch and then tells him, "Great . . . you feel okay? Then get me a cup of coffee before you take off. Black."[5] This is a scene about humiliation and power, but it is also about homosocial bonding. In Chad's understanding of a "company of men," it is about who has big balls, but it is also about *showing them,* both literally and metaphorically.

Chad and Howard do complete their contest with Christine, a deaf, temporary secretary in the office, and Chad even manages to have sex with her and gets her to say that she loves him. He is charming and attentive when he is with her, but he makes fun of her disability constantly when he is with his male buddies. As it turns out, Chad has also been manipulating Howard, who seems to need Chad's approval in order to let his own defenses down with Christine. When Chad tells Howard, "I could actually see myself with this person . . . she's definitely got something," he is doing it primarily to encourage Howard to amp up the competition. Howard mistakenly believes that they are fighting for Christine's affections and so sends Chad off to report to their boss on the project, staying behind so he can take Christine out on July 4 and get Chad out of the picture. The film strongly suggests that Chad is orchestrating the entire thing, however, to get the opportunity to advance himself at Howard's expense. Chad uses the opportunity to "lose" four pages of Howard's report, which eventually leads to Chad's promotion and Howard's demotion.

Howard does tell Christine the truth about the game eventually, but he does so only to hurt her when she refuses the engagement ring he has offered. Howard's own innate meanness and disrespect for Christine comes out here when she pushes the ring away: "You are fucking handicapped! Do you think you can *choose*?" Howard, at least, feels guilty. He shows up weeks later at Chad's apartment, telling him that he can't eat or sleep. When he finds out that Suzanne had never left Chad, Howard wants to know why Chad lied. Chad simply says, "Because I could."

At first, the film suggests that Chad has been rewarded for his cutthroat game. In Chad's mind, he has proven that he has balls because he will cut down anyone in his path to success in the company. Chad, however, is emotionally and psychologically barren. He has cheated on his girlfriend and lost Howard as a friend, and while his girlfriend might be performing oral sex on him in his last scene on-screen, he has been dehumanized to such a degree that his masculinity is hardly reassuring. His masculinity is tenuous, an "act" he will have to keep orchestrating if he is to survive.

Howard is even more pathetic because he feels some sense of guilt about what he and Chad have done, and he is essentially destroyed at the end of the film. After leaving Chad's apartment, Howard throws up in the hallway and then tracks Christine down at a new job in a bank. He walks over to her desk and starts yelling over and over, "Listen! Listen! Listen to me!" but in the closing scene, we see a point-of-view shot from

Christine's perspective. We see Howard yelling, but the film is silent, which is ultimately, I believe, a commentary on the emasculation of the American male.

In *Your Friends and Neighbors,* we see three men, Barry, Cary, and Jerry, all fighting to hold on to a sense of masculine identity.[6] All are professionals with good jobs, but they are having trouble finding (and maintaining) fulfilling personal and sexual relationships. For Barry and Jerry, good jobs and nice houses and clothes cannot mask their problems in the bedroom with their partners. Both men have literally "gone soft," represented by their flabby, overweight bodies and their sexual dysfunction. The third friend, Cary, is even more troubling; his sense of masculine identity seems to come in equal parts from his excessive misogyny and his over-investment in his tightly muscled body's ability to sexually perform. For all three friends, material possessions cannot mask the psychological emptiness of their lives; emasculation is the threat on the periphery of everything that they do and say. If masculinity is predominantly judged according to each man's ability to perform sexually (and it is by these three characters), they are not succeeding very well.

The opening shot of the film shows Cary (Jason Patric) from the waist up, bare-chested, sweating, and having sex, we assume, based on the things he is saying: "I feel special coming inside you. I'm always going to think of you as a very special fuck." Significantly, Cary stops speaking with the words "I only hope that I can . . ." and then he stands up, almost disgusted. As will become clear, this is not a line Cary wants to leave his lips. He is not one to question his ability, and he most definitely does not want to show any signs of weakness. As the camera pulls back, we see that he has a sheet wrapped around his waist but he also has pants on; he is leaning over the side of his bed. Cary's first reaction is to check his watch and to rewind the cassette recorder to make sure that it is getting his monologue. Even more significant, he is trying to decide whether or not it sounds convincing: "If I was a chick I'd believe that." He looks into a small standing mirror he has placed by the table, conveniently positioned for him to obsessively look at himself, and slaps his own face, saying, "Come on, let's pick up the pace. One more time before she gets here . . . ," and then returns to his position over the side of the bed. We will later see him sweating in the gym doing sit-ups and listening to the same cassette of himself pretending to have sex with someone. This sets the stage for the entire film: masculinity and heterosexual prowess need to be practiced and rehearsed to be convincing.

While on the surface Barry (Aaron Eckhart) seems to be the most traditional of the three friends, with a good corporate job, a wife, and a large house, he is the least successful sexually. As Cary makes clear, Barry has gone "soft" as a result of his marriage to Mary (Amy Brenneman); indeed, Barry is so "pathetic" that when asked by his friends about his "best lay," he responds unhesitatingly, "My wife," even though the audience knows that they are having significant problems. Barry works out with Cary, but he clearly does not have the same investment in developing his body, seeing the workout instead as an opportunity to socially bond with his friends. As Bordo notes, "To be exposed as 'soft' at the core is one of the worst things a man can suffer in this culture" (55). Barry's softness is physical, but it is also, as we find out, psychological, since he only wants to please his wife. Part of Barry's problem is that he doesn't recognize *why* this is a problem. Instead of *acting* sexually, Barry and Mary are clearly spending a lot of time looking at sexual advice books.

Barry has his own degree of narcissism, as we see when he tells a co-worker that the "best lay" he has ever had is not his wife but himself: "Nobody gives me more pleasure than I give myself. . . . Nobody makes me come the way I do." Barry has failed according to masculine heterosexist paradigms because his sexual virility has turned in upon itself. Part of the reason he likes masturbation is because there is no demand or expectation of performance. We find out early on that Barry and his wife are having sexual problems. We see him in bed with Mary, unable to perform and asking, "I'm sorry . . . is it me? I've just had a bad go of it." The scene suggests that part of the problem may be the control that Barry has given to his wife to dictate the sexual positions they will try: "Do you really like this . . . sidesaddle thing? I bet Adam and Eve from the Old Testament never did it on their side. It's just not natural." His wife, however, will not reassure him and just turns away from him. Barry pleads, "We could start again; I'm still quite hard," but Mary refuses, making Barry feel impotent. In the next scene, Barry is masturbating beside his sleeping wife, clearly illustrating his sexual incompetence.

When the film opens, Barry and Mary have just recently bought a large house, which they have filled with nice furniture. Part of Barry's problem is that he doesn't know how to fulfill his wife, other than to buy her gifts. In one of the opening scenes, when he and Mary invite Jerry (Ben Stiller) and Terri (Catherine Keener) over for dinner, Barry makes a display of handing Mary a gift. This is obviously something they have discussed because Mary seems put off, saying, "I thought we agreed . . ." The gift has been given in front of an audience, however, so Mary just says, "He likes to spoil me." Inside the box is a lovely antique watch that no longer works, which Jerry starts to question, essentially noting its uselessness if it can't tell time. The watch, of course, is symbolic of the relationship, since the watch is "for show" only—it has no utilitarian value (much like Barry and Mary's marriage).

The film strongly suggests that Barry has allowed himself to be overtaken by consumerism, and it is one that seems largely directed by his wife. In one scene, when Barry is going to meet Cary, we see him in his large walk-in closet asking his wife's advice on which color polo shirt to wear, holding up a pink and a green one: "Should I go for . . . what is this? Loden?" Mary, who is on the phone with Jerry planning a sexual rendezvous, advises him to wear the salmon one. When Barry meets Cary at the bar, Cary's first mocking question is, "What is that? *Pink*?" Barry corrects him, saying, "It's salmon." Cary rolls his eyes and tells Barry to put his jacket back on, asking, "Where'd you get it?" When Barry answers, "My wife," Cary sneers: "Enough said." For Cary, Barry's wearing a pink shirt given to him by his wife is a definitive commentary on Barry's emasculation, and the fact that Barry calls it "salmon" rather than "pink" shows he is a lost cause. Cary represents the judge of the other men in the film, constantly scrutinizing what Barry and Jerry wear and what they say and mocking them for their frailties.

The film suggests that submission to domestication might be the explanation for Barry's inability to have sex with his wife. One day in the grocery store (and even here, the film asks exactly why Barry would be accompanying Mary), Barry can't stop talking about their sex problems: "We need to just do it . . . not make it so special." Mary is embarrassed, but Barry persists: "For right now, we need to treat each other like meat. Didn't we read that? You need to see me as a big . . . a penis. You need to be just this huge vagina." He takes his wife to a hotel one night to try and jump-start their sex life, and again, he fails to keep his erection. Unbeknown to him, it is the same hotel room to which his friend Jerry had taken Mary when they had an affair. Jerry later tells Mary that he deliberately recommended the hotel to Barry because he felt jealous, because he wanted to "be there *first*." As in *In the Company of Men*, the woman is beside the point; the competition is really between Jerry and Barry.

Jerry, played by Ben Stiller, is also having a hard time feeling masculine, given his relationship with Terri (Catherine Keener). The film sets us up to be almost sympathetic for him, when we see him with his shrill and demanding girlfriend, who is described by Cary as "just a touch unfeminine." Terri is beautiful, but she is very thin with small breasts and no hips, which makes her a target for the film's female bashing. She and Jerry fight a lot, and they are also having problems in the bedroom. In one of their first scenes together, Jerry is having sex with Terri, and she gets frustrated with his verbalization of his feelings, saying, "I'm losing a sense of concentration. I don't need the narration—it's not a travelogue." This has obviously been an ongoing debate, and Jerry is furious: "I'm sick of it. I'll talk as much as I like." This is not, however, an option Jerry has, because as Terri tells him, "You won't be fucking me then," a threat she enacts in the next scene by beginning a relationship with Cheri (Nastassja Kinski).

Jerry is the character who seems the most vulnerable of the three male friends because his girlfriend is leaving him for another woman. In the final breakup scene with Terri, he keeps asking her why she is leaving, and Terri gives the final blow to Jerry's ego: "Why do you find it so hard to fathom that I'd want to be with a woman? I mean, I wanted to be with you . . . now I want to be with her; that's all." The fact that Jerry can be so easily exchanged for a woman is an indictment of his masculinity.

While Terri is perhaps blamed for emasculating Jerry, he clearly has to work a little too hard with his nonstop chattering, narcissistically wanting to hear his own voice-over in their lovemaking. It sounds forced and contrived, and the audience can't really blame Terri for getting sick of it. Jerry's need to talk about things—processing them and analyzing them—suggests his feminization, while for Terri, "Fucking is fucking . . . it's not a time for sharing," a far more stereotypic male response. For Jerry, however, fucking is all about *performing*, which he makes clear in one of his acting demonstrations with his students, and the way each word is said, the way it is timed and inflected, will change the meaning of the scene. Each of the men in the film understands this well.

We don't see Jerry with a lot of material possessions, but he still seems to have an over-investment in them. Jerry gets very upset when Terri accidentally splashes his jacket because it's made of doe skin (in LaBute, nothing is insignificant). Terri calls attention to Jerry's distress over the coat, and when he says he needs to go to the bathroom before leaving Barry and Mary's, she mocks him, saying, "Careful not to splash. Remember, it's doe skin." The next scene shows Jerry returning to the house to get Mary's phone number so that they can get together romantically, but Jerry has shown himself to be so fastidious that the audience can anticipate his eventual failure with Mary.

Jerry's problems in the bedroom are even more exacerbated when he tries to start the affair with Mary. Again, the film suggests that the affair is as much about his own feelings of inadequacy as it is about his attraction to Mary. He keeps babbling in the hotel lobby about how "optimistic" he feels until Mary asks him to stop "going over it" so much. LaBute then cuts to the hotel room where Mary is sitting up in bed in disbelief, while off-camera we hear Jerry saying, "It's never been like this ... never. This is not me. I'm much more hard ... or firm than this." His insecure questions sound exactly like Barry: "Do you feel that it was me?" Jerry doesn't want to risk having it happen again, however, and tells her, "We haven't really made a mistake yet. We'll still be good friends," while Mary, with obvious disgust, just asks him to leave. Mary has clearly agreed to the rendezvous because of her husband's sexual problem, and to have Barry replicate the problem is more than she can take. Mary is the commodity exchanged among all three of the friends, and she represents a feminine threat in her expectations. Mary seems to be torn between two impulses: the desire to be with a man who can sexually "perform," and the desire for emotional attention, evidenced when she asks all three men, "Just hold me." When both Jerry and Barry are left impotent at the end of the film (Jerry fails with his student, and Barry can't keep an erection while masturbating), the suggestion is that Mary has been too demanding—she wanted too much from them. The film suggests, then, that in allowing themselves to express their feelings, Jerry and Barry have become "sissies"; therefore, they don't deserve the ultimate "prize" that will eventually be taken by Cary.

Cary is the most interesting of the three friends, and he is almost a caricature of masculinity. He clearly manages to date lots of women, but they are rarely seen in the film, and then only in single brief glimpses. Cary clearly devotes a lot of time to working out, and he seems somewhat obsessive about it. This may reflect Bordo's point that, among gay men, an interest in muscles is "about dispelling homosexual stereotypes, by embodying an ideal of masculinity which announces that one is a real man whether one is a 'top' or a 'bottom'" (58). Cary is a complicated character in the film because, while he is depicted as a womanizer, there are also several hints that he might be deliberately performing an exaggerated heterosexuality to belie a homosexual identity.

Cary gets lots of women, but he also seems to have a genuine dislike for them, bordering on hatred. He demonstrates this to Barry over a beer one night when he describes a co-worker who questioned his authority in front of other people. His "revenge" was to have a "complete revenge fuck," which he describes in detail: "I slipped my cock out, completely jerked it right out, turned her over kind of rough by the hair" and then told her, "Get the fuck out of my place." Cary sees himself as somehow sticking up for men in general: "I told her if she ever crosses *one of us* like that in public—I'll fucking kill her. . . . I think she believed me" (emphasis mine). Cary also describes getting revenge on a woman who broke up with him by getting a piece of medical letterhead and sending her a letter saying she had been identified as the partner of a man who was HIV positive.

Cary's career is a bit unclear, but the film suggests that he works in a gynecology office of some kind, although we never see him with a patient. In the only scene showing him at work, Cary is playing with the clitoris of a half-section medical model. Significantly, he is talking on the phone at this point, trying to set up a date through a friend with a woman who has gone to Harvard Medical School. When Cary asks, "What's her name? Tits like that must have a name," the scene becomes about his genuine fear of women biologically and psychologically. At the end of the scene, Cary pulls out the model baby from the uterus and, after a brief consideration, kicks it across the office like a football. Even Cary's anger, however, is somewhat suspect. As Susan Faludi notes in *Stiffed*, part of the contemporary performance of masculinity includes male anger: "An ornamental culture encouraged young men to see surliness, hostility and violence as expressions of glamour, a way to showcase themselves without being feminized before an otherwise potentially girlish mirror" (37). Most of his anger is directed toward women, but it seems part of his act, one that allows him to constantly have stories for his friends (particularly Barry) to take vicarious pleasure in.

Cary's misogyny is shown explicitly in the film on several occasions. In an early scene, he is in his darkened apartment, jiggling the bathroom door handle and yelling: "You're a tramp! Who *in the fuck* just gets her period all of a sudden . . . and all over my bedding?" Despite his supposed experience with women and (perhaps) his medical training, Cary seems ignorant about their bodies and completely unsympathetic to his partner's inability to control the timing of when she gets her period: "I hope you have a red biohazard bag because you just bought yourself a set of linens—380-thread count!" The camera cuts away only once to a few seconds of a naked blonde woman curled into a ball on top of a toilet, crying as he yells through the door and tries to open it: "Are you feeling sick? Crampy? Try shoving two aspirins up your crack and never, *ever* call me in the morning! I'm going down to grab a beer . . . be gone when I come back." Despite his threatening anger, there is a sense that Cary also has been emasculated by his possessions: referring to his sheets as "linens" and talking precisely about the thread count suggest he might be more invested in his material possessions than he lets on.

Cary seems to be trying to distance himself from a certain kind of masculinity that he recognizes (and, the film suggests, perhaps rightly so) as weak. Cary is the one of the friends who recognizes the value of homosocial bonding, and he actively seeks it out with his two friends. The film never really shows him with a woman, and he never enters into the lives of Barry and Jerry, even though he obviously knows Mary and Terri. He also is the one who "stands up" to the women in the film in what he believes is a defense of his friends and men in general. When he complains to Barry that Jerry isn't calling him any more, Cary blames Terri. Barry asks, "What are you gonna do?" It's a rhetorical question, but Cary decides to act upon it by tracking Terri down at a bookstore and trying to get her to come out for coffee with him. Terri says no, but then she gets angry when Cary is insistent. He corners her in an aisle of the bookstore and says, "You're a real piece of work. I don't get your kind. You give my friend nothing but grief, always coming across like some dyke bitch." He then threatens her: "You keep dicking around the people I know, I'm going to find you and knock you on your ass. You are a useless cunt." Cary walks casually away, but Terri is visibly shaken, standing in the bookstore with tears in her eyes.

We see a somewhat tamer scene when Cary is outside the bathroom door (again), asking his date if she is using his toiletries, although it also calls into question his masculinity. When he hears the toilet flush, he walks to the door in his Calvin Klein underwear, adjusts his penis, and glances at himself in the mirror (the same one in which he had checked himself in the first scene of the movie, when he was practicing his sexual virility). He says through the door, "If you use any towels in there . . . it's a health thing strictly . . . set anything you do use off to one side. I gotta do wash anyway." Again, this fastidiousness becomes even more suspect since we haven't actually *seen* Cary with a woman, but only have seen him talking through locked bathroom doors.

Cary seems to be trying to perform against this stereotype, however, by working out in a small, run-down high school gym because he doesn't want to work out with "those office assholes downtown." He tells Barry that, even though he knows it's a "fucked place to exercise," he does it "to spite them." The question is, *whom* is he really trying to spite? Part of the appeal of the old gym seems to be precisely *because* it does not have women working out there; he is far more interested in jokingly wrestling with Barry over the soap in the shower, a scene which resonates very differently when Cary recounts a childhood shower scene later in the film.

Cary is so narcissistic that he can reminisce about how he and his teenage friends gang-raped a young boy and insist that he and the boy, Timmy, shared an important bond at that moment. He describes this scene in the sauna one afternoon with Barry and Jerry when they ask each other to describe their "best fuck." Cary doesn't seem to have a fear of being perceived as homosexual, however, because he goes into graphic detail: "It was *nice*. It's never been like that with a woman, not even close. Timmy and I are making love like we're on some beach on the Mediterranean. It was amazing." Cary goes on to describe Timmy dropping out of school: "He never turned us in. I admired him for that. The reason he kept silent . . . is that he felt something special as well. Him and me."

The film suggests, however, that Cary is the only male character who has retained his masculinity because he ends up with Mary, Barry's wife, and he is the only one who has been able to sexually perform with her. Mary is far from satisfied, which is suggested when Cary asks her why she cries every time he tries to touch her, but the difference between him and the other men is that Cary really doesn't care. When he asks Mary the same question that Barry and Jerry had previously asked, "Is it me?" he immediately says, "I don't think so," without waiting for her to answer. As with the other two men, Mary asks if he will just hold her, but Cary makes it clear that, while he will give her a few minutes, "We will fuck tonight." It also is made clear in this scene that Cary doesn't want to miss an opportunity to have sex because, in a few more months, it's not going to be so easy, which suggests that Mary is pregnant. Cary, then, has effected the best performance, so his reward is the ownership of Mary's body.

The Shape of Things is set on a college campus, and even here, as LaBute makes clear, American males are facing a crisis of masculinity. Adam (Paul Rudd) is another character who lacks a masculine capability to deal with women. He also lacks the right "look"; he is overweight, with disheveled hair and unflattering glasses, and he wears a worn, brown corduroy jacket. As will become clear throughout the film, Adam's insecurities as a male have everything to do with his bodily insecurities. *The Shape of Things* complicates this, however, by suggesting that Evelyn emasculates Adam at the same time that she transforms him into a more sexually appealing man; he literally becomes a commodity.

Significantly, Adam meets Evelyn (Rachel Weisz) when she is in the museum where he works as she is threatening to paint a "big dick" on a statue of God that has been covered over with a plaster leaf to appease people in the community. Adam immediately shows his masculine weakness because, despite being in a position of authority as a museum security guard, he doesn't want to confront Evelyn and asks her to wait until the next shift comes on duty. As it turns out, this weakness is precisely what Evelyn needs to effect a dramatic change on Adam, whom she has been studying and planning to manipulate. Evelyn starts out seemingly innocently with her "project" by telling Adam that she thinks he is cute— he needs work but he's "definitely cute." This validation is enough to embolden Adam to ask Evelyn out on a date, to which she agrees. In the next scene, Adam is already starting to look noticeably different; his hair is better and he is losing weight.

Adam is still rather insecure at this point, however, and before Phillip (Fred Weller) and Jenny (Gretchen Mol) get there, he asks Evelyn, "Why would you like *me*? I'm not anything." Evelyn is disgusted: "That's the only thing I don't like—the fucking insecurities." As it will turn out, of course, all of Evelyn's feelings for Adam are false. By halfway through the film, Evelyn literally makes Adam into a new person. He slims down, has plastic surgery, and changes his wardrobe to include designer labels in more appealing colors, as Evelyn tries to "help" Adam see the connection between his sexuality and his visual appearance. The film still questions Adam's abilities as a lover, however. He is not particularly adventurous; twice in the film, Evelyn tries to get him to have sex with her in a bathroom, and both times he refuses. In one scene, when Adam and Evelyn are talking intimately in bed, Adam admits that he has not had much experience with women, and Evelyn says that she could "kind of tell," making him further sexually suspect. As in *In the Company of Men* and *Your Friends and Neighbors,* masculinity is tied to sexuality. Failure in this arena will "de-sex the man, make him appear as not fully a man. He will be seen as a wimp, a Mama's boy, a sissy" (Kimmel 137). This is also demonstrated when Evelyn performs oral sex on Adam in front of a video camera, a virtual "judge" of Adam's sexual inabilities.

Adam is commodified by allowing Evelyn not only to change his wardrobe but to physically change the contours of his body; she gets him to wear contacts and he stops biting his fingernails. Adam has also voluntarily gotten a tattoo of Evelyn's initials, E.A.T., on his hip, near his groin. The symbolism is fairly obvious here, but the threat is not just that Evelyn is eating into his flesh, but that she is eating away at his masculinity since he seems to have so little control over the changes she is having him make. Adam seems less certain about cosmetic surgery, but Evelyn convinces him that he should have the end of his nose cut and altered; she reassures him by saying, "Lots of guys do it." Cosmetic surgery is one of the arenas that contemporary men have bought into, and it allows them to perform a different kind of masculinity: it's become far more socially acceptable to be vain about appearance, and having the ability to alter the body points to a class privilege that is part of the male "package" as well. Adam seems more concerned about how he will be judged by his friend Phillip, however.

Phillip *does* notice Adam's change immediately: "What's up with you? Did you lose weight?" As will become clear throughout the film, Phillip seems to care a little too much about Adam's physical changes. Phillip's fiancée, Jenny, is the object of exchange between them, and Phillip continually draws attention to her by saying, "This could have been yours." Like in the other two films, Jenny is really the third side of the triangle, allowing Phillip and Adam to interact. We find out that Adam used to have a crush on Jenny, but he never got up the courage to ask her out, a point in which Phillip seems to take great satisfaction. Evelyn offers a toast to Phillip and Jenny for deciding to have an unconventional wedding by saying, "To people with balls," which Phillip follows with his own toast: "To balls, long may they wave." A little later, when they are talking about the defacement of the statue on campus, Jenny whispers the word "penis." When Evelyn asks why they are whispering, Phillip starts to sing, loudly, saying that in *his* apartment, they can say it as loudly as they want: "Penis! Penis! Penis!" In some ways, Phillip is like an adolescent boy who both wants to shock the women in the room and also remind them who's in charge. Of course, this scene also points to the power that Evelyn has appropriated—unlike Jenny, she can use the words "penis" and "balls" without embarrassment, and her painting of a penis on the statue of God was meant to divest the statue of its symbolic phallic power by putting it right out there for all to see. And this might be why Phillip seems so personally offended by what he sees as vandalism in the museum.

In *The Shape of Things*, Phillip functions as the hypermasculinized male watching and judging Adam's transformation. He shares many of Cary's characteristics: he is handsome, well dressed, with a biting wit. He is also performing, however, as suggested by the sunglasses he wears on his head at all times of the day. He is not as explicitly misogynistic as Cary, although we find out that he has cheated on Jenny at least once before. When Evelyn gets angry at him for cutting Jenny off and not letting her speak, or when he refuses to listen to Evelyn's alternative explanation for why someone might have defaced the statue, his way of putting Evelyn back in her place is to ask Adam, "Which Take Back the Night Rally did you find her at?" If masculinity is defined by the "repudiation of femininity," as Kimmel (136) suggests, Evelyn's behavior threatens Phillip on some deep, fundamental level.

There is also a sense with Phillip that his interest in Adam is a bit too intense, according to a heterosexist script. He seems jealous of the attention Adam is paying to Evelyn, a jealousy which seeps out during one of the first times Evelyn and Adam double-date with Jenny and Phillip. Evelyn comes to his apartment and somehow the conversation turns to the defacement of the statue on campus, and Phillip and Evelyn start to fight. When Adam tries to come to Evelyn's defense, Phillip asks angrily, "Did she give you a blow job and a hair cut, and now you're her puppy?"

Phillip seems threatened by Adam's transformation partly because Evelyn's intrusion into their lives breaks up the erotic triangle among him, Jenny, and Adam. He mocks Adam's changes, and in fact, seems to get genuinely angry with the changes that Evelyn has been able to effect. He is particularly judgmental of Adam's cosmetic surgery. When Phillip sees Adam one day with a big bandage across his nose, he starts goading him: "What'd you do?" When Adam insists that he fell, Phillip keeps pushing: "I saw your girlfriend. She said you were recovering from an operation—some *procedure* you had done." Adam won't admit the truth, however, and just keeps saying that he fell. It is interesting that this is the moment when Phillip decides to confront Adam about kissing Jenny. Phillip seems unconcerned about this kiss and blames himself: "It's all right. I'd been acting weird lately. This whole marriage idea." He also says something strange at this point: "It's no big deal. Better than me having to kiss you," to which Adam responds, laughing, "No kidding." This is meant to be a joke, presumably, but it doesn't make sense within the context of the conversation.

When Phillip realizes that Adam has discarded his corduroy jacket for a light-colored, reversible Tommy Hilfiger designer coat, this pushes him over the edge: "I begged you to throw it out. . . . you lost both of us a lot of dates with that thing on." Obviously, Phillip's reaction is not about missed opportunities, but the fact that Evelyn has more control over Adam than Phillip was able to have when they were roommates. He also seems to want to rise up against Adam's willingness to let his very identity be manipulated by Evelyn. Even though Adam gives Phillip up as a friend at Evelyn's insistence, Phillip is vindicated at the end when Evelyn reveals her game: her performance art project which has involved her "sculpting" of a real human being.

While Adam is emasculated by Evelyn, he is paradoxically empowered to be more of a man in the contemporary consumerized landscape. Jenny, who has initially deflected her attention to Phillip, actually seduces Adam one afternoon, telling him he's a "totally hot guy now." They kiss, and the film strongly suggests that they have sex. Even after Evelyn humiliates Adam at the art show when she reveals that her project has been Adam, when we see the side-by-side before and after posters of Adam, the audience is reminded that Adam *is* better off on some level. His looks will allow him to compete in the marketplace more effectively for jobs and, particularly, for women. Ultimately, however, it is Evelyn who has won the contest: she remains unapologetic, she has completed her thesis project, and she has humiliated Adam to such a degree that presumably he will never recover from this public emasculation.

The question that is frequently raised in critical discussions of LaBute is whether his films and plays *are* misogynistic or if they are *about* misogyny. There is no simple answer to this question, but I would argue that these three films ally themselves with the male characters at the end, stopping short of any real criticism of the sexism and homophobia that prop up these characters' tenuous relationship to their own masculinity. If we walk away from *In the Company of Men* or *Your Friends and Neighbors* thinking that Chad and Cary are despicable for their actions, LaBute also wants us to believe that they are victims of the cultural definition of manhood, which constantly asks men for proof of their masculinity. Both become the schoolyard bully who succeeds by choosing opponents who are weaker than he is (Kimmel 138); there is no doubt that both men will successfully do the same again. If we are to equate manhood with power, both of these characters do have the power at the end. Chad has played his game and walked away without any sense of guilt or responsibility. He has the girlfriend waiting for him in bed in the beautiful apartment, he has the job, and he has a secure sense of his own masculinity. Cary is the same; he wins the competition by impregnating Mary, and his confidence in his own ability to sexually perform has not been challenged.

Adam's problem in *The Shape of Things* is that he did *not* participate in the homosocial arena in which Phillip tried to involve him. Rather than competing with Phillip for Jenny initially, he capitulated and walked away from his own pursuit. Even though he may have had sex with Jenny, she remains with Phillip at the end of the film. Adam made himself vulnerable to destruction at Evelyn's hands because he wasn't trying to prove his masculinity at all, because he was not afraid of appearing as a sissy. Instead, he gave in to consumption masculinity, believing that, if he could improve his outward appearance, his masculinity would be confirmed. He made a grave error, however, and the film suggests he has to pay the price. As Jay Clarkson has noted, "Some critics claim that the blurring of gay and straight by the evolving metrosexual consumer masculinity is a symptom of the current crisis of American masculinity" (244). LaBute, I would argue, completely agrees with this assessment. Adam becomes not a "victim of oppressive male socialization" (Kimmel 146), but a victim of his own refusal to be a man. If, as Kimmel notes, "the willingness to fight" and "the desire to fight" are the key markers of masculinity (141), LaBute's films suggest that men better keep on fighting. The culturally entrenched definitions of hegemonic masculinity remain alive and well in these films, and the sexism and homophobia that accompany them remain a small price to pay for men to stay on top.

NOTES

1. And films such as *Fight Club* and *American Psycho* also demonstrate that the pressure to be a *real* man can be too much for the already fragile masculine ego, and the characters in both films literally go insane trying to live up to an ideal.

2. Bordo notes that gender differences dictate visual instructions: "Women are supposed to care very much about fashion, 'vanity,' looking good, and may be seen as unfeminine, man-hating, or lesbian if they don't. The reverse goes for men. The man who cares about his looks the way a woman does, self-esteem on the line, ready to be shattered at the slightest insult or weight gain, is unmanly, sexually suspect" (200).

3. Eve Kosofsky Sedgwick's seminal introduction to *Between Men* can be helpful here because, while *homosocial* is distinct from *homosexual*, there is a continuum between the two; at the same time, homosocial bonding actually supports heterosexist patriarchy.

4. As Susan Bordo notes of *American Gigolo* in *The Male Body*, straight masculinity usually has to be protected on-screen:

> In every film in which the hero treads just a little too close to what straight audiences might identify as the gay man's world—*American Gigolo*, for example (1980), in which Richard Gere plays a narcissistic male prostitute—extra insure [*sic*] is required to make sure that audiences don't get confused. That might mean making the characters ostentatiously heterosexist—in one scene, gigolo Julian Kay[e] (Gere) says he "doesn't do fags." It may also mean trotting out the stereotypes to do some work. So, in another scene, Gere—trying to protect the reputation of his rich "date" when her friend spies them at an antique store—minces, lisps, and swishes, pretending he is her gay male companion. The pretense establishes not only that Julian's "reality" is straight but that his own attitude toward homosexuality is safely condescending. (157)

5. LaBute himself was surprised by this scene, as he explained in a *Salon* interview by Jennie Yabroff: "So I tried to constantly surprise myself as I was writing it, to keep myself engaged. The intern scene (where Chad forces a young intern to lower his pants), for instance, doesn't really propel the plot, but it adds a certain life. I didn't plan it being in the script, but I'm glad it's there."

6. While the characters are named in this analysis, and they are identified in the film script, not once are the characters named in the film.

BIBLIOGRAPHY

Bordo, Susan. *The Male Body: A New Look at Men in Public and Private*. New York: Farrar, Straus and Giroux, 1999.

Clarkson, Jay. "Contesting Masculinity's Makeover: *Queer Eye*, Consumer Masculinity, and 'Straight-Acting' Gays." *Journal of Communication Inquiry* 29, no. 3 (July 2005): 235–255.

Faludi, Susan. *Stiffed: The Betrayal of the American Man*. New York: Morrow, 1999.

In the Company of Men. Dir. Neil LaBute. Alliance Atlantis, 1997.

Kimmel, Michael S. "Masculinity as Homophobia: Fear, Shame, and Silence in the Construction of Gender Identity." In *The Social Construction of Difference and Inequality*, 4th ed., ed. Tracy Ore, 132–148. New York: McGraw-Hill, 2008.

Lee, Katherine Hyunmi. "The Ghost of Gary Cooper: Masculinity, Homosocial Bonding and *The Sopranos*. Feminist Television Studies: The Case of HBO." *Scholar & Feminist Online* 3, no. 1 (2004). http:www.barnard.edu/sfonline/hbo/lee_03.htm.

Sedgwick, Eve Kosofsky. "Introduction from *Between Men*." In *Feminisms: An Anthology of Literary Theory and Criticism*, ed. Robyn R. Warhol and Diane Price Herndl. New Brunswick, N.J.: Rutgers University Press, 1991.

The Shape of Things. Dir. Neil LaBute. Mepris Films, 2003.

Yabroff, Jennie. "Playing the Game." *Salon*. http://www.salon.com/aug97/entertainment/labute970801.html.

Your Friends and Neighbors. Dir. Neil LaBute. Polygram, 1998.

THREE

THE MIGHT OF THE METROSEXUAL: HOW A MERE MARKETING TOOL CHALLENGES HEGEMONIC MASCULINITY

MARGARET C. ERVIN

"This shaving gel is great because you don't have to keep applying it. And playing baseball outside a lot, I need protection from the sun. I had never used any SPF before, so it's something I pay more attention to now."[1] This is what Derek Jeter, shortstop and team captain for the New York Yankees, had to say in 2007 about the new skin care regimen he embarked on after signing a contract with Avon to promote Driven, his signature fragrance and line of skin care products. He described his teammates as simultaneously mocking him for promoting Avon and asking him for samples of the company's products. In the way Jeter took care to distance himself from too much concern over his appearance, insisting that he was, as Avon wanted him to be, an "average guy" (that is, heterosexual guy) who just needed to look good, he could be said to have marked himself as metrosexual. This metrosexual marketing campaign was a big success for Avon. After introducing the Jeter line in 2007, Avon capitalized on the success of the metrosexual angle by launching a fleet of hyper-heterosexually endorsed fragrances, including a Patrick Dempsey (aka *Grey's Anatomy's* McDreamy) Unscripted line of products in 2008 and a Matt Miller Ironman line in 2009.[2]

The term *metrosexual* denotes a straight man with some stereotypically feminine traits, such as taste in grooming and culture. Though the term was first used with intended irony in the 1990s,[3] it subsequently was taken up quite seriously in the popular press, both by those sympathetic to the concept and by those who saw metrosexuality as a threat to the natural order. In the former category, for example, were those who claimed that metrosexuality was the future of masculinity and that it broke a barrier between straight and gay men.[4] In the latter category were those who, starting in about 2004, began claiming that the fad was over and that women wanted more "traditional," manly men.[5]

A more scholarly reading of the metrosexual phenomenon is that it does not necessarily have any effects but is a reflection of changes that are taking place in society. Sociologist Toby Miller theorizes that the phenomenon of metrosexuality reflects a "historical shift that recodes the male body," which has been brought on, for example, by increasing pressure on men to look young and fit in order to stay employed.[6] Katherine Sender, in reading *Queer Eye for the Straight Guy*, remarks upon the same phenomenon. The show seems to mock the gay makeover team, the Fab Five, but she argues that "the show's joke is on its makeover candidates: now straight white guys have to work harder, in the ways women and gay men have had to work, in order to get and keep their mate, their job, their class position."[7] Metrosexuality is thus a bellwether for the changing socioeconomic position of traditionally privileged straight, white men. Sender further argues that men are being enlisted as consumers in the neoliberal project, which is the "willing participation of citizens in the generation of capital."[8] Men earn their keep, so this theory has it, by buying products and doing their part to keep the capitalist economy in motion.

If metrosexualizing men is about generating capital, it should come as no surprise that most numerous in the metrosexual-enthusiast category in the first few years of the twenty-first century were marketers who eagerly tested for their existence and found that a straight male demographic does exist for items such as high-priced hair products. The term *metrosexual* was later said to fall out of fashion. As one industry reporter put it in 2007, it "died a long, lingering (merciful) death." Yet the same reporter went on to say, "Some of its ideologies still live on, specifically in the form of antiaging products for men."[9] For marketers, even after what some claimed to be the death of the metrosexual, there continued to be a winning tie-in between sports stars and grooming products. Examples of metrosexual sports models, in addition to Derek Jeter and the other Avon men, are Brian Vickers, NASCAR driver, selling Garnier Fructis hair care products; David Beckham, British soccer star, with his own signature fragrance, Instinct; and Andre Agassi, tennis star, promoting Aramis Life. In Jeter's case, the ad campaign featured a website with images of him on a photo shoot for the print ads and a section titled "Meet Derek" that described his "ambition, courage, and passion."[10] The intended audience in these advertisements is not solely women. According to Avon, the company expected to sell directly to men[11] as well as to women shopping for men. The notion of the passionate warrior may have been a fantasy targeted at women buyers, but Jeter's "regular guy" credentials were also counted on to sell the products to men. Men who are Yankee fans are also fans of the team's clean-cut image, and Jeter says Avon is the way to get that look.[12] Thus, metrosexuality did its work in broadening the range of consumer products men were responsible for buying. Beyond grills and cars, the metrosexual sports model lengthens men's shopping lists to include SPF moisturizers and expensive shaving creams. Industry reporters in 2007 cited market analysts who projected that "the $5 billion industry could double in the next two years. It's clear from the big names among the winner's circle—Redken, Clarins, and Clinique, to name a few—that the men's grooming market is being taken seriously."[13] In this way, while some claimed the metrosexual fad was over, the fashion industry raked in billions from metrosexual consumers.

Metrosexuality, often perceived as the queering of regular guys, continues to have an impact, whether or not the term itself is considered fashionable or current. Perceiving the metrosexual as a mockery or threat to "real" masculinity, some have tried to put the notion to rest, but the advent of the metrosexual heralds a very real change in the social construction of masculinity. It isn't just that the concept is useful in furthering the neoliberal project, as Sender eloquently argues, the metrosexual also furthers the wide acceptance of gender as performance and drives a wedge between the notions of sexuality and the "true" self. The more reactionary responses there are to the metrosexual, the more this effect is realized. Attempts to legislate the demise of the metrosexual only serve as markers to locate it. Negation demonstrates presence. Similarly, as social historians search court records for evidence of the lives of people who did not write and were not written about, they look for legislation about those groups and prosecution of those laws. Homosexuality in Puritan New England has been studied through laws and court records. The strongest evidence for what was happening is what was forbidden to happen.[14] Metrosexuality may be a trivial and flippant notion, merely denoting a change in the buying patterns of an already privileged and dominant class, but in the way people have reacted to metrosexuality, it is apparent that metrosexuality is viewed as similarly transgressive and threatening as homosexuality. In this way, what began as a fashion and marketing phenomenon became an oddly powerful and subversive force that may even mark a permanent change in the way we treat and view male sexuality and identity. The more referendums and marketing surveys there are on masculinity, the more what sociologist R. W. Connell calls "hegemonic masculinity" is challenged. In this roundabout way, the heralds of metrosexuality as a subversive arrival are correct.

THE RISE AND FALL OF THE METROSEXUAL

In 2006, *Good Morning America* aired a segment reporting the demise of the metrosexual,[15] but even as the text posted on its website reported that metrosexuality is over, it suggested, consistent with Miller's and Sender's theses, that the phenomenon is based on an actual shift in the perceived role and position of men in U.S. society: real fears and obsessions about masculinity that govern actions, including buying patterns. The reporters describe a study that was conducted to determine men's needs and attitudes, a study that is claimed to be "global" and therefore representative of an essentialized male reality:

> Leo Burnett, a Chicago advertising firm, conducted a global study of masculinity last year, which found [that] half of men say their role in society is unclear and that they feel "less dominant" than in previous decades. More than 70 percent of men said advertising was out of touch with men's "reality," leading company executive Rose Cameron to recommend that advertisers "reassure men of their masculinity."[16]

The marketers react to the survey by assuming that men need to be "reassured" of their masculinity, clearly read as the dominance that mean perceive as lost. The survey does not report that men feel they have lost their masculinity, but the PR industry, seeing a vulnerability or anxiety that can be exploited, advises advertisers to reassure men. An example of an advertising campaign that does this well is a beer commercial in which men sit around making "man laws" and reassuring themselves of their masculinity.[17]

The backlash following the 2000–2004 hype about metrosexuality in popular culture is exemplified by the *Good Morning America* segment. Sometimes, this backlash exceeded the inconsequential realm of marketing and fashion. Anti-metrosexual stories even made headline news. One of the first counter-metrosexual responses was a marketing survey by Dodge trucks conducted in 2005 to prove that women prefer regular truck-buying guys to fashion-conscious metrosexual guys ("Texas Man"). In a Harris marketing poll of women, the so-called regular guys won by a landslide. In response, the *Washington Times,* in April 2005, ran a story *on page 1* that far exceeded the ambitions of the original marketing survey that led to the ad campaign. It read, "Women want the 'man' back in 'manly'. . . . The rough-and-ready attitude is in, women say, while the manicured 'metrosexual' look is on the way out."[18] The *Washington Times* chose to use a corporation's piece of marketing due diligence as the basis for Darwinian claims that go well beyond fashion and marketing. What is natural? What kind of mate will a woman choose? Another interesting feature of the Harris survey used by Dodge is the fact that women were polled. Metrosexuality lost the Dodge trucks contest, but traditional masculinity was forced to parade before the *female* gaze in order to win.[19]

The reactionary response to protect the status of hegemonic masculinity has a long lineage. It has been observed for decades that "contemporary" (post-1970s feminism) men are derided as "soft" in comparison to the rugged men of yesteryear, in particular in comparison to the 1940s warrior or the 1950s breadwinner. Even many liberal and progressive men, those who advocate the equitable sharing of housework and childrearing between men and women, have somehow managed to maintain a nostalgia for a mythic past when "men were men" and oppose that to the fallen state of "narcissistic, fashion-driven" contemporary masculinity, of which metrosexuals would be the ultimate example.[20] In one view, men in modern society can be excused for bending traditional gender roles and embracing the feminine side of their "natures." Nonetheless, in finding the feminine, they become divorced from essential sources of masculine nurturance. This is the case laid out in Robert Bly's *Iron John.* The concept in Bly is that it is natural for men and women to have both male and female "energy." "In every relationship something *fierce* is needed once in a while: both the man and the women need to have it."[21] In *Performance Anxieties: Re-producing Masculinity,* David Buchbinder explicates the way in which Bly's text is subtly hostile to women and to men who are homosexual, while protesting that it is not.[22] In Bly, ultimately the "fierce" element is the essence of masculinity. Bly asserts that men must gain access to a mythic Wild Man order rooted in the past. Another, more conservative view maintains an absolute division between male and female gender traits. From the absolutist position, it follows that men who share in childrearing or take on traditionally feminine roles are weak, with again the belief that men once had their place and must return to it. They have crossed a line, always conceived of in terms of what is natural. Contempt for such "sissies" is strongly encouraged.

This absolutist position best describes the ethos of the PR firm that advises advertisers to reassure men of their masculinity. In this view, there are real or regular men and there are those who have lost both dominance and their masculinity. The historically absolutist position on masculinity, the one that wants to keep masculine and feminine gender traits separate and neatly aligned with sex and sexuality, underlies the increasingly hyperdefensive posture taken in response to metrosexuality. All metrosexuality did at the outset was function as a joke and a boon for the marketers of hair care products. Mark Simpson, in his bitingly satirical column in *Salon*, invented the word as a way to mock specific celebrity figures, such as David Beckham for his self-conscious preening. Far from celebrating metrosexuality, Simpson inveighed against it, but marketers initially were excited about the opportunity to market to straight men who were unselfconsciously interested in consumer goods. When the term *metrosexuality* began to wane in popularity, marketers checked in with their researchers and determined that the notions of "real" and "regular" were more saleable.

In essence, marketers had to marshal new avatars of masculinity to compete with the metrosexual. The two most popular alternatives were "regular guy" and "badass." The regular guy avatar is summoned to sell Derek Jeter and Avon's cologne. Jeter has to show that he doesn't care too much about his appearance in order to be an appropriate regular guy spokesmodel. This is in contrast to earlier metrosexual icons like Beckham, who in some respects is the model for Jeter. Beckham, unlike Jeter, never tried to hide the fact that he cared about his image and that he crafted it self-consciously. (He also owned his own line of products as opposed to lending his name to a company that sells his image and their products.) The badass image, the one sported by the old-fashioned Marlboro Man, is also always an option for marketers. This is not the regular guy. He is more exceptional, the man other men would like to be.

Metrosexual masculinity defines a person who, in contrast to the regular and hyperbolic masculinities, is consciously interested in consumerism rather than in seeming to be oblivious to it. But this marketed set of alternative identities for men—regular, badass, metrosexual—undermines the notion that masculinity is a natural, essential category. There is little that deniers of metrosexuality can do to erase the notion that these identities are as easy to exchange as clothing. How hollow it sounds when Stephen Perrine, editor in chief of *Best Life* magazine, proclaims, "The new macho is the old macho. . . . It is about being competent and feeling traditional, filling traditional male roles."[23] In other words, let's scrap that metrosexual idea and go back to the Marlboro Man. But when the old macho wins out over metrosexuality, one set of trivial surface attributes attractive to women is exchanged for another, while fundamentally what has been achieved is the wide acceptance of masculinity as a shifting, contingent construct.

The origins of the anxiety and backlash surrounding the concept of the metrosexual can be traced to the time of the 2004 U.S. presidential election and the escalation of the war in Iraq. From a celebrity-driven and fashion-focused phenomenon emerging in the late 1990s, the concept of the metrosexual had gained wide enough recognition for a book titled *The Metrosexual Guide* to be published in 2003. From there, the term seeped into the presidential campaign: Howard Dean claimed to be a metrosexual, and John Kerry fled from the label, pursued by George W. Bush, who seemed to easily claim both the regular guy and the badass roles. The 2004 U.S. presidential campaign marked the apex of interest in the metrosexual concept. Afterward, marketers became more and more worried that the metrosexual might be on the way out and mounted a series of marketing surveys, such as the Harris survey used by Dodge trucks and the "global" survey on masculinity conducted by the PR firm Leo Burnett, but whether metrosexuality achieves any lasting prominence or not, the notion that different brands of masculinity are up to a vote indicates a shift in our understanding of masculinity. That metrosexuality is "out" implies that it could, like the goatee, come back. A line has been crossed. Metrosexuality is claimed by Simpson to be the ultimate instance of the queering of the codes that define gender.[24] Thus, it isn't George Bush as real man and John Kerry as not, as sissy. It's Bush and Kerry each representing different versions of masculine drag.

MASCULINITY BY THE BOOK

The boosters and detractors of metrosexuality are often working out of the same assumption that both metrosexual and traditional male roles represent an outward manifestation of a stable, inward psychic reality. Michael Flocker, the author of *The Metrosexual Guide,* does not intend to bring about change through challenging traditional gender roles on the basis of a critique of performativity. He claims to be describing an evolution that has already occurred, a return to a more natural way of being. Metrosexuality is justified as an authentic lifestyle choice, one that expresses a man's essential self. The notion of authenticity is called on frequently throughout Flocker's text. In the realm of fashion, for example, Flocker's advice is to dress in a way that expresses oneself: "If you want to be the Midnight Cowboy, go for it. The key lies in making the decision consciously rather than simply dressing obnoxiously to bring attention to yourself. In the final analysis, however, it is far more impressive to express your sense of style through small touches as opposed to garish choices."[25] Flocker is opposed to performance. He does not condemn a way of dressing that marks the wearer as ambiguously gay, as in the Midnight Cowboy reference. However, he advocates that men adopt a style of dress that is more neutral, that "avoids ridicule."[26] He cautions, "identify which styles look best on you." Here, the sexuality of the "you" is neutral, or at least does not matter.

Much of the advice in *The Metrosexual Guide* about behavior has to do with having good manners and good taste. A word on music, books, and film, for example: "Whether you're living in a New York penthouse or holed up in a cozy little trailer by the sea, the world is at your fingertips and it's your responsibility to explore it."[27] The metrosexual man explicitly avoids shows of violence, a hallmark of traditional masculinity, because his self-proclaimed authenticity is not in question:

> One of the defining characteristics of the metrosexual man is that he is beyond sexual stereotypes. He knows who he is and what he wants. For that very reason, he feels no compulsion to defend his masculinity through posturing or threatening others. The metrosexual man knows that in order to be comfortable with himself, he needs to allow others to be themselves. The heterosexuality, bisexuality, or homosexuality of anyone else does not concern him, unless of course he is romantically interested in that person. Then he needs to know.[28]

The guide promotes a nonviolent approach, one in which several ways of performing gender can exist at once without "threatening" each other. In accepting this plurality of performances and suspending judgment about sexuality, Flocker's brand of metrosexuality (as opposed to Simpson's mocking version) opens the door for a performative theory of gender without actively proposing such a theory.

There is, however, some confusion on the performativity issue in *The Metrosexual Guide*. It asserts that being straight is not the same thing as looking straight, in the traditional macho sense, but that masculinity is nonetheless tied to being straight:

> Secure in his masculinity, he no longer has to spend his life defending it. He has options. The sexual revolution is old news and the new man is free to enjoy his single life and his youthful appeal. If he is married, it is by choice, not by necessity, and the walls separating straight men from their gay, fashion-forward brothers are beginning to crumble.[29]

There is an inherent logic here that, though not explicit in the text, is apparent upon closer examination. Being secure in masculinity is, as tradition has it, synonymous with being secure about being straight, but elsewhere in the guide it is asserted that appearance is supposed to be a natural expression of *self*. So if appearance, which is supposed to emanate naturally from self, is gay or neutral, and the performer is straight, sexuality has become separated from self. Self-aware fashion sense has to reveal the wearer's sexuality if sexuality is part of self, but Flocker elides these.

Simpson, or MetroDaddy as he has called himself, has an explanation for this splitting of self from sexuality. He describes the metrosexual as disempowered by the entry of women into traditionally male roles. He refers to the *Sex in the City* female metrosexuals who are active, while the male metrosexuals are the passive objects of their conquest. "Nowadays straight men are also emasculated. . . . No longer is a straight man's sense of self and manhood delivered by his relationship to women; instead it's challenged by it."[30] Simpson implies that the response from some men has been to become what women want them to become—metrosexuals. Metrosexuals are emasculated through being cast in a passive role. While he backs off from this claim in a later article,[31] the active-passive dualism remains prominent in his description of the phenomenon of the metrosexual.

Picking up on the threat to masculinity represented by a connection to the passive is a guidebook parody titled *The Badass Bible*. It portrays the threats posed to traditional masculinity, or "badass" masculinity as the author, S. K. Smith, terms it, by modern culture. Many of the rules set down in this handbook deal with the necessity to act spontaneously and naturally, just as in *The Metrosexual Guide*, but by virtue of the fact that the book is a parody, the notion is mocked. The text, like much humor, is Janus-faced, both inviting criticism of the nostalgic attitude toward traditional masculine values and making that nostalgia seem logical. In this ambivalent fashion, the text reveals some of the cultural underpinnings of the subject it targets, the rugged individual and the allegedly crumbling culture that threatens his existence. Smith writes:

> The badass is all about fundamentals. That's what makes him stand out like a sore thumb in today's culture of excess—the badass sticks to essentials. . . . Like the Yeti, the badass is hairy, mysterious, seldom spotted. But one sighting will change your life. The badass offers us a glimpse of an earlier, wilder time. It's an encounter with our undiluted, brutal origins.[32]

The joke works because of the juxtaposition of the serious note of concern of "in today's culture of excess," the melodramatic "undiluted, brutal origins," and the absurd "Yeti." Humor is generated through the techniques of exaggeration and juxtaposition. In the text at large, a depiction of the badass, the avatar of hegemonic masculinity, is combined with snatches of half-serious gripes about globalization and illustrated with absurd cartoons that depict a square-headed badass with a perpetually serene smile.

Smith exploits the comic potential of the unattainability of badass stature. A disclaimer at the beginning of the book reads, "This is a joke book, you moron. Don't try this stuff at home."[33] *The Badass Bible* makes it clear that being a badass is all about being ready for a fight, not necessarily starting the fight, but being ready to physically retaliate for the slightest cause. Smith's "badass bar skills" scene, familiar from a number of movies, reveals the nostalgia for the notion of justifiable violence. Yet it's not designed to be taken seriously. We start to laugh as soon as we see it coming. The text advises, "when you feel some bad mojo coming from the dude at the end of the bar with the Cat Diesel hat on, start by not taking it personally."[34] Then it proceeds with steps that move from "offer to buy him a drink" to "Mr. Wise Ass blows it big time. He does stupid and makes another derogatory comment. Blood flows."[35]

This apt parody takes aim at a very real phenomenon, America's love affair with the rough-and-ready man of action. Yet in the twenty-first century, the concept turned into a joke. In 2004, John Kerry was quoted as bragging that he was a metrosexual.[36] Kerry struggled with this throughout his campaign and clearly would have preferred to be seen as a macho war hero. The battle for the role of badass candidate, for which both Kerry, with his Purple Hearts, and Bush, with his proud claim of being a war president, strove, was aptly parodied in the popular web short *This Land* in which Kerry was depicted simultaneously killing Vietnamese with a hand grenade and metrosexualizing himself by getting shots of Botox. The short was so contagious on the internet that it jumped the boundary between mainstream and web media, as portions of it appeared on television news and talk shows. The central joke in the parody centered on Kerry's intellectual, well-schooled manner, which was lampooned in opposition to Bush's tough-guy persona. The Bush caricature sings, "You're a liberal sissy." Kerry returns, "You're a right-wing nut job," with *nut job,* illustrated by camo-wearing Bush riding in a tank, clearly referring to Bush's militarism.[37]

The term metrosexual had come into play earlier, in the campaign leading up to the primaries, when Democratic candidate Howard Dean called himself metrosexual at one fundraising stop, then backpedaled, saying he wasn't really sure what the term meant. Gossip columnist Karen Croft, writing for *Salon,* quipped, "It means you know about hair products but you still like sports, Howie."[38] The later Fox attack on Kerry "quoted" him gloating over his success in the debates, saying, "Didn't my nails and cuticles look great? What a good debate! . . . I'm metrosexual— he's a cowboy."[39] The taunt of "sissy" that lurked within Fox's fabricated news story was evident in an August 2004 article in the *Chicago Sun-Times* in which the author stated her theory that, despite the current hype about metrosexuals, women prefer manly men, and she believed that her theory would be proven by the election. In other words, if Bush wins, metrosexuals lose: "Though we may find some secret satisfaction in the idea of men obsessing over their looks as much as we do, it seems that most women would agree: When it comes down to the battle of the men, evolution does not favor the metrosexual man yet. Let's see what happens in November."[40] Thus, in the eyes of the gossip-columnist pundocracy, the election became a referendum on the metrosexual versus the badass.

HYBRIDIZED METROSEXUALITY

If even a presidential election can be read as a referendum on metrosexuality, there are many other, more explicit referendums in marketing. Once metrosexuality lost in the polls, marketers wanted to get as far away as possible from the term, but they were equally eager to create a new prototype for the hyperconsuming, yet non-metro man. The Dodge trucks marketing survey spawned the creation of one of the first hybridized metrosexuals (Derek Jeter was a later notable example). The new non-metro metrosexual was "Dodge Dakota Ultimate Guy." Although Ultimate Guy was meant to represent the naturalized epitome of masculinity, he had to prove himself through being nominated by his wife. Like the Ivory Girl of the 1970s, the Dakota guys were sponsored by their mates, as in "I think my guy is an Ultimate Guy because . . ." The press release announcing the winner was explicitly about the company's staged nominations for best masculinity. Having shown that "ninety percent of U.S. women surveyed prefer a regular, capable and laid-back guy to just five percent still wanting the hip, fashion conscious 'metrosexual' male,"[41] Dodge wanted to create a forum for introducing him to the public. The release quoted the winner, David Neumann of Valley Mills, Texas, as saying, "I plan to spend the summer enjoying my new Dodge Dakota, camping with my wife and two daughters, dove hunting, and picking up materials for projects around the house."[42] His wife was quoted as saying that he is the kind of guy who always "takes care of the people in his life."[43] Ultimate Guy is caring, all-around nice, good-natured, and dependable. Because, unlike the presidential candidates, he did not have access to badass claims such as having killed people or started a war, Dodge tried to toughen up his image a little by throwing a prize of an "ultimate sports day" into his Ultimate Guy prize package.

Another ad campaign that features the hybridized metrosexual, albeit a parody of one, is the GEICO series in which cavemen, dressed in metrosexual clothing and sporting metrosexual accoutrements (sweaters draped over shoulders, linen sports coats, tennis racquets, tuxedoes, therapist appointments, and other telltale signs of being cultured and manicured), defend themselves against the taunt that they are mere cavemen. The tagline is "GEICO, so easy even a caveman can do it." In one advertisement in the series, the metrosexual cavemen are seen at a party. Two of them are talking on the balcony of what looks like a New York penthouse apartment. One says to the other, "What? You think getting GEICO makes me less of a caveman?" In another spot, the cavemen are at a restaurant with an ad executive who is apologizing to them, saying, "We had no idea you guys were still around." The waiter arrives, and one of the cavemen turns from the apologizer in disgust and places his order, "I'll have the roast duck with the mango salsa."[44] In this instance, the hairy caveman costume represents manliness. The ad campaign plays on the joke that, if you take the idea of the "real" man to its extreme, you end up with a caveman. Insensitive hypermasculine men are often referred to as "Neanderthals."[45] Smith's *Badass Bible* makes use of this joke as well: "Back when early man squatted in caves, naked and malnourished, terrified of his own shadow, there were a select few, an elite handful. . . . They were the originals. They were 'Badass.'"[46] The GEICO cavemen are actually hybrids of the badass and the metrosexual with hairy Cro-Magnon heads atop hip urban outfits. The downside of being a caveman, so the GEICO joke goes, is that everyone thinks you don't understand how to operate in modern society. Presumably, cavemen (real men) are great at bringing down prey, but one wouldn't expect them to be able to order in a restaurant.

In a 2007 publicity stunt, GEICO sent a caveman to "Night of 100 Stars," a fundraiser in Los Angeles, where an amateur camera crew caught the scene and put it on the web on YouTube.[47] The footage shows a beaming caveman with a tall blonde model. The interviewer asks, "How's your life changed since GEICO?" The caveman goes on about how life is great. Then, the interviewer turns to the girlfriend, "What do you love most about this guy? About this caveman?" She replies, "It's that manly, that personality. He's a real animal." The caveman says, "Listen to her. I'm an animal. And you guys at home: stop bleaching your teeth. Stop showering. Stop shaving. Let's be men again." This sounds like Flocker's advice about the irrelevance of sexuality to the self and shows that this implicit,

Butlerian disconnection of self and sexuality seems to be gaining wide acceptance.

Every response to the metrosexual is revealing of the panic that ensues when gender is defined as fluid rather than fixed, or as contingent rather than natural. In her groundbreaking work *Gender Trouble*, Judith Butler describes the way in which this troubling disconnection is related to compulsory heterosexuality. When confronted with bodies, such as the metrosexual, that disrupt "the regular fiction of heterosexual coherence, it seems that the expressive model loses its descriptive force. That regulatory ideal is then exposed as a norm and a fiction that disguises itself as a developmental law regulating the sexual field that it purports to describe."[48] Thus, when the metrosexual who both does and does not act straight is proven by marketing surveys to exist, badass defenders rush to reclaim masculinity as an essential category and to deny the possibility of this other masculinity. Specifically, they aim to delegitimize metrosexuality, with its self-conscious performance of gender, by showing that metrosexuality is feminine and has no claim in the realms of political power or sexual or military conquest that legitimize hegemonic masculinity.

As Simpson observes, metrosexuality is "passive where it should always be active, desired where it should always be desiring, looked at where it should always be looking."[49] He argues in *Male Impersonators* from Freudian theories of sexuality, positing that the metrosexual inverts the binaries of active-passive and male-female. The idea of metrosexuality is that a man, without the excuse of being gay, performs masculinity. Masculinity becomes an act, and the response to the performance is often the argument that men should behave differently, in a manner that calls to mind a "real" man. In this way, metrosexuality sets a trap. Where hegemonic masculinity involves our accepting as natural certain ways of being and doing, the defensive response to metrosexuality (act this way, not that way) makes clear that real masculinity is just another version of drag—"retrosexuality," as Simpson calls it.[50]

Hegemonic masculinity demands a binary, hierarchical view of gender in which masculinity is equated with power, action, dominance, and so on, and femininity with their binary opposites. Within this logic, the badass masculinity portrayed in movies and advertising is easily absorbed into the hegemonic ideal. Logically, it seems that the regular guy and the badass support hegemonic masculinity, and they have been put into service in support of the very real power and world dominance that it represents. Within the popular culture vehicle of marketing, however, these masculinities have been put on stage to parade before a female audience alongside metrosexual masculinity. When George Bush won the election in 2004, carrying a confirmation of the dominance of badass masculinity in his wake, the door was opened for Americans and others to conceive of his performance of masculinity as an act, directed by his political handlers. In the same way, as consumers of popular culture, we are aware that Brian Vickers is posing as a metrosexual for money. His spring-green racing car emblazoned with the Garnier Fructis unisex hair care logo is a means to riches, even as it has earned him the metrosexual label. Bush's cowboy attitude was admired by many Americans, but suspected by an almost equal number as an insincere attempt to curry the favor of those disposed to vote for a badass candidate. Simpson reads Bush's appearance on the deck of an aircraft carrier to announce victory in the "Battle of Baghdad" as an instance of the president in retrosexual drag. Desperate as the anti-metrosexual response has been, culminating in its retreat into a hybridized form, it has furthered the acceptance of plural male identities as opposed to hegemonic masculinity. Badass masculinity, like the feminized masculinities it is supposed to supplant, must compete for the approval of the consumer, whose gender and sexuality are, as Flocker would say, irrelevant.

NOTES

1. Edgar, "Success of Derek Jeter Scent," 11.
2. Avon, http://shop.avon.com.
3. Simpson, "MetroDaddy."
4. See, for example, Flocker, *The Metrosexual Guide.*
5. See Doolittle, "Hold the Quiche."
6. Miller, "A Metrosexual Eye," 116.
7. Sender, "Queens for a Day," 146.
8. Ibid., 135.
9. McIntyre, "I Am Man, See Me Moisturize," 24.
10. Avon, "Derek Jeter: Driven."
11. Edgar, "Success of Derek Jeter Scent," 11.
12. Ibid.
13. Thomas, "Men's Health Spotlights Grooming," 11.
14. Oaks, "Things Fearful to Name."

15. "Metrosexual Is Out."
16. Ibid.
17. Ibid.
18. Doolittle, "Hold the Quiche," A1.
19. Simpson, "MetroDaddy."
20. Beynon, *Masculinities and Culture,* 127. See also Connell, *Masculinities,* 27.
21. Bly, *Iron John,* 4.
22. Buchbinder, *Performance Anxieties,* 29–47.
23. "Metrosexual Is Out."
24. Simpson, "Meet the Metrosexual."
25. Flocker, *The Metrosexual Guide,* 82–83.
26. Ibid., 83.
27. Ibid., 69.
28. Ibid., 131.
29. Ibid., xiii.
30. Simpson, "Meet the Metrosexual."
31. Simpson, "MetroDaddy."
32. Smith, *The Badass Bible,* 10–11.
33. Ibid., front matter.
34. Ibid., 92.
35. Ibid., 92–93.
36. Lichtblau, "Fox News."
37. Spiridellis and Spiridellis, *This Land.*
38. Croft, "The Fix."
39. Lichtblau, "Fox News," 32.
40. Berman, "Language of Love," 44.
41. "Texas Man."
42. Ibid.
43. Ibid.
44. "GEICO Caveman Series."
45. From October to November 2007, ABC aired a sitcom written by the originator of the Martin Agency's GEICO ad series, Joe Lawson. The show was not only canceled quickly, it also generated some anger over the notion that the cavemen were playing up stereotypes of African Americans. No one seemed to pick up on the metrosexual joke in the sitcom version. See also Defamer, "Defending 'Cavemen II.'"
46. Smith, *The Badass Bible,* 14.
47. "GEICO's Caveman at the Night of 100 Stars."
48. Butler, *Gender Trouble,* 173.
49. Simpson, "MetroDaddy."
50. Ibid.

BIBLIOGRAPHY

Avon. http://shop.avon.com (accessed May 20, 2009).
———. "Derek Jeter: Driven." 2006. http://shop.avon.com/shop/driven/driven_home
.html (accessed June 27, 2007).

Bellafante, Ginia. "They Put on Their Pants a Leg at a Time; It's Just That Their Legs Are Hairier." *New York Times*. October 4, 2007. http://query.nytimes.com (accessed May 20, 2009).

Berman, Laura. "The Language of Love." *Chicago Sun-Times*. August 23, 2004.

Beynon, John. *Masculinities and Culture*. Philadelphia: Open University Press, 2002.

Bly, Robert. *Iron John: A Book about Men*. New York: Da Capo, 2004.

Buchbinder, David. *Performance Anxieties: Re-producing Masculinity*. Sydney, Australia: Allen and Unwin, 1998.

Butler, Judith. *Gender Trouble: Feminism and the Subversion of Identity*, 2nd ed. New York: Routledge, 1999.

Connell, R. W. *Masculinities*. Berkeley: University of California Press, 1995.

Croft, Karen. "The Fix." *Salon*. October 29, 2003. http://www.salon.com/entertainment/col/fix/2003/10/29/wed.

Defamer. "Defending 'Cavemen II': The Racial Insensitivity Question." *Gawker*. http://defamer.gawker.com/hollywood/sitcom-stereotypewatch/defending-cavemen-ii-the-racial-insensitivity-question-282577.php (accessed May 20, 2009).

Doolittle, Amy. "Hold the Quiche: Manly Men Are Back." *Washington Times*. April 7, 2005.

Edgar, Michelle. "Success of Derek Jeter Scent Drives Brand's Expansion." *Women's Wear Daily*. May 11, 2007.

Flocker, Michael. *The Metrosexual Guide to Style: A Handbook for the Modern Man*. Cambridge, Mass.: Da Capo, 2003.

"GEICO Caveman Series." *YouTube*. Posted February 11, 2007, by "mtubero." http://www.youtube.com/watch?v=3F3qzfTCDG4 (accessed May 20, 2009).

"GEICO's Caveman at the Night of 100 Stars." *YouTube*. Posted March 5, 2007, by "Newsvideoweb." http://www.youtube.com/watch?v=H1YRgaLtzM4 (accessed May 20, 2009).

Lee-St. John, Jeninne. "NASCAR Goes Metrosexual." *Time*. February 7, 2005, 18.

Lichtblau, Eric. "Fox News, Citing 'Bad Judgment,' Apologizes over a Made-up Posting about Kerry." *New York Times*. October 3, 2004.

McIntyre, Megan. "I Am Man, See Me Moisturize." *Beauty Biz*. March 16, 2007, 24.

"Metrosexual Is Out: Macho Is In." *Good Morning America*. ABC, June 19, 2006. http://abcnews.go.com/GMA/story?id=2092965&page=1.

"Metrosexual Man Embraces Feminism—UK." *Euro RSCG Worldwide*. Press release. June 16, 2003. http://www.eurorscg.com/press/press_203.htm.

Miller, Toby. "A Metrosexual Eye on *Queer Guy*." *GLQ: A Journal of Lesbian and Gay Studies* 11, no. 1 (2005): 112–117.

Oaks, Robert F. "Things Fearful to Name: Sodomy and Buggery in Seventeenth-century New England." *Journal of Social History* 12, no. 2 (2001): 268–281.

Sender, Katherine. "Queens for a Day: *Queer Eye for the Straight Guy* and the Neoliberal Project." *Critical Studies in Media Communication* 23, no. 2 (2006): 131–151.

Simpson, Mark. *Male Impersonators: Men Performing Masculinity*. New York: Routledge, 1994.

———. "Meet the Metrosexual." *Salon*. July 22, 2002. http://www.salon.com/entertainment/feature/2002/07/22/metrosexual.

———. "MetroDaddy Speaks." *Salon*. January 5, 2004. http://www.salon.com/entertainment/feature/2004/01/05/metrosexual_ii.

Smith, S. K. *The Badass Bible*. New York: Red Brick, 2004.

Spiridellis, Gregg, and Evan Spiridellis, dirs. *This Land*. 2004. http://www.jibjab.com (accessed May 20, 2009).

"Texas Man Named a Dodge Dakota Ultimate Guy." *PR Newswire*. May 10, 2005. Press release. http://www.prnewswire.com.

Thomas, Brenner. "Men's Health Spotlights Grooming." *Daily News Record*. April 16, 2007, 11.

FOUR

FATHERS, SONS, AND BUSINESS IN THE HOLLYWOOD "OFFICE MOVIE"

LATHAM HUNTER

Much has been written on how Hollywood has represented the contemporary social climate in order to shore up, reinforce, or shape U.S. culture's perception of what it is to be a man. Postwar films tended to emphasize the role of the father at home (think Vincente Minnelli's 1950 *Father of the Bride*) to solidify the traditional family after its disruption (dad at war, mom at the factory). The über-male action films of the 1980s (with stars like Arnold Schwarzenegger and Sylvester Stallone) are often read as a reaction to the feminist boom of the 1970s, or to the sagging U.S. economy. In the 1990s, an entirely new subgenre emerged to reflect the position of the "disempowered" middle-class, white, heterosexual male—the drone of the new corporatized, managerial culture. *Falling Down* (1993), *In the Company of Men* (1997), *Very Bad Things* (1998), *American Beauty* (1999), *Being John Malkovich* (1999), *Office Space* (1999), and *Fight Club* (1999) are a few of the films which seem part of the male disempowerment awareness campaign arising from the much-debated and so-called 1990s masculinity crisis. Each highlights the self-estrangement and repressed anger of men lost in the alienating ranks of management culture and cubicle grids. I call these films "office movies," not because they all take place in an office, but because the films let us know that the protagonists are caught in the middle rungs of an increasingly corporate culture, usually somewhere in the cubicle class. This position is depicted as symptomatic of how the middle-class white man has become alienated and disenfranchised: he is as grey and lifeless as his surroundings, caught in a deadly boring routine doing he's-not-sure-what or he-doesn't-care-what (Hunter 72).

Ideologically, then, these films (as with any other ideological apparatus) invite their viewers in with a shred of reality: picking up on a renewed social anxiety about the shifting fortunes of the white, middle-class male, office movies convincingly depict one of the focal points of that anxiety (the office). Under the pretense of being movies for regular guys about regular guys (stories that men tell themselves about themselves), these films use the promise of transformation to impose fixity. In other words, office movies claim to be about something current—a men's movement rumbling for change in the face of an alienating late capitalist system—but they offer little that is new. Ergo, the supposedly new movement only reaffirms the essential, intrinsic, and inevitable nature of society's existing power structure. Perhaps Robyn Wiegman puts it best in "Bonds of (In)Difference," where she studies the male—specifically, the white male—power structure and how it solidifies through a posture of victimization. She writes that the illusion of "man" forms "that materially violent abstraction that perversely gathers strength by offering itself now as a struggling, innocent, and singular voice" (222). It works as simply—and as insidiously—as the basic hegemonic model, by incorporating even the idea of resistance so as to consolidate its own power. Central to the structure of patriarchy are, of course, the succession of son to father, and the transformation of son into father—the longest-standing mechanisms of patriarchal control. It therefore comes as no surprise that the identities of father and son—and the relationship between them—are key elements of office movies and are bound tightly to another mainstay of patriarchal society: capitalism. Put simply, office movies suggest that failure in one realm (i.e., being a bad father, or having only daughters, or not being a father at all) leads to failure in the other, and vice versa.

A prominent father-son connection exists in office movies, but this is not particularly unique to this subgenre. In the 1950s, for instance, American film promoted "the breadwinner ethic" (Cohan 34–78). In the 1970s and 1980s, the "father bond" was prominent in *Kramer vs. Kramer* (1979), *Ordinary People* (1980), *On Golden Pond* (1981), *Mr. Mom* (1983), and *Nothing in Common* (1986), among many others.[1] In the next decade, "the more sensitive, loving, nurturing protective family men of the 1990s" emerged, so much so that Susan Jeffords declares that "1991 was the year of the transformed U.S. man," given the release of films like *Regarding Henry* and *One Good Cop* (Jeffords 197).[2] I cannot make such an assertion: the truth is that the 1990s gave us as many violent models of masculinity as it did sensitive ones, which is also the case when one looks at the films of the 1980s. I do think, however, that there is something different about how office movies represent fatherhood because never before has such a large group of films produced in such a small span of time depicted a male protagonist's success or failure as a father as being so closely linked to his success or failure as a late capitalist worker.

In her book *Bringing Up Daddy: Fatherhood and Masculinity in Post-War Hollywood*, Stella Bruzzi argues that many 1990s Hollywood films featuring father-son relationships (such as *A River Runs Through It, Quiz Show, Legends of the Fall, Gladiator,* and *Apollo 13*) are "set in the past, indicating a shared nostalgic desire to return to older values" (158). Others that aren't set in the past still achieve the feel of the "old-fashioned" through retro associations (such as the Cold War feel of *A Few Good Men*) or the burdensome reminder of a dead father's legacy (as in *Backdraft*) (159). Though Bruzzi finds that the 1990s offered a greater "diversity of representations of the father" that "suggests the fragmentation—or at least the dissipation—of the traditional paternal role model that has hitherto underpinned Hollywood's pre-occupation with the father" (153), she concludes that "ultimately [Hollywood film] seems to protest that the traditional father is what we want" (191). Though she doesn't discuss office films per se (mention is made of *Falling Down, Fight Club,* and *American Beauty*), I think a similar frustration with and then recapitulation of the traditional model of fatherhood is evident in them, only with the added dimension of traditionality through the assertion of a kind of breadwinner ascendancy. And these are films set unequivocally in the current moment, produced and circulated during the crisis of masculinity, rife with the irony and cynicism Bruzzi finds absent in other films' representations of the "omniscient, guiding father" (158). I wonder if what we have in 1990s office movies, then, is a group of films which perform the cinematic equivalent of stretching an elastic band to its absolute and utmost extension. How thoroughly can they divest themselves of the respect and sincerity accorded to the traditional Hollywood model of fatherhood and the father-son bond before snapping back to form? How far can these ideological limits be pushed before they are permanently misshapen?

Using socially situated ideological critique and close textual analysis, this chapter will investigate two central ideas in 1990s office movies. The first is the notion that American males' sense of masculinity is in crisis because they have suffered a disconnect from their fathers or from their own fatherly potential. The second is that fatherhood truly cements masculinity when it is concomitant with business success and, conversely, that business success is empty or incomplete without a correspondingly successful position as a father ("successful" being graded according to largely essentialist, traditional patriarchal notions). What comes out of these films is a "pan-masculine" sense that masculinity can and should be at the head of both families and businesses and that society works most profitably and happily when such is the case.

Stiffed: The Betrayal of the American Man is feminist Susan Faludi's exploration into the 1990s masculinity crisis. In it, she writes:

> From the start, I intended to talk to the men in this book about such matters as work, sports, marriage, religion, war, and entertainment. I didn't go to them originally to ask about their fathers. But they insisted that I do so. Over and over, the breakdown of loyalty in the public domain brought my male guides face-to-face with the collapse of some personal patrimony. Behind all the public double crosses, they sensed, lay their fathers' desertion. (596)

Faludi certainly doesn't wrap up her study by blaming the crisis of masculinity on the postwar generation of fathers; her conclusion rests more in the argument that men must find a sense of social responsibility (something to do, rather than a masculinity to be) in the face of the increasing market for their glamorization and ornamentalization and the late capitalist loss of middle-class agency. However, she points out very deliberately that, throughout her research, men often discussed how they had been abandoned by their fathers, and in so doing, revealed a key issue in the 1990s crisis of masculinity. In *White Guys*, Fred Pfeil comes to a parallel conclusion:

> There is one area of discussion [in men's meetings inspired by the 1990s men's movement] around which the question of what men want masculinity to be comes closest to focusing: when the subject of fathers comes up. There is lots of talk, lots of witnessing, at these meetings about our baby-boom generation's fathers, almost regardless of whatever the official stated topic of the meeting might be; and almost all of it is freighted with disappointment, guilt and rage. (192)

I am similarly struck by Anthony Easthope's frequent return to the issue of fatherhood in his seminal book, *What a Man's Gotta Do: The Masculine Myth in Popular Culture*. Despite tackling a range of subjects related to popular culture's construction of masculinity, Easthope makes clear that the father-son relationship deserves special attention. He observes that *Hiawatha* (1855), *The Jungle Book* (1894), *Tarzan of the Apes* (1914), and the ever-present and evolving Superman stories can be linked to "the greatest foundling story in the Western tradition, that of Jesus, who is the son of God and not of his ordinary parents, Mary and Joseph" (28). Therefore, Easthope presents us with a long history of sons born of conditions and circumstances and fathers, but not mothers. "Women," Easthope says, "are simply written out of the script" (118), while boys become men out of their "wholly self-sufficient masculine will" (20). There is a sort of "in-the-beginning-ness" to all of this, not only because it can be traced back to the Bible, but because it seems to speak so directly to the issue of how men are created. Finally, Easthope concludes, "masculinity must find itself in the place of the father or not at all" (118). How pertinent, then, to find the following: in *Fight Club*, Tyler Durden (Brad Pitt) sits in a bathtub while the Narrator (Edward Norton) sits on the floor beside him. They are amicably nursing their wounds after a fight:

> Tyler: If you could fight anyone who would you fight?
> Narrator: I'd fight my boss, probably.
> Tyler: Really?
> Narrator: Yeah. Why? Who would you fight?
> Tyler: I'd fight my dad.
> Narrator: I don't know my dad. I mean, I know him, but he left when I was like six years old. Married this other woman, had some other kids. He, like, did this every six years—he goes to a new city and starts a new family.
> Tyler: Fucker's settin' up franchises. [Pause] My dad never went to college, so it was real important that I go.
> Narrator: That sounds familiar.
> Tyler: So I graduate. I call him up long distance, I say "Dad, now what?" He says, "Get a job."
> Narrator: Same here.
> Tyler: Now I'm twenty-five, I make my yearly call again. Say, "Dad, now what?" He says, "I don't know. Get married."
> Narrator: God. I mean, I can't get married. I'm a thirty-year-old boy.
> Tyler: We're a generation of men raised by women. I'm wondering if another woman is really the answer we need.

This scene reveals the Narrator's and Tyler's alienation from their fathers. The first father has left town and left his family. The second father is always a "long-distance" call away. Neither son can share the experience of college with his father, nor acquire any knowledge or wisdom from his father. Consequently, the Narrator and Tyler have stagnated in boyhood (indeed, Tyler turns out to be an imaginary friend of sorts), unable to attain a truer, more developed masculinity. The film uses this exchange to explain how it is that a generation of men could be so lost, so in crisis (so literally beaten up and bloodied and living in squalor), and it seems to indict these absent fathers. But the film also suggests that the only way boys can learn to be men is from men, through that "wholly self-sufficient masculine will," as Easthope puts it (20). Immediately following this scene, we see the Narrator making coffee. In voice-over, he says: "Most of the week we were Ozzie and Harriet." Tyler walks in, dressed for his catering job, and the Narrator turns to straighten Tyler's bow tie. The film, therefore, answers Tyler's question: he and the Narrator have created a domestic space without a woman—they're actually Ozzie and Ozzie, and quite content about it. Despite the fact that fathers are clearly blamed for this generation of men not being able to grow into manhood, it is actually women who are subordinated, or made redundant. Therefore, while there is clearly a problem with boys depending entirely on fathers to teach them how to grow into men, the solution the film posits is to depend even more on men—to circle the wagons more assiduously around the gender.

Another interesting element regarding the above bathroom scene is how business and fatherhood are depicted as coterminous. First, the Narrator chooses to fight his boss, while Tyler chooses his father: a natural association between the two roles is thus suggested. Second, the Narrator's father isn't starting new families—he's setting up franchises. Third, what little information in common ("same here," "that sounds familiar") that seems to have passed between these two men and their fathers has concerned going to college and getting a job: the desire for professional advancement from one generation to the next. It is not enough to solidify the gender by pinning its survival on the exclusion of women; masculinity must exemplify the mores and ubiquity of capitalism.

Perhaps *Jerry Maguire* doesn't spring to mind as an office movie; it is so thoroughly washed in male bonding, romance, humor, and Tom-Cruise-ness that the protagonist's initial crisis gets a bit lost. The film introduces Jerry (Tom Cruise) as a slick sports agent: we see him confidently working a crowd and brokering deals at a conference. But this is not, apparently, where he works. The camera zooms in on a high-rise, while Jerry says in voice-over, "Inside that building—that's where I work. S.M.I. Sports Management International." Next, we're shown a boardroom full of men in white shirts and ties, having a meeting around a table. Of the eight shots in this sequence, women appear in the periphery of only two. The film clearly establishes, therefore, that Jerry—though he resembles a Hollywood movie star and seems to be a successful, popular man in a glamorous job—is, after all, part of the world of white male office workers. And he's not happy. He began "a few years ago" to notice the chronic insincerity and greed of his business, but this isn't what really pushes Jerry over the edge. "Lately," he says in voice-over, "it's gotten worse." The jolt that tips off Jerry's crisis comes when he tries to finesse the fourteen-year-old son of a concussed client, a hockey player. The son, standing in the hospital corridor, reminds Jerry that this is his dad's fourth concussion: "Shouldn't somebody get him to stop?" Jerry offers a glib, patronizing retort: "Hey hey hey. . . . It would take a tank to stop your dad. . . . Right? Right?" The boy sees through Jerry's patter: "Fuck you." This creates a moment of reckoning for Jerry: "Who had I become? Just another shark in a suit?" It is not just that he is defined by his suit—his identity as a profit-hungry businessman. This exchange with the hockey player's son opens up the idea that Jerry has failed as a father figure. Essentially, the boy looks to Jerry to protect his family while his own father is debilitated, and Jerry cannot perform in such a role.

Jerry's feeling that he's drowning in corporate greed gestures toward a critique of corporate culture, but ironically, his solution is expressed in a classic corporate idiom: Jerry feverishly writes a mission statement (a typical component of corporate image making) which extols the virtues of better client service, of "caring for them." And he fashions this statement using a distinctly paternalistic language. As he begins to write, he recalls, "Suddenly, I was my father's son again. . . . I was remembering even the words of the original sports agent, my mentor, the late great Dicky Fox who said, 'The key to this business is *personal relationships.*'" The shot of Dicky shows a kindly old man in a suit, behind a desk, dispensing his brief words of wisdom. Jerry's conversion to a paternalistic role can only happen under the guidance of his two father figures: his biological father and his professional mentor. What is created, then, is a patriarchal continuity through generations that overlaps the spaces of family and business and somehow supersedes the critique of the "shark in a suit." The next step for Jerry, of course, is to grow from a son to a father himself, and his urge to do so is expressed by the design for the cover of his mission statement: "Even the cover looked like *The Catcher in the Rye.*" The "even" suggests that both the contents and the cover of the mission statement can be connected to Holden Caulfield's one wish: to catch children in a field of rye, to become their older male protector, their father figure.[3]

Jerry Maguire anticipates Tyler Durden's suggestion that what men need is *not* a woman. When Jerry meets the film's romantic interest, Dorothy (Renee Zellweger), it is because she has lost her five-year-old son, Ray, at an airport. She moves helplessly, calling out for her son; Jerry approaches her, they recognize each other from the office (she's an accountant with S.M.I.), and Jerry promptly points out Ray's location, only a few yards away from where Dorothy had been standing all along. This scene sets a pattern that recurs throughout the film: Jerry and Dorothy do not fall in love as much as they are pulled irresistibly toward the idea of Jerry being a much-needed father to Ray as Dorothy becomes Jerry's assistant, and then wife.

Jerry's unexpected visit to Dorothy's house indicates that, in fact, it is Jerry and Ray who complete each other (to borrow the oft-quoted line uttered by Jerry to Dorothy: "You complete me"). While Dorothy and her sister busy themselves in the kitchen, Ray slips out of bed and into the living room, where Jerry is waiting alone. The two share a giggly, bonding exchange. They talk about—what else—fathers and sons:

> Jerry: My daddy worked for the United Way for thirty-eight years. Do you know what he said when he retired? "I wish they'd given me a more comfortable chair." Thirty-eight *years* he sat—
> Ray [eagerly jumping in]: Wait wait wait—when my dad died my mom took me to the zoo and I love the zoo. Do you love the zoo?
> Jerry: No, wait wait—'cause I want to tell you more about my dad.
> . . .
> Ray: Let's go to the zoo now!
> Jerry: Ray, the zoo, you know—the fuckin' zoo's closed.
> Ray [whispering]: . . . You said fuck.
> Jerry [taken aback]: Yeah . . . I did . . . is that—?
> Ray: I won't tell.

Jerry: Now I'm going to have to take you to the zoo.
[Female voices are now audible and getting closer]
Ray: I gotta go to bed. My mom's coming I gotta go to bed. I hear my mom I
gotta go to bed. [Ray quickly pads out of the living room]

It is important to note that Ray and Jerry seem to instantly pick up on each
other's characteristics. Jerry reassures Ray that he "won't tell" about Ray
circumventing his bedtime, and Ray reassures Jerry that he "won't tell"
about Jerry cursing. When Jerry starts talking about his dad, Ray starts
talking about his own dad. They both interrupt the other by repeating
the word "wait." We understand that these two share a kind of father-
son language, woven of repeated words and shared memories of what it
means to be a son and to have or need a father. While this is going on,
Dorothy reminds her sister that while other women her age are at parties
and bars trying to get a man or keep a man, Dorothy is "trying to *raise*
a man." The suggestion is that this is a struggle for her—she's "trying"
rather than succeeding. Accordingly, Dorothy's and Laurel's actions and
words—busy, uncoordinated, flustered, contradictory, cautionary—are
in direct contrast with those of Jerry and Ray, who are connecting easily
and comfortably. The film is telling us why Dorothy struggles to raise a
man: she is not a father. It takes a father to raise a son. It takes a man to
raise a man.

 In stark contrast, Dorothy and Jerry's initial courtship is marked by
awkwardness. After a drunken advance and abrupt breast grope, Jerry
compares himself to Clarence Thomas,[4] and thus emphasizes the unnatu-
ralness of his attempt at connecting with Dorothy: for men and women
to bond within the sphere of business is a risky venture in the age of
the sexual harassment lawsuit. This is also expressed by their respective
props: the sunglasses create a kind of shield for Jerry, while the fire poker
implies Dorothy's wariness and defensiveness. Jerry also keeps banging
his head on a low-slung lamp; in more ways than one, he doesn't have
enough clearance. Dorothy and Jerry's attempt at having a relationship
that is both business *and* pleasure (both professional and personal) is
altogether wonky, stilted by all those restrictions and dangers that make
a workplace shared by women and men seem more cautionary than col-
legial. A sense of desperation and distance characterizes Dorothy and
Jerry's ensuing relationship. A sense of utter devotion characterizes Jerry
and Ray's relationship.

It seems as though Jerry might actually have fallen in love with Dorothy by the end of the film; when Rod finally achieves the kind of success
that nets the big money, Jerry feels incomplete because he can't share the
moment with his estranged wife. He rushes home to restore his marriage,
and Dorothy is easily persuaded ("You had me at 'Hello'"). But this is
not the happy ending. The happy ending of *Jerry Maguire* is established
in the next three scenes—the last three scenes. First, Jerry and his family are in a studio, watching Rod on a sports program being told that he
has succeeded in securing a high-paying contract with his current team.
This financial success for Rod and Jerry is the background for the tab-
leau of Jerry and his wife and son, gathered closely together as a family,
and a close-up of Ray, standing against his dad's legs, holding his dad's
hand, on which a wedding ring shines brightly. Dorothy's legs are visible behind Ray, but she seems secondary in the arrangement, given the
frequent shots of Jerry as he is congratulated by others in the studio and
thanked by Rod. I am particularly intrigued by the shot of Ray holding
Jerry's hand, with Jerry's wedding ring so close to Ray's face, glinting
with Ray's bright blond hair and glasses, in the center of the frame. The
union between father and son, therefore, is central and is cemented as
such while Jerry's career takes off before our eyes. But there is more: in
the next scene, Jerry and Dorothy walk with Ray in a park after a trip to
the zoo (of course—from the loss of a father to the acquisition of a father,
things have come full circle). An errant baseball drops in front of Ray, who
throws it back to the waiting Little League players with such power that
Jerry immediately latches on to the business potential here. As with the
previous scene, Jerry's happy family must finally focus on the father and
son as central players, and they must exist as such within the sphere of
work as well as family. Jerry and Ray's relationship is further solidified by
the possibility of them working together one day as agent and client. And
to make even more clear that this is a story about how men become men
through business and fatherhood, the final scene is another shot of Dicky
Fox (the first real sports agent and one of Jerry's father figures) delivering
his final piece of advice from behind his desk.

Jerry Maguire is not a terribly serious office movie. Its manifesto for
office men—its mission statement—is referred to with some degree of
irony, and it contains no violence or angry resentment. Its office setting
is left behind early on, as are its protagonist's suit and tie. It is, however,

an exception that proves a rule: happy endings are rare in office movies, and I wonder how much that has to do with the fact that so few of them feature father-son relationships like that between Jerry and Ray. Most of the protagonists in office movies have daughters. Ray's lightning-quick attachment to Jerry suggests that there was a hole in Ray's life that desperately needed to be filled despite two loving women and a male nanny tending to him. These people are not fathers, and a father is what Ray needed. By joining together as father and son, Jerry and Ray solve their crises and set themselves up professionally: the film gives us a hint of where Ray will end up working and how his dad will help him get there and shows us the first in a long line of father figures who have established how to succeed in this line of work and in life.

And what of the male protagonists saddled with daughters instead of sons? In *Falling Down,* D-Fens (Michael Douglas) spends the whole film trying to get to his daughter, who remains in his ex-wife's custody. By the time he does finally see her, he realizes that the only way he can provide for her is to set up his own shooting death so that she can inherit his life insurance. In *Glengarry Glen Ross,* Levene (Jack Lemmon) is failing to sell real estate shares—his status as "Levene the Machine" is all but forgotten—and he becomes desperate enough to steal some "new leads" in order to provide for his sick daughter. In the original 1984 play *Glengarry Glen Ross,* Levene has no daughter. He steals the leads because he is desperate to regain his status as a "machine," churning out sale after sale. It is highly significant that the Hollywood film version of this Pulitzer Prize–winning play not only adds the daughter as Levene's impetus for the theft, but begins the film with a shot of Levene on the phone to the hospital, assuring them that the money is on the way. The fact that Levene fails at his job and fails at the theft ensures that he has failed his daughter. If he was isolated from her while she was in the hospital, he will lose her completely once he is in jail. Her survival—how good a father he is, how well he can look after her—is directly linked to how well he performs in his business. In *The Insider,* Jeffrey Wigand (Russell Crowe) has two daughters, but they too end up in his ex-wife's custody. In the latter two films, the protagonists have lost their jobs and their daughters, and neither succeeds in getting either back. In all three of these films, what happens to the daughters is a direct result of the fathers' employment statuses. D-Fens and Wigand have lost their jobs, and both have watched their daughters leave with their wives. Levene loses his job and his daughter at the same time. While *Jerry Maguire* is nowhere near as dark as these three films, it still critiques its protagonist for the clumsiness with which he fumbles his marriage, and it treats his mission statement with a definite sense of irony, but in the end he recovers completely, creating a new, more successful career for himself and acquiring a son. In different ways, with varying degrees of censure, each film suggests that, when all is said and done, things just seem to turn out better when a father has a son.

American Beauty is primarily about Lester Burnham (Kevin Spacey), a cubicle worker who sells advertising for a magazine. But the movie doesn't start with Lester; it starts, and therefore places emphasis on, his questionable abilities as a father. The film begins with a digital camera shot of his daughter, Jane. She is reclined on her bed: "I need a father who's a role model. Not some horny geek boy who's going to spray his shorts whenever I bring a girlfriend home from school. What a lame-o. Someone should put himself out of his misery." The voice from behind the camera—a young male—asks, "Want me to kill him for you?" She sits up and leans forward slightly, cunningly: "Yeah. . . . Would you?"

The narrative structure of *American Beauty* is tightly knit around two families: the Burnhams and their next-door neighbors, the Fittses, made up of eighteen-year-old Ricky and his mother and father. The Burnhams and Fittses reveal, in many ways, mirror opposite characteristics of dysfunction. Caroline Burnham (Annette Bening) reacts to her loveless marriage with a kind of nervous hyperactivity—she is constantly moving and doing and talking. Mrs. Fitts is catatonic, sitting and staring blankly, hardly connecting with her husband and son. Ricky, who once acted out violently, is not the picture of self-confidence and has an almost religious devotion to the "beauty" he sees around him. This puts him at constant odds with his militantly military and sexually repressed father. Jane— Ricky's gender opposite—has never acted out, but is plagued by low self-esteem and cynicism. This puts her at constant odds with her (newly) rebellious, sexually liberated father. Even before his rebirth, Lester offers a kind of opposite reaction to Colonel Fitts: whereas Lester deals with his dysfunction by letting everything go—becoming "sedated," in his words—Colonel Fitts hangs on tighter, trying to increase his control over his family and himself. Ricky acts as a kind of pivot between these two fathers, offering them both a chance at redemption. Their failures to assume traditional paternal roles by the end of the film are highlighted by the fact that they—the two fathers—come together and witness each other's undoing.

Certainly, Lester and Ricky's first meeting doesn't exactly typify traditional paternalistic behavior. Caroline drags Lester to one of her real estate business social functions, where he meets Ricky, who is working at the event as a waiter. Ricky introduces himself *and* his business to Lester by asking him if he likes "to party." Lester follows him outside to share a joint, and they get along immediately, laughing about a movie they both like. When the cantankerous caterer comes out to send Ricky back to work, Ricky quits. Lester is impressed: "I think you just became my personal hero. Doesn't it make you nervous to just quit your job like that?" It doesn't, Ricky replies: he takes random jobs to keep his father from finding out how he really makes money (he deals marijuana). Ricky, who works for himself and only at what he likes doing, is Lester's hero. Lester learns from him, and therefore has lost a good deal of paternal capital, but the film doesn't suggest that this is a bad thing (not in the beginning), and it therefore challenges the traditional notions of patriarchal distance and leadership. It reveals, like so many other office movies, the male desire to have closer relationships with other men without the artifice and rigidity of the paternalistic hierarchy at home and in the office. Ricky teaches Lester about his career and acquires him as a client; they achieve an easy, instant camaraderie (like Jerry and Ray) which goes further than simple business transactions.

Ricky inspires Lester to become a teenager again (flipping burgers, playing with a toy car, lifting weights in the garage, smoking pot), but Lester's version is only a narrow reflection of Ricky's life. Lester sees the marijuana, the music, the freedom, and the consumer goods in Ricky's life, and pursues them. He fails completely to see the pain and abuse in Ricky's life brought on by his father, Colonel Fitts, despite the evidence. Fatherhood is the last thing on Lester's mind. This might act as a subversion of traditional middle-class perceptions of the family and patriarchal authority, but the film urges us to see that Lester's abandonment of his paternal role is to the detriment of both Jane and Ricky.

After Lester leaves his job and assumes his more juvenile identity, he cruelly insults Jane and leaves her to her abusive mother: without Lester on deck, Caroline delivers harsh realities about the isolated life she expects Jane to live and slaps her vehemently when she feels Jane is ungrateful for those harsh words. In the next scene, which is a complement to the former, Fitts beats Ricky for opening his wall cabinet without permission. The ensuing exchange between father and son is pathetic:

> Fitts: This is for your own good, boy. You have no respect for other people's things. Or for rules. You can't just go around doing whatever you feel like. You can't. There are rules in life.
> Ricky [ardently]: Yes sir!
> Fitts: You need structure. *You need discipline!*
> Ricky [still in a military tone]: Yes sir! Thank you for trying to teach me! Don't give up on me dad!

Ricky's response to his father is bewildering: we do not know whether he is trying to gain his father's confidence to make his life easier in the long run, or if he is actually trying to reach out to his dad and asking for his paternal devotion. Fitts and Ricky have none of the easy, genuine connection shared by Lester and Ricky. However, though Lester and Ricky do share an honest and disarming kind of bantering, there could be much more on the table. Perhaps if Ricky had practical, parental guidance, he would not be dealing drugs, which is a risky line of business, and perhaps he would not obsessively film other people and things, trying to inject himself into other people's lives. Perhaps the guiding force in his life would not be the inhuman "benevolent force" he sees in a dancing, wind-blown plastic bag. There is artistry and poetry in Ricky, but there is also an aching sadness, as there is in Jane.

The film offers us two teenagers who turn to each other, perhaps because they have no one at home to care for them. The two scenes I have described suggest that, more specifically, it is because Lester is not there to care for them, and thus the film reinforces the importance of the father. After all, we do not see any evidence that Mrs. Fitts, Colonel Fitts, or Caroline are capable of providing comfort and guidance to their children, but the film tells us more than once that Lester has it in him. He resists making love to Angela, Jane's friend, and instead wraps her in a blanket and comforts her. When Colonel Fitts comes over to Lester's garage late one rainy night, soaking wet, shivering, and obviously in turmoil, Lester hugs him and tries to comfort him. But Lester has crossed too many lines to save himself and assume the role that he was, as an adult male, meant to play. These two fathers, both flunking at adult masculinity for different reasons, come together to highlight the central reason behind their failures and demises. Fitts's masculinity is empty and repressive: he has worn the mask of homophobic disciplinarian to hide his homosexuality. Lester's masculinity is stunted and regressive, relishing irresponsibility and disconnection. Their ends—as murderer and murdered—offer a warning to those who might shun the traditional models of father and breadwinner.

As with the other films discussed here, we can see how *American Beauty* sets up a correlation between failure at fatherhood and failure at work. It is interesting that, though we see Fitts driving an expensive truck and living in an upper-middle-class house, and though he introduces himself as "Colonel Frank Fitts, U.S. Marine Corps," we never see him work or go to work; we aren't shown what he *does* for a living. Maybe this is the film's commentary on government-funded work, or public, noncapitalist work. Can a real man be funded by the government, or is this too dependent? Too much like having a benefactor? Too much like being a kept woman? It certainly lacks that self-made man, capitalist spirit. *American Beauty* shows us the other side of *Jerry Maguire's* coin: Jerry is always driven toward professional success, which he must and does achieve on his own, as he is driven toward becoming a father to a son. Lester and Fitts show no evidence of being committed to careers, least of all individualist, capitalist careers, and even less commitment to connecting with and guiding their children into a secure future. There is, of course, no happy ending here.

I believe that *American Beauty* has several transgressive qualities which, given its unexpected and immense popularity, might indicate a public willingness to acknowledge the stultifying nature of the dominant ideologies surrounding our notions of gender, family, and work. In a general way, the film seeks to uncover the unhappiness beneath a commercialized, cold suburbia. Its popularity marks a tacit public acceptance of its critique of a lifestyle which forces authentic emotions underground. The slippage between this critique and its more traditional, patriarchal leanings (which ultimately resolve the film) indicates perhaps why it was so successful at the Academy Awards (and with virtually every other film-awarding institution).

What emerges as we look at the depictions of fatherhood in these films is the sense that to shift masculinities—to change roles—is to cast oneself into a chaos from which one might not return. The Narrator in *Fight Club* exchanges his nebbishy, workaday masculinity for a militant, rebellious masculinity, and ends up a witness to mass destruction of which he suddenly finds himself in charge. When he shoots himself in the face at the end of the film, the point is well taken: the man he once was has been irrevocably altered, and the new man he has become is a mangled, uncontrollable replica of his former self. In *American Beauty*, Lester and Fitts both let slip their long-standing performances of masculinity, and are drawn into a violent conclusion as a result. Contrast this with Jerry Maguire, who doesn't change as much as he evolves, improving on what he already was in a very traditional way. In effect, the sports agent with a fiancée turns into a more successful sports agent with a family. It is a logical, traditional progression wherein Jerry goes from single man to family man, embracing all those desires that his father and male mentors had long ago planted in him. I am also reminded of *The Family Man*, wherein Jack (Nicolas Cage), "a credit to capitalism," a corporate king complete with penthouse, thinks he has "everything." Magically, he is proven wrong by being transported to a parallel universe where he chose family over career. By the end of the film, Jack has not only learned to embrace his newfound family of a wife and three kids, he has managed to work his way into the company that he worked for in his previous life! Like Jerry, he goes from single man to family man without altering too much of his life: he takes part in that logical, traditional progression that truly gives him "everything." If a man can't be happy at work and at the head of a family, is random, violent chaos the best he can expect? What are the alternatives to an essentialist, traditional conception of the breadwinner masculinity? What happens to men who seek alternatives, as opposed to those who find everything? For Lester, death happens.

One could argue at this point that I am crossing genres without making allowances for their inherent differences. *Jerry Maguire* and *The Family Man* are feel-good family flicks—romantic comedies where a man falls in love with a woman and child(ren). *Fight Club* and *American Beauty* are not comedies. They're not romantic, either. However, they still support the ideologies put forth by romantic comedies, in that they offer a binary opposition that is completely untenable, like the destructive extremes exemplified by Fitts and Lester. Put another way, films like *Fight Club* and *Jerry Maguire* stand on opposite sides of the same ideological depiction of the importance of fathers and jobs, each tapping into what has been established as a credible social dissatisfaction with as much critique as is possible within the confines of their genres, and then shoring up the archetypal father by underlining his ultimate necessity.

Even films that have the veneer of the cutting edge (more so than *Fight Club* and *American Beauty*, which were ultimately too popular to be considered edgy) warn against alternative masculinities. *Being John Malkovich* is part social satire, part romance, part comedy, part drama, and part science fiction. The plot is complex and absurd and will take some explaining before it can be examined. The protagonist, Craig (John Cusack), is a puppeteer who is passionately devoted to his work, but can't make a living from it, which makes him despondent and aimless. He's reduced to busking, during which he often gets punched out by passersby who object to the sometimes-sexual nature of his performances. His wife, Lotte (Cameron Diaz), suggests that Craig get a job: "You know, I was thinking, maybe you'd feel better if you got a job or something. Until this puppet thing turns around." At home, Lotte has assembled a veritable menagerie of surrogate children: a chimp, a dog, an iguana, a ferret, a bird. Not to put too fine a point on it, Lotte discusses the chimp's therapy sessions and "childhood trauma," and then asks Craig, "So honey, have you thought any more about having a baby?" But Craig feels that things are "too tough economically" to have a (human) child. The busking knockouts, the menagerie, the beseeching wife, and particularly the popularity of another puppeteer, whom Craig deems inferior, all crowd in on him at the outset of the film. These pressures lead him to the want ads, where "Lestercorp" is "Looking for a man with fast hands." Craig's puppeteering skills get him the job easily, and he becomes an office filer among rows of cubicles, chairs, and filing cabinets. It is here that he meets Maxine (Catherine Keener) and is instantly smitten. He makes a marionette of her and acts out a scene in which the Craig doll tells the Maxine doll why he loves puppetry: "Well, Maxine, I'm not sure exactly. Perhaps the idea of becoming someone else for a little while . . . being inside another skin. Thinking differently, moving differently, feeling differently." The puppet Maxine is, of course, entranced, but the real Maxine rebuffs him in her brutally honest, emotionless fashion: "You're not somebody I could get interested in, Craig. You play with dolls." But Craig finds something to get Maxine interested: while retrieving a file from behind a cabinet, he discovers a tiny door which opens onto a long, dark, circular, muddy tunnel. He passes through the door and is swept down the tunnel, where he enters John Malkovich's mind. He sees, through a slightly narrowed frame (portal vision, if you like), what Malkovich (played by Malkovich himself) sees, for fifteen minutes, whereupon he is dumped beside the New Jersey Turnpike. When he feverishly relays his discovery to Maxine, she devises a scheme to turn the portal into a business, "JM Inc.," that will charge people $200 to "be someone else for fifteen minutes." But the film is much more than a statement on people's desperate desire for fifteen minutes of fame.

When Craig tells Lotte about his new business venture and business partner, she demands to try the portal herself. As Malkovich, Lotte is changed: "Being inside *did something* to me. I knew who I was. . . . it's like everything made sense. I knew who I was." She soon realizes how, exactly, things have begun to make sense: "It's kind of sexy that John Malkovich has a portal, you know . . . sort of like he has a vagina. Sort of vaginal, you know. Sort of like he has a penis *and* a vagina. Sort of like John Malkovich's feminine side." Lotte decides that she's a transsexual. Craig tries to dissuade her, claiming that her transgendered awakening is "just a phase," but Lotte is emphatic: "Don't stand in the way of my actualization as a *man*." Maxine supports Lotte, somewhat bemusedly, right away: "Let her go, Craig." Craig is quickly pushed aside; Lotte reenters Malkovich and meets Maxine, and falls in love with her. Maxine is attracted to what Lotte brings to John—the "feminine longing" behind his eyes. We are shown a shot of Craig, alone in his bed, while Maxine meets Lotte-as-John, this time for a sexual encounter revealed mostly through Lotte's portal vision. But Craig puts his foot down. He locks up Lotte with her chimp and enters Malkovich permanently, learning to play him like a puppet until he controls his speech and movements. Craig wears John like "an expensive suit" and seduces Maxine. The chimp frees Lotte, but Maxine likes the idea of a permanent resident in Malkovich—of manipulating his image and bank account. Craig likes the idea of using Malkovich's fame to advance his puppeteering career. And so it goes.

Eight months later, Maxine is very pregnant and Craig/Malkovich has become a virtuoso puppeteer with his own master class at Juilliard. But Maxine misses Lotte. Malkovich is too much like the bumbling, guileless Craig she initially rebuffed. Meanwhile, Lotte has found out that Craig's former boss, Dr. Lester of Lestercorp, has been using portals to stay young. When Malkovich turns forty-four, he will be "ripe," and Lester and a few other old people will move into him. If they try to enter Malkovich after midnight on his forty-fourth birthday, they will end up in the next available unripened vessel, only an infant, where they will be "absorbed . . . trapped, held prisoner if you like, in the host's brain. Unable to control anything, forever doomed to watch the world through someone else's eyes." Lester, working with Lotte, kidnaps Maxine in order to force Craig to abandon the Malkovich vessel. Maxine tells Lotte that Lotte is "the father" of her baby, or "the other mother," because it was Lotte inside Malkovich when Maxine's baby was conceived. They reconcile, leaving Craig (wailing in despair) in the rain on the side of the turnpike. He attempts to get Maxine back by reentering the Malkovich portal, but it is too late. Lester and his friends have inhabited the vessel just prior to the deadline, and as a result, Craig is thrust into an unripe vessel: Emily, Lotte and Maxine's daughter. Craig is absorbed, forced to helplessly watch his wife and his beloved raise his puppet's child. He sees Maxine and Lotte, through a little girl's eyes, holding each other and laughing together. In voice-over, we hear his agony: "Maxine . . . Maxine . . . I love you Maxine. Oh, look away . . . look away . . . look away . . . look away . . ."

This detailed plot summary is necessary in order to establish just how many identities are exchanged and/or altered in the film. The film begins with Craig and his puppet alter ego. In voicing not only himself, but puppet versions of Lotte and Maxine, Craig is trying on other personas. This is a safe kind of impersonation, given that Craig remains in control of all the characters at play. But when Craig takes on a male puppet which is not carved in his own image (Malkovich), he is transgressing a significant boundary, more dangerous even than the gender boundaries Lotte and Maxine cross with so much ease and confidence. Craig is no longer "playing with dolls," he is playing with masculinities. He leaves behind his invisible, weakling masculinity for Malkovich's imposing, distinguished masculinity, and in so doing, creates a new masculinity that is a somewhat conflicted compendium of the two. One could also argue that Malkovich himself is a collection of masculinities: in the film, we are reminded several times that he is an "actor," a "performer," and therefore a collection of all those male roles he has inhabited. At one point in the film, Malkovich himself—shocked and enraged at the discovery of JM Inc.—enters the portal and finds himself in his own subconscious: he is at a table in a restaurant, where all the patrons and employees are different versions of himself. He sits across the table from his own head on a woman's body. And all anyone (any Malkovich) can say is "Malkovich." His subconscious is crying out that there are too many Malkoviches: he has tried on too many masculinities and stretched his own identity, as a man, too far. He stares in horror at the sight of himself as a woman. As Lotte notes, Malkovich's portal is another expression of how his gender boundaries have been broken down: it is like he has both a penis and a vagina. Finally, Malkovich is simply a vessel for others, with no identity of his own. It should come as no surprise, then, that his role as a father is taken over by a woman; Maxine completely subverts Malkovich's role in the conception of Emily, declaring that Lotte is the "father." Malkovich's flexibility—his identities and masculinities—twists the father right out of him.

The same is true for Craig. He, too, has toyed with masculinities for too long—worn too many identity "suits." Perhaps even more debilitating is his unwillingness to provide Lotte with the children she so desperately wants because, he says, they don't have enough money. Craig's twin failures, then, are linked: he cannot earn money, ergo he cannot be a father. Lotte and Maxine, on the other hand, are employment-minded. Until Craig gets an office job at Lotte's urging, it is she who has been the sole income earner in their marriage. When Maxine begins her relationship with Craig/Malkovich by telling him to "stay in [Malkovich] forever," he looks to her to make the financial decisions: "My darling how will we make a living if our clientele doesn't have access to our product?" But Maxine goes beyond simply living off Malkovich's bank account and acting jobs. She becomes Craig/Malkovich's manager and is identified as an "entrepreneur" by the media. Lotte and Maxine are not artists like Craig and Malkovich; they are workers and providers.

The ultimate reward comes in the form of Maxine's pregnancy: the three females—Lotte, Maxine, and Emily—make up a family of their own with Craig's pathetic pleas droning in the background. The white male has been imprisoned in, and by, the female as a result of his conflicting and alternative masculinities. The women are skilled shape-shifters— they embrace the chance to change sexualities and gender identities—but for men, such flexibility is a dangerous prospect. And let us not forget that Craig betrays his wife before she betrays him, which Lotte so handily points out to him when she suggests he go and play with his "Maxine action figure." With one line, she sums up Craig's most damning flaw: he has abandoned his role as husband and aspiring father (albeit to a menagerie, but still) and become a child. His "work" is not art, it is child's play.

As radically different as this film is, it comes to the same conclusion: men whose gender identities get messed around are doomed. That traditional masculine role comprising breadwinner, nine-to-fiver, and father, at the helm of both the economics and the social order of the family, is rigid and cannot be bowed or modified. Certainly, a critique of the rigidity of male gender roles is a valid and necessary social commentary; however, to privilege men's suffering is to set up a dangerous and selfish victimhood which obscures a parallel suffering in truly marginalized groups. The film seems uncertain as to whether Craig's banishment is justified by his warped and cruel treatment of the women in his life, or whether he's been manipulated and ousted unfairly by them. Ultimately, *Being John Malkovich*'s strength may lie in the uncertainty suggested by its final scene, leaving us to struggle with our own notions of all the players in the gender war being represented on the screen.

Tyler Durden's suggestion that the solution to the crisis of masculinity isn't more women is a reflection of the political (both Democratic and Republican) and social atmosphere in America throughout the 1990s and into the 2000s that lamented the absence of fathers and heightened their importance as the determining factor in a child's future.[5] The question in these films is not how to change the patriarchal system or devise new, healthier configurations of the family; the question is how to prop it up, and frequently, how to prop it up in spite of or because of threatening female figures. Perhaps we can see this reluctance to cinematically imagine a new model of fatherhood/masculinity/late capitalist worker as a reflection of America's stagnant and predictable approach to the father dimension of the so-called masculinity crisis. The representation of a nation in crisis due to a lack of fathers in families was publicized by both the Bill Clinton and George W. Bush administrations. Various states incorporated the "father crisis" into their government agendas; the Wisconsin Fatherhood Initiative, for example, was kicked off in 1998, leading to its Fatherhood Summit in 1999. The Wisconsin state government allocates state funds as "seed money for local communities to utilize for fatherhood activities" (www.dwd.state.wi.us/wifatherhood). It does not specify what these activities are. In 1998, Pennsylvania's governor launched the Governor's Fatherhood Task Force Event. Moving a little further up the U.S. political ladder, in 1999 a Senate bill called the Responsible Father Act was introduced by Indiana's senator. Also in 1999, a House bill was put forth and passed: the Fathers Count Act. In his June 7, 2001, address to the Fourth National Summit on Fatherhood (sponsored by the National Fatherhood Initiative), George W. Bush outlined how his federal budget would promote fatherhood: he would set aside $64 million in 2002, and $315 million over five years, for "programs designed to strengthen fatherhood." Again, there was no stipulation as to what these programs might be, but it appears as though none of them would have dared investigate how it is that fathers have fallen so far and so hard, nor propose to study new ways of perceiving and enacting fatherhood which might avert any further occurrences of a father crisis.

This reluctance in public policy to articulate the causes of a masculinity crisis or any new ideas about solving the problem can be read in office movies' tendency to revert to traditional cinematic tropes and social constructs of gender, power, and work. Dominant ideas being circulated through mainstream venues seem incapable of writing a new script. The protagonists' inability to take on the role of father signals the debilitation of their masculinity, rather than the first step in discovering a new kind of masculinity that is not quite so closely tied to a more traditional, family- and work-centered, essentialist, and exclusionist conception of the male gender. As Fred Pfeil has written in *White Guys:*

> [U]ntil the glacial drift of this deadlock within and around the normative terms of gender is altered by a collective political will that, as of this moment, does not seem to exist here, there is no reason to think we will find anywhere in the popular culture that gets made for and peddled to us any answers to the question of what's left of white straight masculinity after and aside from the protector-provider role. (238)

Now that we are in the second decade of the twenty-first century and urgent public debate over the masculinity crisis has been replaced by the familiar rhetoric of American male heroism and might reborn through 9/11, the wars in Iraq and Afghanistan, and, more recently, a massive economic recession, so too has the more sardonic and critical office movie been replaced by the office-movie-lite. While no office movie really follows through on envisioning an alternative to the traditional linkages between masculinity and capitalist work, most are marked by a brooding darkness—a cynicism, unease, and/or even anger—regarding the rigid confines of work and manhood in the United States and by some kind of calamity, destruction, or moment of reckoning to express anxiety about the effects of these confines. And in most, there is also a sense of responsibility for the protagonists. As Jerry puts it: "What had I become?" In more recent films featuring abused male office workers, this sense of unease and culpability has disappeared.

How fitting, then, that *The Incredibles* (2004) is an animated children's film. It is the story of parents, Bob and Helen, who are former superheroes forced into hiding in the style of witness protection programs. Bob has supernatural strength, but has become a deadened office worker—an insurance adjuster—trapped in a maze of bureaucracy that, like the tiny cubicle he's squished into, severely handicaps his desire and ability to help others. The son, Dash, is supernaturally fast, but must curb his talent and dwell under his mother's disappointing platitudes about everyone being special. Dash sulks: "That just means *no one's* special." Helen's superpower—extreme flexibility and elasticity—and daughter Violet's invisibility are sad statements indeed on the traditional gender roles still being represented in our culture. Significantly, it is not Helen and Violet who chafe under the normalcy of their suburban anonymity—it is Bob and Dash who argue that they should be allowed to express their superpowers and be the winners they were so clearly destined to be. When Bob secretly begins to work as a superhero again, he brings in more money (new car, new suits) and magically begins to spend more time with his children. When he is captured, he forces a reluctant and indignant Helen back into her superhero role. And it is Dash who discovers, and then drags his sister into, the rescue mission. Essentially, Bob's high-paying, high-octane job—for it is, indeed, portrayed as a job complete with pay and assignments and bosses—as a superhero leads to a happier home life for his entire family. They are brought closer through their super-exploits, whereas before they were bickering and distant. What emerges is the sense that the desire to outperform others in a competitive playing field is inherently a more masculine trait and that, when encouraged and let loose, this competitiveness and dominance leads to a closer, more loving family. The capitalist spirit—in an archly patriarchal form of Social Darwinism—breathes through this family, as those most naturally gifted in dominance and competition win the money, the glory, and the happiness, and do so thanks entirely to the fact that such gifts apparently will not be hidden or squelched in men and their sons. The film ends with the climactic discovery that Jack Jack, the baby of the family, has superpowers too: he can burst into flames and morph into steel, and thereby take his place with his father and older brother in their spectacular examples of might, fairly exploding off the screen with bulging muscles, flying limbs, and bursting flames.

The father-son business bond is similarly strong in *The Pursuit of Happyness* (2006), in which a homeless father, Chris (Will Smith), and his son, Christopher (Jaden Smith), cling desperately together as Chris doggedly pursues the bottom rung in the stock-trading business. The only two female characters in the film—the heedless, faithless wife and mother and the lazy daycare provider—are outshone by the beneficent upper-class men working the money-making magic of the stock exchange; they recognize Chris's raw talent and give him a chance. This film seems to alternate between two basic scenarios: Chris and his son bonding despite their hardship, and Chris working his way toward a good, steady income. The idea that Chris is motivated to succeed (success here means getting a job that typifies the late capitalist economy: stock trader) out of his love for his son (and vice versa) is clear.

In yet another feel-good film, *In Good Company* (2004), a hot young executive, Carter (Topher Grace), replaces and subsequently demotes a man twice his age, Dan (Dennis Quaid). The film reassures us, however, that capitalism is a fair system that rewards the most worthy: Carter may be a young Turk, but in the end he learns from Dan, the wise father figure who demonstrates that humanized business practices (personal contacts, the ability to read people, an old-fashioned handshake) still outshine the new, flashy, callous promises of globalized conglomerate synergies. The most salient feature of *In Good Company* is its focus on these two men, who are brought together by the grace of corporate competition. Dan has no sons—only daughters—and Carter is personally adrift and without a father figure. The two are thus drawn into an inevitable bond that strengthens their sense of place in the business world: Carter decides to leave and find something he enjoys more, and Dan's original position within the company is not only reinstated, it is strengthened. The final scene is a reconstruction of the classic shot of lovers riding off into the sunset together: Carter, now on the West Coast, is jogging along the beach into a gorgeous sunset, chatting to Dan (still on the East Coast) on his cell phone. This is really a love story between a father figure and his surrogate son; it revives traditional notions of a son's need for a father so that he can be molded into a man and then go out into the world and succeed and be happy. The fact that Carter jogs into a western sunset makes the film all the more reflective of the inherently American nature of this patriarchal capitalist project. It doesn't matter that the West was conquered long ago; notions of gender, power, and work have changed little since that frontier fell.

Ultimately, I would argue that, in the 1990s, Hollywood films acknowledged another masculinity—that of the disempowered late capitalist office worker—and yet failed to articulate that masculinity or a concomitant social critique in any sustained way. Rather, these films updated the ideologies shoring up the traditional breadwinner ethic by connecting them to contemporary experiences of middle- and upper-class work in late capitalist, globalized management culture. One might wonder, would the critique barely begun in office movies have progressed further if not for 9/11? Might it even have been expanded to include other experiences of men at work that are not, after all, crisis or no, the most privileged in the world? What is it about America's political economy that necessitates the circulation and then containment of messages about masculine crisis that divert attention from other more oppressively marginalized masculinities?

NOTES

1. For more on this trend, see *Papering the Cracks: Fantasy and Ideology in the Reagan Era* by Robin Wood; and "Fathers, Sons and Brothers " by Neil Rattigan and Thomas P. McManus.

2. See also Van Fuqua's "'Can You Feel It, Joe?'"

3. The complete text of Jerry's mission statement, entitled "The Things We Think and Do Not Say," has been published on the film's website and was released on the 2002 special DVD edition of the film. It contains even more evidence of the film's assertion of patriarchal consistency through the generations of family and business. The first paragraph quotes his dad: "My father once said, 'Get the bad news over with first. You be the one to say the tough stuff.'" Jerry quotes his father along with his first boss and his business mentor throughout his mission statement; moreover, Jerry notes that his life is "neutral" because, among other reasons, he's never "fathered a child." He also notes that "an agent can be a father, a friend, an inspiring force in the life of a young man or woman," and that he is "the most successful male in [his] family," but not the happiest

(his brother wins that prize, for his NASA work). In keeping with Anthony Easthope's observation in *What a Man's Gotta Do* that women tend to be written out of the process of creating a man, Jerry's mission statement reveals that women have been eliminated from his recollections of his family and upbringing—there is only a father, two older male mentors, and (to a much lesser degree) a brother.

4. In 1991, when Judge Clarence Thomas was nominated for a position on the U.S. Supreme Court, Anita Hill—a law professor—publicly accused Thomas of sexual harassment. A media frenzy ensued.

5. In 1994, the National Fatherhood Initiative was formed (www.fatherhood.org). Its assertions that children without fathers are significantly at risk and disadvantaged have been repeated and circulated in publications like the *Journal of Marriage and Family* and through various government-funded studies like the 1997 *Federal Interagency Forum of Child and Family Statistics*. The NFI and similar government bodies frequently omit the fact that a mother's education level and the family's socioeconomic level are the greatest predictors of a child's success. Several studies have also established that children from single-father households are at a disadvantage (www.gate.net/liz/liz/017.htm).

BIBLIOGRAPHY

Bruzzi, Stella. *Bringing Up Daddy: Fatherhood and Masculinity in Post-war Hollywood.* London: BFI, 2005.

Cohan, Steven. *Masked Men: Masculinity and the Movies in the Fifties.* Bloomington: Indiana University Press, 1997.

Easthope, Anthony. *What a Man's Gotta Do: The Masculine Myth in Popular Culture.* 1986. Rpt., Boston: Unwin Hyman, 1990.

Faludi, Susan. *Stiffed: The Betrayal of the American Man.* New York: Morrow, 1999.

Hunter, Latham. "The Celluloid Cubicle: Regressive Constructions of Masculinity in 1990s Office Movies." *Journal of American Culture* 26, no. 1 (March 2003): 71–86.

Jeffords, Susan. "The Big Switch: Hollywood Masculinity in the Nineties." In *Film Theory Goes to the Movies,* ed. Jim Collins, Hilary Radner, and Ave Preacher Collins. London: Routledge, 1993.

Pfeil, Fred. *White Guys.* London: Verso, 1995.

Rattigan, Neil, and Thomas P. McManus. "Fathers, Sons and Brothers: Patriarchy and Guilt in 1980s American Cinema." *Journal of Popular Film and Television* 20, no. 1 (Spring 1992): 15–23.

Van Fuqua, Joy. "'Can You Feel It, Joe?': Male Melodrama and the Feeling Man." *Velvet Light Trap* 38 (Fall 1996): 28–38.

Wiegman, Robyn. "Bonds of (In)Difference." In *The Masculinity Studies Reader,* ed. Rachel Adams and David Savran. Oxford: Blackwell, 2002.

FILMOGRAPHY

American Beauty. Dir. Sam Mendes. DreamWorks; Jinks/Cohen, 1999.

Being John Malkovich. Dir. Spike Jonze. Gramercy Pictures; Propaganda Films; Single Cell Pictures, 1999.

Falling Down. Dir. Joel Schumacher. Warner Brothers, 1993.

Fight Club. Dir. David Fincher. Alcor Films; Le Studio Canal; Regency Enterprises; Warner Brothers, 1999.

Fun with Dick and Jane. Dir. Dean Parisot. Imagine Entertainment; Sony Pictures Entertainment; Columbia Pictures; JC 23 Entertainment, 2005.

Glengarry Glen Ross. Dir. James Foley. New Line Cinema; Zupnik Cinema Group II, 1992.

In Good Company. Dir. Paul Weitz. Universal Pictures; Depth of Field, 2004.

Jerry Maguire. Dir. Cameron Crowe. Gracie Films; TriStar Pictures, 1996.

Kramer vs. Kramer. Dir. Robert Benton. Columbia Pictures, 1979.

Mr. Mom. Dir. Stanley Dragoti. Sherwood Pictures, 1983.

Nothing in Common. Dir. Gary Marshall. TriStar Pictures, 1986.

One Good Cop. Dir. Heywood Gould. Hollywood Pictures; Silver Screen Partners IV, 1991.

On Golden Pond. Dir. Mark Rydell. Universal Pictures, 1981.

Ordinary People. Dir. Robert Redford. Paramount Pictures; Wildwood Enterprises, 1980.

The Family Man. Dir. Brett Ratner. Beacon Communications; Howard Rosenman Productions; Riche-Ludwig Productions; Saturn Films, 2000.

The Incredibles. Dir. Brad Bird. Walt Disney Pictures; Pixar Animation Studios, 2004.

The Insider. Dir. Michael Mann. Blue Light Productions; Forward Pass; Kaitz Productions; Mann/Roth Productions; Touchstone Pictures, 1999.

The Pursuit of Happyness. Dir. Gabriele Muccino. Columbia Pictures; Relativity Media; Overbrook Entertainment; Escape Artists, 2006.

Regarding Henry. Dir. Mike Nichols. Paramount Pictures, 1991.

Very Bad Things. Dir. Peter Berg. Ballpark Productions; Initial Entertainment Group; Interscope Communications, 1998.

PART TWO

BEYOND GENDER ALONE: DEFINING MULTIDIMENSIONAL MASCULINITIES

POPULAR MEMORY, RACIAL CONSTRUCTION, AND THE VISUAL ILLUSION OF FREEDOM: THE RE-MEDIATION OF O.J. AND CINQUE

JOHN KILLE

To put pen to a text is to begin the movement away from the original.

EDWARD SAID, *BEGINNINGS: INTENTION AND METHOD*

That night I dreamed I was at a circus with him and that he refused to laugh at the clowns no matter what they did. Then later he told me to open my briefcase and read what was inside and I did, finding an official envelope stamped with the state seal; and inside the envelope I found another and another, endlessly, and I thought I would fall of weariness. "Them's years," he said. "Now open that one." And I did and in it I found an engraved document containing a short message in letters of gold. "Read it," my grandfather said. "Out loud!"

RALPH ELLISON, *INVISIBLE MAN*

THE O.J. SIMPSON INCIDENT

On Monday, June 13, 1994, Nicole Brown Simpson, a white female, and her friend Ronald Goldman, a white male, were found dead outside Goldman's condominium in the lush and extravagant Brentwood section of Los Angeles. During the course of the following week, the Los Angeles Police Department pieced together enough evidence to arrest its primary suspect, former football star O.J. Simpson, a black male and Nicole's former husband (they had been divorced two years prior), for the double murder. On Friday, June 17, a warrant was issued for Simpson's arrest, and his lawyer, Robert Shapiro, a celebrity criminal defense attorney who had once defended Johnny Carson, indicated that Simpson would turn himself in to police custody. As this information became public, reporters flocked to hear Simpson's statement. However, after Simpson failed to show, it was rumored by many that he had committed suicide or was hiding at his house. Confusion set in, and later that afternoon, in a hunt for the former football star, a sheriff's patrol car spotted his 1993 white Ford Bronco traveling north on Interstate 405. Al Cowling, Simpson's long-time friend, was driving while Simpson rode in the passenger seat.

As people returned home from work on Friday evening and turned on their televisions, they saw a classic chase scene: police cars, or signifiers of authority, cruising down the highway (in this case, at a low speed), pursuing an "outlaw" vehicle (in this case, a white Bronco with two black males inside). Since most television stations had centered their evening broadcast on the Simpson case, this visual spectacle *became* the evening news. The live broadcast, a type of transmission that viewers perceive as closer to reality since it is unrehearsed and anything can happen, brought over 95 million people to the sidelines as the Bronco rolled down the highway (Furno-Lamude 23). Television viewers, jaws agape at this bizarre occurrence, watched the live action closely for an hour and a half, eager to know the fate of the Heisman Trophy winner, pro football Hall of Famer, Hertz spokesperson, sports commentator, and Hollywood actor, O.J. Simpson. Then, viewers saw the Bronco wind slowly through the glorious Brentwood neighborhood and pull carefully into the driveway at Simpson's home; more confusion arose—a standoff, a confrontation, and the Los Angeles police arresting Simpson.[1]

This imaging of O.J. Simpson, an extremely popular and well-liked African American celebrity, in a car chase and standoff launched a continuing spectacle that would soon develop into a televised trial, allowing viewers to tune in every day, as if watching a soap opera or courtroom drama, to witness firsthand—with little effort since all they had to do was turn on the television—a black man, sitting in a courtroom, on trial for a violent crime. Like the heightened mediation of the *Amistad* Africans' trial in 1839–1840, Simpson's trial received a surplus of public attention. But since in the 1990s, television was, as it still is now, such a popular medium through which to obtain information and entertainment, the visual spectacle of moving pictures and the realism that this medium creates re-mediated Simpson as the representation of blackness in the audience's view.

As Simpson sat in the defendant's chair and, along with the television audience, watched the trial unfold, viewers witnessed his live reactions to the words and actions in the courtroom, deciding for themselves whether he "did it" or not. Johnnie Cochran, who had previously represented singer Michael Jackson in a child molestation trial; Reginald Denny, the white truck driver who had been beaten by a black mob during the height of the Los Angeles riots in 1992; and former Black Panther Party member Elmer "Geronimo" Pratt, defended Simpson, along with prominent attorneys Robert Shapiro, F. Lee Bailey, and Alan Dershowitz.[2] Footage of the trial was continuously scrutinized during the evening news, keeping viewers up to date with the story, and talk show hosts, such as Jay Leno and David Letterman, created additional narratives concerning the Simpson trial and the persons involved, such as Judge Lance Ito and prosecuting attorney Marcia Clark. The O.J. Simpson visual narrative continued into other forms of popular culture and visual media. Debates on whether or not Simpson murdered Nicole Brown Simpson and Ron Goldman became popular at bars, supermarkets, and other public spaces. On July 27, 1994, shortly after the arrest, and only five days after Simpson's hypermediated July 22 statement to the court that he was "100 percent not guilty,"[3] *Time* magazine featured Simpson's LAPD mug shot on its cover. In the photo, Simpson's clothes hang wrinkled and misshapen, his mouth is straight and expressionless, his eyes look tired and stare directly into the camera or toward the viewer. In addition, the magazine's graphic designer had darkened Simpson's face significantly.[4] This image stood miles away from the much lighter, happier, and heroic popular image of Simpson that had been portrayed for years in magazines, such as *Sports Illustrated,* and on television and in films, such as the Hertz commercials and the *Naked Gun* series.[5]

As the trial progressed, other visual media re-mediated Simpson's popular image. A play concerning the incident and trial opened at the Ibis Club, a dinner theatre in midtown Manhattan, which promoted viewer interaction. At the end of the night, each table at the theatre, through a selected foreperson, turned in a verdict indicating whether or not Simpson was guilty (Kilgannon CY6). Fox television aired *The O.J. Simpson Story,* a film concerning the initial part of the spectacle, during the midpoint of the highly publicized trial.[6] It focused mainly on the car chase and stand-off, but helped to produce additional visual images to re-mediate the hero.

As more and more visual narratives re-mediated the incident, Simpson's image transitioned from all-star athlete to black criminal on trial for a double murder of two white people, one of the victims his former wife, before a national (and international) audience. This imaging launched a discourse on post–civil rights movement black deviance (Morrison, "Official Story," xxvii). His "race-neutral" and heroic image had been transformed into one signifying danger, domestic violence, and murder (Crenshaw 97–103). Thus, in popular culture as well as popular memory, Simpson's image as a black male became less focused on heroism and strength, and more on violence, danger, and criminality.

In this chapter, I will analyze director Steven Spielberg's *Amistad*, a popular Hollywood film produced and released soon after the highly publicized O.J. Simpson incident (and also the Rodney King incident and nationwide urban riots) created a heightened awareness of racial conflict due to mediated moving pictures and further public reaction. I will examine how the beginning of the film, which sets the movie's tone for the audience, constructs whiteness in opposition to blackness—a racial identity formation re-mediated in a similar way as the O.J. Simpson narrative. I will also examine the viewer spectacle of O.J. Simpson and Joseph Cinque within the courtroom, as they both were quickly detained and then placed in front of a large (television and movie) audience. As viewers watched the two men detained within the walls of the courtroom (and legal system), they witnessed the incarceration of the black man. I will address how the narratives concluded, and how they projected a visual illusion of freedom: both men won their trials, but they could not return to their original "homes," Brentwood and Sierra Leone, because the economics of race displaced both individuals in some way. Simpson, after having been re-mediated for media profit as a violent black man,[7] which altered his former identity as a powerful athlete, could not return to his Brentwood home for various reasons relating to the trial, and relocated to Florida.[8] However, this information is less widely available than the actual trial, which concluded with Simpson's release from the confines of the courtroom. In the Spielberg narrative, after Cinque's release and during his journey home, subtitles inform the audience about Cinque's future, indicating that, as he returned to his home, he discovered that his village had been destroyed and his family was probably enslaved. He also had been displaced through the modern institution of race and must move on. Thus, although Cinque and the other Africans and O.J. Simpson won their cases, generating a visual illusion of freedom in a post–civil rights movement society, the places of residence for both men were destroyed in some way. Both black men have been displaced.

Spielberg's film *Amistad* and the O.J. Simpson television coverage create a visual illusion of freedom, similar to the illusion of freedom created at the end of the 1960s civil rights movement when the Voting Rights Act was granted, a historical moment that cultural theorists, such as Michael Brown and Martin Carnoy, argue has divided the United States concerning the future equality of the oppressed races (Brown et al. 4–5). Since the 1960s, asserts Brown and other critics discussing post–civil rights movement society, people on all points of the political spectrum have grown to believe that race relations have moved in three ways. The first is the belief that the civil rights movement was successful and that racial segregation no longer exists. The second assumes that, if there are still racial inequalities, it is because blacks have not taken advantage of opportunities given to them through the civil rights movement and other government and public policy efforts. The third is the belief that America is rapidly becoming a color-blind society and there is no need for affirmative action or other color-conscious policies (Brown et al. 1–5). The *Amistad* film, a visual narrative couched in the ideologies of racial construction and conflict, re-mediates for a post–civil rights movement society notions related to the O.J. Simpson incident. I will argue that the film re-mediates not only the bodies of Cinque and the other Africans, but also the body of O.J. Simpson in 1990s American culture.

VISUAL ILLUSION OF FREEDOM

As cultural theorist Diane Furno-Lamude argues, "metaphorically, the O.J. Simpson trial may be equated with a spectacle, and media coverage of the trial, to a pair of spectacles through which the public sees, interprets, and translates information presented as news" (19). In other words, what is visually and aurally mediated via television news is what readers tend to consume and believe. Media theorist Ana Celsing states that "the information we get from the picture is neither 'independent' as it is highly influenced by the accompanying text, nor a 'source' in the sense of direct unmediated information" (129). The mediated image, especially on television news, produces notions of an "independent source," thus making whatever is being transmitted more believable. The news image, or its rhetorical function, creates an objectivity factor, appearing to the viewer that it is reality. However, since there are countless subjective functions, this is not actually the case (Celsing 127–129). But, to the reader of the television text, the idea of the subjective producer can sometimes be forgotten.

The Simpson incident, as a spectacle, transmits a visual narrative through the medium of television's moving pictures, which appear realistic to readers. Since the identity of the reader will always differ, the production of the event will differ as well, according to how the reader sees the event. Carl Gutiérrez-Jones notes in *Critical Race Narratives* that a nationwide poll conducted by the *Los Angeles Times* in 1997, immediately following the civil trial that declared Simpson liable for the murders and fined him $8.5 million, found that 76 percent of whites agreed with the civil case's verdict while only 25 percent of blacks agreed (1). This large difference in perception draws attention to the multiple viewpoints that one event can create and recreate. The Spielberg film, produced during a time in which racial conflict was visually renewed through the screen with the Rodney King incident (resulting in nationwide televised urban riots) and the O.J. Simpson incident, works to create a visual illusion of freedom. It does this by moving the black male body from violent criminal to docile prisoner to freed man while white bodies are the primary movers of these actions. Compared to other *Amistad*-centered narratives throughout the twentieth century, the film focuses more on the heroic actions of the white abolitionists as defenders of freedom, although the fictionalized black abolitionist Theodore Joadson, played by actor Morgan Freeman, is included as a defender. Thus, by focusing on the heroic actions of the white men, the film works to mute the heroic actions of the *Amistad* Africans, particularly the hero, Cinque, who literally broke the chains of captivity. This filmic image is a largely different visual interpretation of the *Amistad* event than Hale Woodruff's 1939 three-part mural in which Cinque and the other Africans are the prominent men throughout the series.[9] After a mediated spectacle of race surfaced once again in popular culture, Spielberg used a historically significant incident couched in issues of racial identity and racial conflict, an incident unknown to most, including historians, to create a mediated illusion of the freedom of African Americans.

In the popularized filmic representation of the *Amistad* incident, the illusion of freedom becomes a newly constructed trope concerning the *Amistad* story in the mid-1990s. In addition to Cinque winning the trial in the Supreme Court, this trope uses images of black men running free alongside white men in Africa, the Hollywoodized destruction (yes, complete with explosions) of large seaside slave-trading houses in Africa, and the onset of the Civil War, which again, with constant cheering as an auditory backdrop as freedom is granted to the black captives through the legal system, suggests the end of racial conflict. As the *Amistad* film mirrors the narrative of the O.J. Simpson spectacle—an alleged criminal act followed by a mediated chase, an arrest, indefinite jail time and a trial, a verdict in favor of the black defendant(s), and then release—the blacks at the end of the *Amistad* film seemingly become as free as the white men who helped them through the trial. In other words, in the Spielberg film, which was released in the late 1990s and is available on video and DVD today, the end of the slave trade/slavery creates an illusion of freedom which seems to illustrate what race theorist Stephen Steinberg calls the "liberal retreat from race during the post–Civil Rights era."[10] In addition, the *Amistad* film re-mediates the *Amistad* story and the O.J. Simpson story, retelling the stories of racial conflict, creating images of the violent and criminal black man, constructing the docile black man confined in the legal system (courtroom and jail), and, at the end, re-mediating a visual illusion of freedom and drawing the post–civil rights movement's color-blind ideology.

HOLLYWOOD, THE MIDDLE PASSAGE, AND STEVEN SPIELBERG

During the first century of film production, Hollywood nearly managed to avoid publicizing any aspects of the Middle Passage, not only one of the most important events of cultural and racial history, but also one of the most dehumanizing and torturous portions of modernity. Although John Berry's *Tamango* (1958), starring Dorothy Dandridge; Alex Haley's *Roots*, launched on television as a mini-series in January 1977; and Guy Deslauriers' *The Middle Passage* (2000) all contain visual elements of the Middle Passage, the American audience has been denied a cinematic view pertaining to an important element of its own identity. Thus, directing a film concerning the *Amistad* incident, a Middle Passage event centered on a black rebellion during one of the thousands of ship passages, Steven Spielberg, an American director well known for such films as *Jaws*, the *Raiders of the Lost Ark* series, *Schindler's List*, and *Saving Private Ryan*, was breaking new ground as he attempted to project American historical racial struggles at sea onto the screen.

Although Spielberg is credited with popularizing to a wide audience a little known but highly important event centered on the often-buried Western cultural truths of racial struggles and black retaliation, he has also been criticized for the film's shortcomings. Scholars reviewing and critiquing the film, such as Stefani Barber, Joseph K. Adjaye, and Peter Hinks, agree that it brought much-needed attention to the historic event, but also note that the film contains too little information on the rebellion and heroism of the Africans and places too much attention on the courtroom drama and the white abolitionists.[11] Media and communication scholars Marouf Hasian Jr. and A. Cheree Carlson argue that the *Amistad* Hollywood film, since it introduced the subject to the public, should have displayed a multitude of legal positions rather than forcing the incident as the turning point of the history of slavery, including the launching of the American Civil War (58–60). I argue that, by focusing the film very little on the captives' uprising and mainly on the courtroom drama, where the *Amistad* Africans sit quietly while white lawyers fight for their human rights, this version of the *Amistad* story centers more on the abolitionists' power to free the captive Africans than on the heroic actions performed by the Africans. In addition, at the end of the film, although the captives are freed and able to travel back to Africa, they are ultimately displaced as they find their villages ransacked and their families absent: the film creates an illusion of freedom after the Supreme Court victory.

Because of the film's power and popularity as a box-office hit in the post–civil rights movement society and, even more specific, in the post–O.J. incident society, it forces a popular memory of the *Amistad* incident as one that seemingly corrects or even extracts racial conflict, supplanting it with a visual illusion of freedom; as F. C. Bartlett argues in his pioneering study of memory and the retaining of an idea, "remembering seems to be far more of an affair of construction rather than one of mere reproduction" (205). Public memory and popular culture are fused and interlinked, so what becomes popular culture plays a large role in what is publicly remembered (Lipsitz, *Time Passages*, 3–20).

Historians and other scholars have discussed racial construction in a text and the making of that text, or authorship. For example, Henry Louis Gates Jr., in *"Race," Writing, and Difference,* discusses the racial differences that are reflected and that occur in the varying productions of media and literature, asserting that, from the beginning of modernity, the viewpoints of blacks and other minorities were scarce regarding certain events for multiple sociopolitical reasons. For example, since blacks and other people of color were banned legally from reading and writing, which are physical and mental acts that help to create popular memories within a society, whiteness and the ideologies of whiteness prevail in the popular memory of various events that have been created through the use of media (7–10). Toni Morrison, in *Playing in the Dark,* argues that, historically within American literature, the constructed identity of whiteness has always been dependent on the construction and identity of blackness. She says, "because American literature has been clearly the preserve of white male views, genius, and power, those views, genius, and power are without relationship to and removed from the overwhelming presence of black people in the United States" (5). Sociologist Darnell M. Hunt, in *Channeling Blackness: Studies on Television and Race in America,* argues that this same ideology is created by contemporary visual media, such as television, as it is widely viewed and creates popular memories. The construction of whiteness and the notions of power that come with it depend on the creation of blackness on the screen (3–5). Constructions of the ideologies of blackness and whiteness within a specific text depend on who produces the text.

FILM REALISM AND RE-MEDIATING AN EVENT

African American co-producer of the *Amistad* film, Debbie Allen, a well-known dancer, choreographer, and actor, discovered the *Amistad* incident in a Howard University bookstore in the mid-1970s, after picking up Charles F. Harris and John A. Williams's two-part book series, *Amistad I and II: Writings on Black History and Culture,* and reading the one-page narrativization of the *Amistad* incident inside the front cover of the first text (Spielberg et al. 9). Realizing the importance of the unpopularized story within the context of American cultural history, she felt it needed to be told (ibid.). In 1984, Allen optioned the rights to William Owens's *Amistad*-incident-based novel, which was published as *Slave Mutiny* in 1953 and *Black Mutiny* in 1968 and 1997. During the next ten years, she researched for the film and searched for a director who could create the *Amistad* story as a Hollywood film. After viewing *Schindler's List*, a film about German businessman Oskar Schindler who, by bringing in 1,100 Jews to his factory to create unusable military equipment during the Holocaust, managed to save them from being gassed at the Auschwitz concentration camp, Allen decided to approach Steven Spielberg with the film idea. After Spielberg, who had some knowledge of the *Amistad* story, understood her idea and her reasons for making the film, he agreed to direct it (ibid., 13–16).

There were other visual creations of the *Amistad* incident produced around the time of the O.J. Simpson incident, some in film form, such as Karyl K. Evans's *The Amistad Revolt: "All We Want Is Make Us Free"* (1995), *Cinque: Freedom Fighter* (1997), and H. D. Motyl's *Voyage of La Amistad: A Quest for Freedom* (1998), and one as a staged opera, Anthony Davis and Thulani Davis's *Amistad: An Opera in Two Acts* (1997). But since a Hollywood film is more likely to produce public memory than an opera which was staged for only a few weeks in 1997 or smaller film productions, which do not have nearly the audience as a DreamWorks picture, I believe that the Spielberg film has created more of a public discussion from its narrative than the other visual creations of the *Amistad* incident in the late twentieth century. Thus, Spielberg's *Amistad* film is important in understanding the construction of public memory concerning such an important event in racial history (Hasian and Carlson 42–44). In addition to the film's popularity, the use of filmic narrative, a medium that appears on the surface to be objective, neutral, or realistic (Fabe 8), is central in creating a popular and collective memory of the event. The opera, staged in Chicago's beautiful and famous Lyric Theater, only ran a short time in 1997, and in any case it functions as a different type of medium than film; its stage, lights, songs, and dance movements create a narrative quite different from the objective or realistic-appearing film narrative, and therefore create a different memory. The other three films, although they re-mediate the *Amistad* incident, function on a more minor scale and cannot compete with the draw of a DreamWorks film.

Though these four visual pieces are important to the history of *Amistad* re-mediations, I have chosen to exclude them from the main analysis of this chapter.

Early twentieth-century filmmaker D. W. Griffith, with his landmark film, *The Birth of a Nation,* changed film narrative and the creation of the film story significantly: he made the visual image of the motion picture less theatrical and more realistic (Fabe 1–4).[12] This fabrication of reality through the medium of film draws readers closer to the narrative as it becomes a more realistic adventure. During the course of the twentieth century, this style of filmmaking was adapted and adopted by various directors and cinematographers. Film became a major tool for the creation of the realistic narrative.

Spielberg, in the film's companion book, *Amistad: "Give Us Free": A Celebration of the Film by Steven Spielberg,* also produced by DreamWorks, discusses how he focused on recreating the *Amistad* incident as "realistically" as possible. In addition to using real chains for the captives to wear, he found places to shoot which resembled mid-nineteenth-century New Haven, Connecticut. He hired West African men to play the captives' roles and had designers research and create authentic clothing for them to wear. And to create the visuals, he recruited Janusz Kaminski, the cinematographer who won Oscars for his work on *Schindler's List* and on *Saving Private Ryan,* another World War II period piece focused on racial and national identity. Spielberg and Kaminski used few complicated camera moves. As Kaminski says, "by not having the dolly and the crane and the camera move, you allow the viewer to focus on the story as it unfolds. We're making a movie, but I tried to make it look less like a movie" (Spielberg et al. 56). The cinematographer and Spielberg, in making the film look "less like a movie," re-mediated the *Amistad* story by creating an illusion of "reality," more specifically, the "reality" of the mid-nineteenth-century *Amistad* incident. Says Spielberg: "I shot it completely different[ly] than my other movies. I did not want the camera to fly, as I customarily have it do, through the scenes. I wanted the camera to lock off, then tilt and pan—but not crane, not dolly, not track. I didn't want to bring modern times—which I equate with long, slick dolly shots—into the nineteenth century" (ibid.)

Spielberg projected a long-absent and important historical event to the forefront of American popular culture in order to grant viewers an imagined and what he refers to as a "realistic" experience of the *Amistad* event. Although this filmic creation launched the American historical moment into popular culture, the reading/writing of the incident re-mediates tropes of the violent and dangerous black male, the docile/happy Negro, and other stereotypes of black masculinity, which are not only historically conveyed in Hollywood films in general, but also historically created in other *Amistad* narratives and cultural artifacts. Thus, by marginalizing and stereotyping the black characters in the film, such as rebellion leader Cinque and the fictional character, Theodore Joadson, who alone represents the entire black abolitionist population, the heroism pertaining to the incident falls mainly on John Quincy Adams, Roger Baldwin, the white abolitionists, and the Supreme Court—white male judicial representations of America.

In cinema, the visual image is one of the most important parts in the system of discourse. Films were initially constructed with only moving pictures and no sound; the foundational element of film is the visual image. Movie houses create the largest screen possible to allow the largest view, and television sizes have increased dramatically since their 1940s introduction. In creating a film, the director spends countless hours trying to achieve the perfect frame, lighting, and material (Metz 45). In doing so, the creator of the film forms a narrative of moving pictures which, deriving historically from photography—which also attempts to create a reality—mediate an illusion of reality. However, unlike the photograph, the film creates a sense of motion for the reader. Photography, as Roland Barthes emphasizes in *Communications*, presents the image to the reader as "a reality in which we are sheltered," but film seems to present more than this since there are additional cues, such as motion, sound, and changing light, that create an illusion closer to reality (Metz 6).

America is fascinated with viewing various true stories through the medium of film. President Woodrow Wilson, after a private screening of Griffith's *Birth of a Nation* at the White House, was reported to have said, "It is like writing history with lightning. And my only regret is that it is all so terribly true."[13] The recreation of history through film, or what is called the historical film, has proved popular in the United States, and in the 1990s the genre included *Malcolm X* (1992), *Forrest Gump* (1994), *Panther* (1995), and *Titanic* (1997) (Landy 10). Cable television stations, such as Biography and the History Channel, devote much or even all of their broadcasting to historical events. Narrative theorist C. Behan Mc-Cullagh asserts that the function of a historical narrative is to give a fair representation of history and of its central subject and that authors should use their creative license when interpreting history into a workable narrative (320–346). Furthermore, cultural analyst John Passmore points out that good historical narratives must be imaginative in order to keep the reader's attention (68–74). Although I agree with both scholars, I believe that there are crucial elements to the construction of racial identity that interpreters should consider when recreating texts that arise out of events involving racial history. Spielberg's interpretation through film, a medium which creates a heightened illusion of reality, re-mediates and popularizes the *Amistad* story with an emphasis on the tropes of violent, dangerous savagery and criminal black masculinity—ideas also created in the O.J. Simpson mediated narrative—and then moves to extract racial conflict altogether by the end of the film. Thus, as the film narrativizes the *Amistad* incident, it also conveys an imagined set of pictorial and auditory cues as to "what happened" during a time in which the O.J. Simpson and Rodney King incidents were redrawing black masculinity (in opposition to white masculinity), and creates a visual illusion of freedom by the film's end.

In performing a close reading of Spielberg's film *Amistad*, examining the construction of black masculinity in opposition to white masculinity within the film narrative, a popular text which conveys the popular culture of the time in which it was produced, I will first look at the film's beginning and the initial constructions of blackness and whiteness within the text, since, as cultural theorist Edward Said asserts in *Beginnings*, the beginning is the first step in the intentional production of meaning of the text (5). In addition, I will read the film's plot as a whole, since, as semiotician and film theorist Christian Metz notes, viewers mainly retain plot and a few images after watching a film since they see dozens of films each year and see multitudes of other media each day (46). Thus, the plot of a popular film has an effect on the viewer's memory and what is retained. By examining closely the beginning and the plot of the film narrative, I will show how the *Amistad* film re-mediates not only tropes and ideologies from the *Amistad* event, but also tropes and ideologies present in the O.J. Simpson spectacle. Also in my analysis, I will pay attention to important film elements as discussed by film theorist Marilyn Fabe: mise-en-scène, or what the camera (viewer) sees; editing, or how the film is put together; and sound, including dialogue, noise, and music.[14] The re-mediation is reflective not only of the past, but also of the time in which the event was (re)produced.

With the O.J. Simpson incident, American viewers once again experienced racial conflict as a prominent, visually mediated image. Three years prior to the Simpson spectacle, viewers saw televised racial conflicts when stations aired shaky amateur camera footage, with its visual grit and grime, displaying four white Los Angeles police officers brutally beating a working-class black male, Rodney King. Shortly after this incident, after a mostly white jury acquitted the four officers, audiences saw on their television screens the worst urban riots in U.S. history.[15] These LA riots visually demonstrated the exploding post–civil rights anger of poor, urban, mostly minority, disenfranchised groups.

Through visual re-mediations, Simpson's former "color-blind" image, in which viewers saw him not as an African American, but as a "race-neutral" celebrity, soon became raced as the trial progressed.[16] His face was literally blackened in the famous Time magazine cover, a visual mediation and re-mediation of Simpson. By darkening his features in the mug shot, a crime-related photo, the alterations accentuated blackness and what it connotes in American society: violence, sexual violence, and danger. The popular visual image, reproduced on television newscasts, re-mediated Simpson's muscular, sculpted, over six-foot-tall black body. Thus, at the beginning of the O.J. Simpson incident, visual media, such as Time magazine and the reproduction of his image on television newscasts, re-mediated Simpson's imaged body from the heroic Heisman Trophy–winning, All-American running back to one with the power and capabilities to slash, with a large knife, two persons at the same time. Simpson, in the visual narrative, represented the embodiment of black criminality, violence, and danger as he was re-mediated as the black man so enraged by another (white) man's fondness for his former wife that he had to kill them both. Although the almost all-female jury, consisting of nine African Americans, two whites, and one Hispanic, acquitted Simpson on

October 3, 1995, debates continued in the popular culture and popular media concerning the Simpson trial. Moreover, in the less popularized, nontelevised civil case that followed, Simpson was found liable for the murders by the mostly white jury and fined $8.5 million,[17] information which again made national headlines.

Once again, during a time of heightened racial awareness (after the televised Rodney King incident and LA riots), a prominently mediated trial divided the nation along racial lines, refocusing national attention on race relations, racial identity, and most important, racial conflict.[18] As legal scholar and critical race theorist Kimberlé Williams Crenshaw asserted: "Race, suspended in the buffer zone, remains ready to reappear as an interpretive frame to justify racial disparities in American life and to legitimize, when necessary, the marginalization and the circumvention of African Americans."[19] The O.J. Simpson incident was drawn and redrawn in visual form continuously during the mid-1990s; thus, television and other forms of visual media displayed historic racial tropes, such as the sexual power and beastliness of the black man, the violent and dangerous black man, and other rhetorical attempts to "keep the black man down."

Since the beginning of a narrative decisively seats the viewer in the point of intention, or direction, in which it will move, the narrative's beginning is the first step in what Edward Said calls the "intentional production of meaning" (5). How the narrative's authors and producers construct the opening sequence holds high importance since the beginning of the narrative points the viewer in a direction in accordance with the plot, character development, setting, time, and other elements that transmit meaning to the viewer's mind. How we view characters in the opening portion of a narrative is powerfully connected with how we view the characters later in the narrative. Thus, the beginning of a narrative, using the medium of either film or television, has significant purpose in the intentional production of meaning. Since the *Amistad* story is couched in meanings of racial identity and racial conflict, the notions of race constructed at the beginning of the narrative are going to affect the reader's ultimate perception of race and racial identity throughout the remainder of the film.

Amistad opens in almost total darkness in the lower portion of the ship before the onset of the rebellion. Cinque, played by Djimon Hounsou, works to remove a large nail from the wooden floor, which will provide him with a pick to help unlock his chains. Cinque is initially portrayed as sweating, working, straining, and concentrating. Using a close-up shot, the film shows the viewer the intensity in Cinque's face, mainly his eyes. His breathing is prominent and labored as the sweat rolls down his brow. Thunder is barely audible, as the focus of sound at this point of the film is on Cinque's breathing. A lightning storm provides only short bursts of light in which the viewer strains to see Cinque's actions. After removing the nail, bleeding from the effort and creating a strong red color amid the darkness of the hold, Cinque unlocks his hand and leg cuffs, and then begins unlocking the chains of the other Africans. The Africans, after being unchained, break open a box of cane knives and push open the hatch leading to the upper deck. Cinque, as the leader, tiptoes over to one of the sailors in the pouring rain and staccato light and hacks down on his right shoulder blade. This action is quick and difficult to perceive, since, with the short bursts of bright light in high contrast to the dark theatre or room in which the reader views the film, the pupil is naturally disrupted in its light intake, causing some eye irritability as the iris muscle works to expand and contract.

At the first point of bloody, brutal violence—the barely clothed *Amistad* Africans breaking out of the hold and wielding huge knives, their muscular bodies glistening in the rain—a trope of black danger and violence (linked with sexuality) is introduced to the audience through the bodies of the black men within the first two minutes of the film. During the beginning of the Simpson narrative, Simpson's body was used for a similar trope with his image on the *Time* magazine cover, which was also re-mediated on television. The non-blacks in the film, as they are attacked, begin speaking Spanish to one another and fight back with guns and swords. At this point of the film, the struggle between the blacks and non-blacks on the ship becomes raced: Hispanic men are introduced as slavers and black men are introduced as the enslaved. A race riot between Hispanic men and black men within the limited space of the ship becomes the initial image of the film, presenting a spectacle of black and non-black violence and a struggle for power. The non-blacks in the film, although Hispanic, become whitened and the Africans become blackened within the binary trap.[20] As the Spanish is translated most of the time into English with subtitles for the audience and as the Mende language is seldom translated, language familiarity (English and Spanish) and nonfamiliarity (Mende) helps to create the white and black binary of masculinity and to distance the audience from blackness. The Hispanic characters, Ruiz and Montes, after being positioned through the binary as not black, are moved off the screen after the Africans are arrested and jailed, so that the audience focuses on the American white abolitionists and legal system helping the African men.

The body imagery of the black and non-black men at the beginning of the film creates a construction of racial identity within the film's world. Although the *Amistad* Africans had eaten very little and moved even less as they were trapped, first, aboard the *Tecora* ship for two months; second, in the slave-holding pens in Cuba; and third, aboard the *Amistad,* their bodies appear on-screen to be muscular and strong, as if they had been recently lifting weights. Thus, what the audience sees breaking out of the ship's hold are not undernourished, under-exercised black bodies holding cane knives, but the equivalent of protein-shake-drinking, Gold's-gym-frequenting, muscular black bodies gripping large murder weapons. Thus, like Simpson's, the black body is transformed into a weapon using re-mediated tropes of the black man. White bodies are covered—both clothed and bearded—creating a sense of civility in opposition to the savagely portrayed, unclothed, and muscular black men. Although Woodruff's 1939 painting of the rebellion portrays the bodies of black men as strong and muscular, the painting focuses on the even struggle between blacks and whites since it reveals an even number of black men and white men feuding over power.

The lack of lighting and the darkening of various *Amistad* Africans during the opening sequence affect the reader in a similar way as the darkening of Simpson's mug shot—the darkening of the features helps to create the trope of violence. The opening of the film reveals the blacks rising up, literally and figuratively, and rebelling against slave trading, slavery, and all notions of commodification of the black body tied to those concepts. But since the lighting is weak and strobe-like, the men are blackened like Simpson in the beginning of the O.J. Simpson narrative. In addition, one part of the killing action is suppressed as a large sail on the ship covers the audience's eyes for them, so that the uprising of black men against white men is shielded. By shielding the audience's eyes from the rebellion, the uprising of black men against white men, the key element of the *Amistad* incident (the civil rights trial in the film would not exist without this particular incident) becomes muted.

In addition to the lighting and the large sail shielding viewers' eyes from the uprising, the element of time works toward suppressing the attacks as well. Since only five minutes of the well over two hours of film narrative are devoted to the actual rebellion, the act becomes minuscule compared to the actions of the white men who will soon defend the blacks in court. However, because the rebellion is discussed throughout the remainder of the film in the courtroom drama, the image of the violent black man is retained in memory, just as the *Time* magazine image of Simpson as the black criminal was sustained during his trial. Film theorist Christian Metz asserts that audiences watching a film usually only remember a few images and the plot line. The images of the criminal black men in both narratives, television and filmic, are most likely to be retained since the discussion during the courtroom drama, or the remainder of the narrative, constantly refers back to criminality and "what happened."[21]

The camerawork within the opening sequence introduces the realistic film technique that Spielberg uses throughout the movie. The shaky camera technique attempts to place the reader on the ship—first, below the deck with the Africans and then on the deck during the rebellion, capturing the action as if it were included on the ship. This technique works to create the realistic effect that we, the audience, are on the ship, much like the often shaky, often visually skewed, realistic camerawork of the Rodney King beating or the white Ford Bronco cruising slowly down the freeway allowed viewers to be up-close participants in those occurrences. The unsteady camera simulates the viewer's head and body movements on the ship or viewing the Bronco driving down the road from the point of view of the helicopter or roadside. It creates a sense of realistic viewership, an illusion that what the audience sees on the screen is what really happened. With the realistic style of camera movement, the incident becomes more "real," more objective, as if what flashes on the screen is "what happened" on the ship.

Close-up shots, which make it possible for the viewer to better observe the intensity in the subject's face (Fabe 4), are used quite frequently throughout the film's beginning. Four minutes into the film, during the rebellion's end, Cinque fights with the captain one on one, since he is seen as the primary captor of Cinque and his fellow African captives. The fight represents a struggle for power, since Captain Ferrer is head of the ship and must be overthrown in order for the captives to attain a semi-free state (in the middle of the ocean). Cinque, in the center part of the ship, grabs the captain's sword, and stabs him all the way through his body while blood gushes out of his mouth. Cinque alone kills the captain. At this point, the viewer sees an extreme close-up of Cinque's face—screaming in anger at the man seemingly responsible for his captivity. This type of extreme close-up creates a heightened sense of emotion for the viewer, who sees the intensity and anger in Cinque's face; although he is barely visible due to the low, sparse lighting, the shots work to place and racialize Cinque at the beginning of the film as the violent, angry black man. The scene ends with the camera facing upward, creating the viewpoint of Captain Ferrer looking up at the man who just stabbed him: the viewer sees Cinque through the eyes of the captain. Cinque, holding the bloodied sword, appears extremely tall and warrior-like in this final shot due to the upward angle.

After the initial racial struggle, the film continues to create ideologies of whiteness and blackness using a variety of elements. In the next scene, it is now daybreak and the Africans are struggling to make sense of the Western materials. One African helps another as the first, not used to floating on a ship or eating Western food, vomits over the side; a third struggles for meaning in a telescope, while some try on clothes and others hungrily eat food. Thus, the trope of the savage black male continues to be expressed and exploited. In the verbal bout, the Mende language is not translated, whereas the Spanish language is subtitled. The camera places the audience in the perspective of Ruiz and Montes as the two Cubans struggle to make sense of the Africans' language. Thus, language becomes important at the film's beginning in socially constructing blackness and whiteness. Although it is a worthy attempt at portraying the Middle Passage and the elements of racial identity that are created on this crucial voyage, translating one language but not another seems to distance the audience more from the Africans than from the Cubans.

At the same time that Yamba and Cinque, two of the Africans, are arguing over leadership in front of Ruiz and Montes, a third African moves into the frame and begins an odd dance for no apparent reason other than to disrupt the intensity of the argument. Because the camera angle situates the audience alongside Ruiz and Montes, the viewer, necessarily adopting the perspective of the two whitened men, sees a docile and playful African happily dancing on the ship. In addition, after the rebellion, a Spanish man comments that Cinque should take a bath, thus displacing the qualities of dirt and lack of cleanliness onto the black man and distancing him from the white man. When the Africans and Cubans anchor and row to land to fill water jugs and attempt to find food, a white man is shown riding his bike along a path near the Africans; he speeds up the second he sees the large number of black men nearby, suggesting and presenting the idea of white fear. Race, at the beginning of the film, has been constructed as white slaver and black slave.

The beginning of the *Amistad* film operates as a point of masculinity division as the black men are portrayed as mostly violent, uncivilized, dangerous, the creators of white fear, and, at times, docile and playful. In opposition to this, the Cubans, the white abolitionists, and the U.S. Navy men are imaged as clothed, clean, and civilized, signifying a constructed whiteness in opposition to the constructed blackness. This constructed perception of reality, as Darnell Hunt discusses in *Channeling Blackness*, creates the ideologies of blackness and ideologies of whiteness into a binary, rather than constructing race as more multicultural (5). In this beginning portion of the film, the Hispanic men are forced into whiteness, in opposition to the black men's savagery, dirty bodies, danger, captivity, badness, and violence. Whiteness becomes civilized, clean, good, noncaptive, and rational. By moving the black bodies into captivity and portraying them as savage, dangerous, and violent, in opposition to the free, rational, and civilized white bodies, the beginning of the film creates a binary of racial construction (black-white), allowing the reader to understand the intentional production of meaning.

THE INCARCERATED BLACK MAN AS SPECTACLE

Within the first eight minutes of the film (which runs two hours and thirty-five minutes), the *Amistad* Africans revolt on the ship, compete for power both with each other and with the whites as the ship moves up the eastern seacoast, are chased by American authority figures in Long Island Sound, are arrested by U.S. Navy officials, are led through New Haven as spectacle, and then returned to captivity in the New Haven jail and courtroom. As television viewers came home on Friday, July 19, 1994, they witnessed American authority figures—the Los Angeles police—chasing Simpson's white Bronco with him and his friend inside. Like Cinque and the others, Simpson was pulled over by the authority figures, arrested in spectacle form (on television, Friday evening), and placed in the custody of the Los Angeles Police Department. Simpson, after being chased, arrested, and detained, soon became part of a viewer spectacle in the courtroom—docile, waiting, and sitting—in a similar manner to how the *Amistad* Africans are treated in the film. Within the first eight minutes of the *Amistad* film, approximately 5 percent of the overall contents, the *Amistad* Africans move from captivity to a semi-free state and then back to captivity (as a spectacle). Cinque and the other Africans, like O.J. Simpson, remain on trial for viewers to see for a significantly long duration of time and a large percentage of the overall narrative.

In the film, after the initial rebellion, the power exchange on the ship, and the arrest and jailing of the black men, the Africans are introduced to Roger Baldwin who, in the Spielberg film, is a young real estate lawyer played by Texas native Matthew McConaughey. Baldwin views the case as related to the commodification of the black body as he equates the black bodies with real estate: he is interested in discovering who owns the Africans and wants to help the abolitionists with the case. Baldwin, excited to understand more about the captives, such as who owns them, if anybody, works with Theodore Joadson, a fictional character who alone represents the entire black abolitionist population. Joadson the abolitionist, played by veteran actor Morgan Freeman, is interested in solving the mystery of the Africans as well, but for different reasons. The two go into the prison to talk to Cinque and the other Africans about what happened, find an interpreter who speaks both Mende and English, and go aboard the *Amistad* ship and find hidden logbooks with important information pointing toward the African (not Cuban) identity of the men. Although the two men, one white and one black, work together to solve the mystery of the Africans and what happened on the *Amistad,* Joadson's character as an abolitionist, who represents the black man who overcame all odds and established himself (the self-made man), is pushed to the side by the end of the film as John Quincy Adams, played by Anthony Hopkins, is introduced and then relied upon to free the Africans from captivity. Just as the three men, Adams, Joadson, and Baldwin, work to free Cinque and the others, F. Lee Bailey, Johnnie Cochran, and Robert Shapiro, part of a similar team, worked to free Simpson. Cochran, like the invented character Joadson, worked as part of the legal team to free the black man for stronger reasons than economic, and he, like Joadson, represented the fate of the black race within the courtroom.

From the film's beginning, the Africans are seated as captives or bound by heavy, clanking chains, as well as the New Haven jail and the American legal system, similarly to how Simpson was seated and bound by the Los Angeles jail and courtroom during most of the O.J. Simpson narrative. The *Amistad* Africans are represented as captives through over 90 percent of the film, and their own struggle is cast aside as the focus of the narrative rests on the white male articulation in court. Each time the Africans are brought into the courtroom, chains clank and rattle to highlight the imprisonment of the black men, which Woodruff highlights with the courtroom re-mediation in his paintings. The six or so minutes of semi-freedom at the beginning of the film between the time the Africans rebel and are jailed again (which in reality was over two months) becomes lost in the midst of the courtroom drama, jail images, and chain noises. In addition, since most of the discussions between Baldwin and Cinque occur within the confines of the New Haven jail, the representation of white hero and black captive works its way through the film. The representation of the black captive sitting and waiting was prominent in the Simpson televisual spectacle. O.J. Simpson's body movements, facial expressions, and place within the courtroom presented him as confined within the arms of the law for the lengthy duration of his televised trial.

The final trial scenes of the mediated *Amistad* incident and the O.J. Simpson case, in which the black men win their cases and attain freedom, bear striking resemblances. In the final trial scene, Cinque, dressed in Western attire—a white shirt, tie, and vest—sits patiently in the midst of Baldwin, Joadson, and Adams. Simpson, dressed similarly—a white shirt, tie, and sports jacket—sat patiently in the midst of Shapiro, Cochran, and Bailey. Both men raise their hands in victory and shake hands with their entourage, as this is the high point of the narrative—the ruling for freedom. Simpson cracked a smile, as does Cinque. However, neither smile lasted long.

ILLUSION OF FREEDOM AND THE
DISPLACEMENT OF THE BLACK MAN

The black captive/white hero image works on a microcosmic level with the courtroom scenes, but toward the end of the film, it is pushed into a macrocosmic form after the trial victory, when the British army rescues African captives from the Sierra Leone slave fortress in a dramatic display. In this scene, the British army runs into the fortress, grabs barely clothed Africans, and helps to free them from the clutches of slavery. During this process of freeing the Africans, words flash on the screen that present a visual voice-over, allowing the reader to understand this global reaction, the destruction of the slave fortresses, after the *Amistad* Supreme Court decision. During the scene just described are the words "Liberation of Lomboko Slave Fortress." Thus, the reader understands and connects, with the word *liberation,* that notions of freedom have been extended across the Atlantic after the *Amistad* case ended. In addition, as part of the grand spectacle of the slave trade/slavery literally being crushed by the court decision, the American navy, working with the British army, shoots cannonballs at the Sierra Leone slave fortress, destroying it in a grand Hollywood film ending complete with fire and smoke. Thus, as the white abolitionists have assisted in freeing the black captives during the major part of the film, the British army and American navy are portrayed as freeing the black captives on a larger scale at the end of the film. The scene at the closing of the film creates a vision of the striking down of legal segregation (in the form of slavery in this era) with the freeing of the blacks in the *Amistad* legal disposition, the destruction of the slave fortress, and the onset of the Civil War images; the audience most likely knows that this event foreshadows the destruction of slavery in the United States and the passing of Amendments 13, 14, and 15.[22]

This film's plot directs the reader's attention on both a microcosmic level, with the courtroom drama, and a macrocosmic level, with the destruction of the slave fortress in Sierra Leone, currently one of the poorest countries in Africa, toward the ideology of freedom. Although the civil war in Sierra Leone and the loss of Cinque's family to slavery are mentioned at the film's end in subtitles, the focus of the spectacle rides heavily on freedom after the civil rights trial. As Darnell Hunt asserts in *Channeling Blackness,* "against a backdrop of increasing racial diversity, a white-controlled industry [television and film] continues to channel blackness in ways that affirm whiteness, while at the same time promoting the fiction of an America beyond race" (300).

At the end of the twentieth century, the ideology of color-blindness lingered even after America witnessed a black man receiving a harsh beating from four Los Angeles police officers; Latinos, Koreans, and blacks rioting and looting in the streets of Los Angeles on the evening news; and O.J. Simpson, formerly portrayed as a race-neutral male, becoming blackened on the stand as his case unfolded in a racial matter. In Spielberg's remediation of the *Amistad* incident, marginalizing the black men as violent, dangerous, savage, and criminal from the opening of the film and creating a plot line that focuses mostly on the trial and white heroism in assisting the "helpless" Africans, and less on the actual rebellion, creates an illusion within the film's "realistic world" that racial conflict was conquered with the destruction of the slave fortress and the Civil War's sociopolitical results. Emphasizing the ideology of freedom throughout the film and then creating images of blacks running alongside whites and slave fortresses crumbling down seem to project a color-blind ideology in which minorities have won their freedom, and race is no longer a problem.

By using a historical incident couched in issues of racial conflict and by "solving" the conflict by the end of the narrative, Spielberg's film creates a visual illusion of freedom as Cinque and the others win their Supreme Court case and the slave fortresses are destroyed in a glorious spectacle. However, like the *Brown v. Board of Education* Supreme Court victory ended in disappointment (black bodies in America were continuously displaced from 1954 to 1989), Cinque's and Simpson's trials ended in disappointment. Both men, after winning their trials and attaining freedom, attempted to return home, but both were displaced by the economics of race.

At the end of the *Amistad* film, after the visual spectacle of the fortresses being destroyed, which symbolizes the end of slavery and the return of freedom for the blacks, Cinque is displayed on a ship returning to Africa, peering into the distance while subtitles, or the printed word, reveal his future. The audience understands, by reading the subtitles, that after Cinque returned to Africa he discovered that his village had been destroyed by the institution of slavery, Sierra Leone was in a state of civil war, and his family was missing. Thus, Cinque was displaced by the modern institution of race. But, as this notion is only revealed in subtitles in the final seconds of the film, it becomes buried. Similarly, at the end of the Simpson narrative, O.J. Simpson, who as a famous spectacle earned media companies millions of dollars,[23] could not return home because his mediated reputation as a murderer (despite his acquittal) disallowed his return to Brentwood. He moved to Florida to protect his children and pension.[24]

Although the mediated trial victories of both men created a visual illusion of freedom for viewers, the black body again was displaced. After the legal bout, Cinque could not return to his original home, nor could Simpson, as the economics of race, whether in the slavery form for Cinque or in the media spectacle form for Simpson (television stations, magazines, and newspapers increased their sales while Simpson sat on display for almost a year), work to, as Ralph Ellison states, "Keep This Nigger-Boy Running" (33).

NOTES

1. This information was taken from Walter Goodman's front-page article, "Television Meet Life, Life Meet T.V.," in the June 19, 1994, edition of the *New York Times*; Dan Meyer's front-page article, "O.J. Simpson Surrenders," in the June 18, 1994, edition of the *Philadelphia Enquirer*; the *Kansas City Star*'s Associated Press article "Escape Shocks Simpson's Fans: Many Find It Difficult to Think of Hero as a Fugitive from Justice," on June 18, 1994; and the *Kansas City Star*'s Associated Press article "O.J. Simpson Flees, Gives Up: Chase Ends with Arrest after Murder Charge," on July 18, 1994.

2. Reporters dubbed Simpson's group of defense lawyers the Dream Team before the trial began. For more information, see Joel Achenbach's "O.J. Simpson's Defensive Linemen: The Dream Team of Attorney's [*sic*] Ready to Tackle Whatever Comes Its Way," *Washington Post*, January 21, 1995, D1; "Dream Team Feud," *New York Times*, January 16, 1995, A8.

3. "Simpson: '100%' Not Guilty: Defendant Emphatic at His Arraignment on Two Murder Charges," *Kansas City Star*, 1.

4. For more information, see Chet Whye's "*Time* Magazine Willie Hortonized Its O.J. Simpson Cover," *Denver Post*, July 1, 1994, B7.

5. Prior to his arrest and detainment in 1994, Simpson had acted in a number of films and television shows, including *Roots* (1977) and the *Naked Gun* film series (1988, 1991, 1994), and had been highlighted in countless articles, including the September 8, 1977, cover shot of *Rolling Stone* magazine (Simpson was the first pro football player to be so featured); and the October 8, 1990, cover shot of *Sports Illustrated* magazine and the story "Why Can't They Run Like Simpson," which reminded the public that Simpson was one of the best running backs ever to grace the NFL. After retiring from football,

Simpson also produced and starred in a few made-for-TV movies, including *Detour to Terror* (1980). For more information, see Simpson's entry in the Internet Movie Database at www.imdb.com/name/nm0001740.

6. This information was obtained through the Fox archives at www.fox.com.

7. Court TV, CNN, mass circulation magazines, and other media profited from the spectacle of the Simpson trial. Thus, Simpson's body became a tool for capitalist gain. See George Lipsitz, "The Greatest Story Ever Told: Marketing and the O.J. Simpson Trial," in Morrison and Lacour's *Birth of a Nation 'Hood*, 3–29.

8. Simpson, in a 2004 interview with CBS, informed viewers that he was comfortable in Florida. More important, under Florida law, his pension cannot be touched. For more information, see "OJ: Media Made Me the Heavy," *CBS News*, June 8, 2004, http://www.cbsnews.com/stories/2004/06/05/national/main621242.shtml (accessed February 23, 2006).

9. Hale Woodruff's *Amistad* paintings focus highly on the heroic actions of Cinque. For more information, see Hale Woodruff and Studio Museum in Harlem, *Hale Woodruff: 50 Years of His Art* (New York: Studio Museum in Harlem, 1979).

10. Steinberg argues that white liberals, after the civil rights movement "freed" blacks from harsh voting restrictions and therefore social problems, have pushed away from examining the race problems in the United States. A large part of the argument is that, since America is too racist to support programs targeted at blacks, any suggestions toward this would drive a wedge in the liberal coalition and ultimately break up the Democratic Party. Thus, liberals after the civil rights movement began to "retreat from race," or turn a blind eye to racial problems. For more information, see Steinberg, "The Liberal Retreat from Race during the Post–Civil Rights Era," in *The House That Race Built*.

11. For more information, see Barber's "Steven Spielberg's *Amistad*: Chained by Liberalism," *Freedom Socialist* 19.1; Adjaye's "*Amistad* and the Lessons of History," *Journal of Black Studies* 29.3, 455–459; and Hinks's "'What Is Your Story?': Howard Jones and Steven Spielberg on the History of the *Amistad* Conflict," at http://www.AmistadAmerica.org.

12. Before the film's 1915 debut, films mimicked stage plays, with long shots that placed the actor as a small body on the large screen (like way a viewer sees a body from a distance when sitting in a theatre), long takes (up to ninety seconds) with the camera at a fixed distance from its object, again mimicking the perception of the audience member at a live play, and poorly spliced together scenes, all of which failed to tell the story well. Griffith, in creating his movie, wanted to improve the way stories were told through the medium of film. In casting and creating a scene, he placed more emphasis on costume and background, which added to the overall cues delivered to the reader to enhance the feel of the story. He also discovered that the close-up shot, a technique that allows audience members to see the intensity on the actor's face, provides additional cues that creates more emotional involvement with the story. Most important, he discovered that smoother transitions between shots create a more realistic narrative. Because of the realism that photography, both still pictures and moving pictures, seems to create, the film narrative can appear on the surface as an objective or neutral story to the reader (Fabe 1–9).

13. This information was taken from the film's website at http://www.filmsite.org/birt.html.

14. Fabe's initial discussion focuses on how D. W. Griffith helped to define standard film techniques, such as mise-en-scène and editing in order to create the story and a realistic feel. She stresses how these techniques and, later, the introduction of sound help to create the overall realism of film. For more information, see Fabe's *Closely Watched Films*.

15. The 1992 Los Angeles riots have been cited as the worst in U.S. history, exceeding in death toll and overall destruction the Watts riots in 1965 and the Detroit riots in 1967. There were 58 deaths and almost 2,300 injuries reported in LA. Of the 58 dead, all but 1 were male, and all were between the ages of eighteen and fifty. Twenty-seven were black, 17 were Hispanic, 11 were white, 2 were Asian, and 1 was of unknown ethnicity. Out of the 9,400 people arrested, about one-half were Hispanic, one-third were black, 11 percent were white, and 2 percent were listed as "other." More than 1,150 structures were destroyed, and approximately 10,000 small businesses were damaged. Most of the rioters made little distinction between stores owned by whites, blacks, Hispanics, or Koreans. For more information regarding the LA riots, consult Dennis Gale's *Understanding Urban Unrest: From Reverend King to Rodney King*.

16. Crenshaw, "Color-blind Dreams and Racial Nightmares," discussed the often unhinged anger and irrational reactions of many Americans in regard to the O.J. Simpson trial.

17. Transcripts of the 1997 civil trial, including the amount that Simpson had to pay, were released by CNN. For more information about this trial, see the transcripts at http://www.cnn.com/US/OJ/simpson.civil.trial/transcripts.february/02.6.transcript .html.

18. S. Dale McLemore and Harriett D. Romo, *Racial and Ethnic Relations in America*, discuss how the nationally televised videotape of the Rodney King beating followed by nationwide race riots and then the entire O.J. Simpson spectacle signify, in popular media and the wider culture, "the renewed visibility of the black-white conflict" (184–187).

19. Crenshaw, "Color-blind Dreams and Racial Nightmares," 103.

20. Darnell Hunt, in his chapter "Making Sense of Blackness on Television," in his edited book *Channeling Blackness* discusses how racial identity on television (and this can be applied to film as well since film is a part of television) pushes an element of binary thinking. Black characters in the Western world are usually placed in opposition to non-black characters in order to define elements of racialized blackness (savage, unclean, uneducated, nonrational) in opposition to what becomes whiteness (civilized, clean, educated, rational). In the twenty-first century, when U.S. demographics no longer privilege the black-white racial binary sociologically, "meanings of other raced positions in a white supremacist America are continually defined and redefined in relation to black and white poles" (5). Thus, in this sense, multicultural identity, whether created on the ship or in contemporary life, although closer to reality, is buried or lost.

21. For more information, see Metz's *Film Language: A Semiotics of the Cinema*, 44–49.

22. Amendments 13–15, passed by Congress between 1865 and 1869, directly after the Civil War (and all implemented by 1870), rework the Constitution to convey the idea that slavery has been abolished in the United States; Amendment 15 states, "The right of citizens of the United States to vote shall not be denied or abridged by the United States or by any State on account of race, color, or previous condition of servitude." For

more information on these three amendments, see http://www.archives.gov/national-archives-experience/charters/constitution_amendments_11-27.html.

23. Court TV, CNN, mass circulation magazines, and other media profited from the spectacle of the Simpson trial. Thus, Simpson's body became a tool for capitalist gain. See George Lipsitz, "The Greatest Story Ever Told: Marketing and the O.J. Simpson Trial," in Morrison and Lacour's *Birth of a Nation 'Hood*, 3–29.

24. Simpson, in a 2004 interview with CBS, informed readers that he was comfortable in Florida. More important, under Florida law, his pension cannot be touched. For more information, see "OJ: Media Made Me the Heavy," *CBS News,* June 8, 2004, http://www.cbsnews.com/stories/2004/06/05/national/main621242.shtml (accessed February 23, 2006).

BIBLIOGRAPHY

Bartlett, Frederick Charles. *Remembering: A Study in Experimental and Social Psychology.* Cambridge: Cambridge University Press, 1932.

Brown, Michael K., et al. *Whitewashing Race: The Myth of a Color Blind Society.* Berkeley: University of California Press, 2003.

Celsing, Ana. "Seeing Is Believing." In *The Focused Screen: Studies in Culture and Communication,* ed. Jose Vidal-Beneyto and Peter Dahlgren, 93–108. Strasbourg, France: Council of Europe Publishing, 1987.

Crenshaw, Kimberlé Williams. "Color-blind Dreams and Racial Nightmares: Reconfiguring Racism in the Post–Civil Rights Era." In *Birth of a Nation 'Hood: Gaze, Script, and Spectacle in the O.J. Simpson Case,* ed. Toni Morrison and Claudia Brodsky Lacour, 97–168. New York: Pantheon, 1997.

Ellison, Ralph. *Invisible Man.* 1952. Rpt., New York: Vintage, 1995.

Fabe, Marilyn. *Closely Watched Films: An Introduction to the Art of Narrative Film Technique.* Berkeley: University of California Press, 2004.

Furno-Lamude, Diane. "The Media Spectacle and the O.J. Simpson Case." In *The O.J. Simpson Trials: Rhetoric, Media, and the Law,* ed. Janice Schuetz and Lin S. Lilley, 19–35. Carbondale: Southern Illinois University Press, 1999.

Gates, Henry Louis. *"Race," Writing, and Difference.* Chicago: University of Chicago Press, 1986.

Gutiérrez-Jones, Carl. *Critical Race Narratives: A Study of Race, Rhetoric and Injury.* New York: New York University Press, 2001.

Hasian, Marouf, and A. Cheree Carlson. "Revisionism and Collective Memory: The Struggle for Meaning in the *Amistad* Affair." *Communication Monographs* 67, no. 1 (2000): 42–62.

Hunt, Darnell, ed. *Channeling Blackness: Studies on Television and Race in America.* New York: Oxford University Press, 2005.

Kilgannon, Corey. "The O.J. Simpson Trial: As Not Seen on T.V." *New York Times.* May 7, 1995, CY6.

Landy, Marcia. "Introduction." In her *The Historical Film: History and Memory in Media,* 1–23. New Brunswick, N.J.: Rutgers University Press, 2001.

Lipsitz, George. *Time Passages: Collective Memory and American Popular Culture.* Minneapolis: University of Minnesota Press, 1990.

McCullagh, C. Behan. "The Truth of Historical Narratives." *History and Theory Studies in the Philosophy of History* 26 (1987): 320–346.

Metz, Christian. *Film Language: A Semiotics of the Cinema*. Trans. Michael Taylor. New York: Oxford University Press, 1974.

Morrison, Toni. "The Official Story: Dead Man Golfing." In *Birth of a Nation 'Hood: Gaze, Script, and Spectacle in the O.J. Simpson Case*, ed. Toni Morrison and Claudia Brodsky Lacour, vii–xxviii. New York: Pantheon, 1997.

———. *Playing in the Dark: Whiteness and the Literary Imagination*. Cambridge, Mass.: Harvard University Press, 1992.

Morrison, Toni, and Claudia Brodsky Lacour, eds. *Birth of a Nation 'Hood: Gaze, Script, and Spectacle in the O.J. Simpson Case*. New York: Pantheon, 1997.

Passmore, John. "Narratives and Events." *History and Theory Studies in the Philosophy of History* 26 (1987): 68–74.

Said, Edward. *Beginnings: Intention and Method*. New York: Basic, 1975.

Spielberg, Steven, dir. *Amistad*. DreamWorks, 1998.

Spielberg, Steven, Maya Angelou, and Debbie Allen. *Amistad: "Give Us Free": A Celebration of the Film by Steven Spielberg*. New York: Newmarket, 1998.

SIX

OBAMA'S MASCULINITIES: A LANDSCAPE OF ESSENTIAL CONTRADICTIONS

MARC E. SHAW AND ELWOOD WATSON

In *The Audacity of Hope,* Barack Obama recounts his experience on the day he was sworn in to the Senate, when the longest-serving member, Robert C. Byrd of West Virginia, spoke to the new senators. As one of the few African Americans elected to that body, Obama writes, "Listening to Senator Byrd speak, I felt with full force all the essential contradictions of me in this new place, with its marble busts, its arcane traditions, its memories and its ghosts."[1] Obama goes on to discuss Senator Byrd's oft-recounted involvement with the KKK as symptomatic of the time and place he was raised, but the phrase "all the essential contradictions of me" is worth focusing on for our purposes here, and not only with the racial allusions that Obama first intended.

"All the essential contradictions of me" functions as a point of entry into something more general than just Obama's Senate induction that day. The phrase shows an awareness concerning identity, and differing aspects within one individual. In Obama, we currently have a president who is fully aware that identity is an ongoing construction and, more specifically, that the self is actively gendered as it is presented to the world. And that identity, Obama's masculinities, is full of essential contradictions. Obama is both a black man and a white man, but also neither completely. He is both feminized and masculinized in the popular media. He plays the part of both nerd and athlete, guy next door and Harvard elite. He has shown his Zen-like calm but also his relentless attack mode. He is aware of his self-construction but maintains a refreshing authenticity. He is familiarly presidential but refreshing and new.

In a notable passage of Barack Obama's first book, *Dreams from My Father*, he asks about the complexity of the term *family*. Obama's examination of this term is important because it shows his ability to navigate and think through complexities of identity, in which we might include the subset of masculinities:

> What is a family? Is it just a genetic chain, parents and offspring, people like me? Or is it a social construct, an economic unit, optimal for child rearing and divisions of labor? Or is it something else entirely: a store of shared memories, say? An ambit of love? A reach across the void? I could list various possibilities. But I'd never arrived at a definite answer, aware early on that, given my circumstances, such an effort was bound to fail. Instead, I drew a series of circles around myself, with borders that shifted as time passed and faces changed but that nevertheless offered the illusion of control.[2]

Those changing borders and circles make the landscape of an individual, just as contradicting masculinities evolve over time. This fluidity in construction marks Obama's attitude toward identity, whether familial or masculine. While Obama is not speaking overtly of masculine identity here, his attitude toward identity reveals complexity and nuance.

The notion of contradiction is nothing new to masculinity studies. R. W. Connell asserts, "Masculinities are not fixed. They are not homogeneous, simple states of being. They are often contradictory desires and conduct" even in the same individual.[3] In addition to contradiction, those same masculinities live up to the Obama mantra of "change": Connell reminds us that "[m]asculinities change. Masculinities are created in specific historical circumstances. Circumstances change."[4] So when we talk about America becoming America again—to paraphrase a Langston Hughes poem—we know that in every new contradiction there is something of the old. Certainly, in contradicting old ways of thinking, change is manifest. The "arcane traditions" that Obama experienced during his Senate swearing-in are mirrored in the arcane traditions of gender expectations for our leaders and society at large. Identity is not static, and Obama's identity influences and potentially changes our conceptions of the black male, men in general, the office of the presidency, fatherhood, the middle-aged body, and the professional male body, among other aspects of masculine identity.

NECESSARY CONTRADICTIONS: RISING ABOVE
BINARY MODELS OF MASCULINITY AND RACE

This exploration of Obama's contradictory masculinities stands in contrast to Frank Rudy Cooper's simplifying assertion that Obama is the first "unisex president"—"a candidate designed to be suitable to either gender."[5] Cooper uses *gender* in the sense of biological sex, and this binary is indicative of his pared-down and polar thinking. Yes, polarities, opposites, spectrums, and continuums *do* exist—above, we listed some binary contradictions about Obama—but they coexist with a multiplicity of gender relationships to create an ever-changing gender process. Cooper argues that Obama has constructed a "Good Black Man" identity by feminizing himself—as opposed to the angrier, hypermasculine "Bad Black Man" construction. Historically speaking, African American men have had to contend with both extreme stereotypes. There has rarely been any middle ground or room for depictive ambiguity. This traditional binary is evidenced in a short documentary by Byron Hurt, *Barack & Curtis: Manhood, Power, & Respect.* The film contains a series of reflections on the influence of two iconic, contrasting African American men: Barack Obama and Curtis Jackson (better known as the rapper 50 Cent). Esther Armah, a radio host and playwright, notes that, historically speaking: "Barack equaled Harvard; someone like 50 Cent equaled 'hood. 'Hood equaled virility. Harvard equaled impotence."[6] Armah admits that this binary is "dangerous" because gangster rap "had begun to shape the definition of black manhood to the degree that it made certain middle-class men lose their place in manhood in the eyes of women."[7] By making black men either one or the other, "right" and "wrong" identities are created. Therefore, one of the goals of racial and gender equality must be to move past simple binaries. Black-or-white thinking creates linear models that regulate us all into opposing camps.

One contradiction for Obama is that he seeks a postracial masculinity while fully and unavoidably navigating the terrain he seeks to transcend. From the point of view of many Americans, for years our nation has indeed fashioned two extremes: at one end, the stereotypically big, bad, violent, menacing, oversexed black buck and, at the other end, the docile, accommodating, subdued, nonthreatening, sexually emasculated black man. While Obama's contradictions of masculinity do not allow him to fit comfortably in either category, in the eyes of many mainstream journalists and of radicals of all races, he is more aligned with the latter one. Yet, importantly, Obama seeks to expand the possibilities of what African American masculinity can be and what the masculinities of the presidency can be. But this can be accomplished only by facing the given reality: Obama must deftly navigate the staid, conventional thought on masculinity and race.

From the moment that he delivered the keynote speech at the Democratic National Convention in July 2004, calling for an end to divisive politics and an embracing of bipartisanship, Obama aggressively and shrewdly cultivated the image that he was a safe, reliable, even-tempered African American man who gave middle America (read: white America) no reason to fear.[8] And this cultivation contains the main contradiction in Obama's construction of self: while one might read it as a rejection of a specific black masculinity, it can also be read as progressively postracial. In a word, during his breakout 2004 speech, Obama wanted to appear *senatorial*—a goal which two or three years later would grow to *presidential*. As a biracial man who came of age during the late 1970s and early '80s in a racially polarized America and who had lived with both races as a child, Obama was well aware of the sinister, retrograde images associated with African American men. Thus, he knew that he could not afford to lose his temper in public or be seen as disrespectful to women (his "sweetie" comment to a female journalist notwithstanding). He could not be combative, loud, undisciplined, or perceived as embodying traits associated with the wrong type of black man.[9] Obama took great pains to present himself as a congenial, admirable everyman with whom people, particularly middle (white) America, would feel comfortable enough to have as a co-worker, a drinking buddy, a next-door neighbor, and maybe even a son-in-law.[10]

There is no doubt that, just like any shrewd politician, Obama knows his public persona—including his masculine self—to be a contradictory creation and also that his masculinity-in-public is established, negotiated, and renegotiated between him, the media, and the world at large. In *The Audacity of Hope*, Obama relates a telling anecdote about that process. While campaigning for the Senate, Obama and his aide Dan

Shomon were eating at a T.G.I. Friday's in southern Illinois. The waitress brought Obama's cheeseburger and the future president asked for some Dijon mustard. Shomon immediately told the waitress: "He doesn't want Dijon," as he handed Obama some regular yellow mustard instead: "The waitress looked confused. 'We got Dijon if you want it,' she said to me. I smiled. 'That would be great, thanks.' As the waitress walked away, I leaned over to Dan and whispered that I didn't think there were any photographers around."[11]

In this anecdote, there is an element of postmodern play, or reflectiveness. Obama knows his persona to be a persona, yet his act of telling us the anecdote makes him not a persona but a *person*. Despite the constructedness of this narrative—we know we are being given a story that will present Obama in a good light—pathos still comes through. In relating the anecdote, Obama grounds himself in authenticity. To those taking the time to read his book, he is saying, "I like Dijon, but I will eat yellow mustard when I have to." He establishes that he will not be like John Kerry in the 2004 election, who tried to order Swiss cheese with his Philly cheesesteak. The connotation, of course, is that Dijon mustard is too upscale and "French," and therefore lessens one's blue-collar masculinity and everyman-ness. Ironically, choosing the yellow French's brand mustard is *less* French and *more* "manly" and "of the people." Through the relation of the narrative, we identify with Obama's awareness and openness, which makes him human and authentic in the process. It is reassuring to have a president who can navigate between social strata because he has lived at all levels of the middle class.

Concerns over masculinity and racial identity were not limited to Obama himself. During the presidential run, his first-rate campaign team—David Axelrod, David Plouffe, and Valerie Jarrett—were aware of the necessity of defining the issues and framing the identity or identities of their candidate. A unifying, postracial, transcendent male image was particularly evident in the race-focused "A More Perfect Union" speech, which Obama delivered in Philadelphia in March 2008:

> It's a story that hasn't made me the most conventional candidate. But it is
> a story that has seared into my genetic makeup the idea this nation is more
> than the sum of its parts—that out of many, we are truly one. Throughout
> the first year of this campaign, against all predictions to the contrary, we saw
> how hungry the American people were for this message of unity. Despite

the temptation to view my candidacy through a purely racial lens, we won commanding victories in states with some of the whitest populations in the country. In South Carolina, where the Confederate flag still flies, we built a powerful coalition of African Americans and white Americans.[12]

This unifying rhetoric was designed to appeal to both men and women. Obama was well aware that, after the Jeremiah Wright controversy, his presidential candidacy was in jeopardy. Something had to be done to limit the criticism he was receiving from various quarters. David Plouffe, Obama's campaign manager, admitted that the controversy was "a direct torpedo to the hull" that could sink Obama's chances.[13] Obama knew that he had to distance himself from Jeremiah Wright or he might be reduced to another hostile black man who may secretly harbor an anti-white agenda. Something had to be done to stem the tide. The "A More Perfect Union" speech was the perfect response to reassure white America that he was still a reliable, safe, and trustworthy black man who was not to be feared. But, simultaneously, it also looked to move beyond race. As expected, the responses to Obama severing his ties with Wright varied. In some quarters, he was praised as courageous for breaking away from a man who was seen as divisive by a number of Americans. Others saw it as an example of Obama making another calculated effort to prove to white America that he was a decent, moral black man who, like Bill Clinton, "felt their pain." Those from the latter group also argued that there seemed to be a double standard in the media due to the fact that John McCain was barely called upon to distance himself from the Reverend John Hagee, who made incendiary comments about Adolf Hitler and Jews.[14]

The balancing act that Obama attempted to perform was a tight, tricky one, indeed. There were some media pundits who argued that, in his efforts to be a racial everyman, Obama was venturing into a racial twilight zone. He was too white to be black and too black to be white.[15] But Obama ran at a fortuitous time: he faced opposition from a Republican Party that was the weakest it had been since the mid-1960s. His GOP presidential opponent was a seventy-two-year-old moderate who never had the solid support of the Republican base. Obama sought to lead a nation that was in one of its worst crises since the Great Depression—and hungry for radical change. These facts aside, it is still safe to say that many whites would have probably dismissed Obama had they seen him as being a "typical" black candidate or even a black conservative.[16] For most moderate whites and some left-leaning ones as well, both types of black men are to be distrusted.

In his article that asks if Obama is the first "unisex president," legal scholar Frank Rudy Cooper reports the findings of his research, which was conducted on media representations of African American men. Interviewees asserted:

> [Different outlets in the media] depict us as either the completely threatening Bad Black Man or the Fully Assimilationist Good Black Man. The Bad Black Man is animalistic, sexually-depraved, and crime-prone. The Good Black Man distances himself from Black people and emulates White views. The images are bipolar in that they swing from one extreme to another with little room for nuanced depictions. Threatened with the Bad Black Man image, Black men are provided with an "assimilationist incentive" to pursue the Good Black Man image.[17]

Depending on your point of view, Obama either sought to capitalize on this acceptable black man image by regularly mitigating any reference to his ethnicity, or he sought to move past the race questions altogether. He accomplished both points of view by focusing his campaign on economic and universal issues. Some black scholars found the former position problematic because by adopting it, Obama was saying, in essence, that in order to be considered a Good Black Man by mainstream America, one must either obscure or negate one's blackness as much as possible. This was evident in his 2004 Democratic Convention keynote address. Throughout his speech, Obama made comments such as "There's not a black America or a white America, a Latino America or an Asian America—there's the United States of America."[18] This was another effort at assuaging any white fear that might exist. It was also Obama's effort to move past the tensions and binaries of the past in order to create a post-racial, transcendent identity.

Another example of Obama's effort to embrace the Good Black Man image was his criticism of irresponsible black fathers. This act gave Obama the opportunity to promote his "safe black man" image, but also to be perceived by some as a leader who spoke the truth, no matter the circumstances, even if it meant offending people of the same race.[19] In a Father's Day speech to a predominantly black audience, Obama criticized black men who were neglecting their children. While Obama mentioned that his remarks were directed toward men of all races who were not actively involved in their children's lives, he specifically targeted black fathers as being deficient in their responsibilities.[20] While a considerable number of Americans, including African Americans, were in agreement with Obama and his message, there were a number of black leaders from the old civil rights establishment—among them, Jesse Jackson Sr.—who were livid with the presidential candidate for engaging in perceived grandstanding and saw him as placating a segment of white America who already harbored negative views of black Americans. Jackson was caught on tape making inflammatory comments about Obama and later apologized for his crude remarks.

But often in the political realm, individuals polarize viewpoints and frame enemies for their own benefit. This binary mode of thinking is dangerous. Black conservative academic Shelby Steele offers this type of controversial critique of Barack Obama in his ill-titled book, *A Bound Man: Why We Are Excited about Obama and Why He Can't Win*. Steele argues that African Americans can be classified into two categories: bargainers and challengers. Bargainers, according to Steele, are blacks who tell white America that they will not use the sordid history of American racism against them if whites will not use the fact that they are black against them. Challengers are blacks who declare all whites to be guilty of racism until proven otherwise.[21] Moreover, Steele argues that both sorts of blacks manipulate whites to some level. Steele sees Barack Obama as the epitome of a bargainer. In stark contrast to his civil rights predecessors of the 1960s, '70s, and '80s, Obama and some of his younger black political cohort have adopted a message of racial inclusion that transcends the bipolar debates of black and white. In short, they have adopted the postracial, "we are all Americans" mindset. Steele believes that, given his upbringing and life experiences, it is not surprising that Barack Obama is a bargainer:

> So it was fate that made Barack Obama a natural bargainer. His interracial background, in itself, assuages considerable racial anxiety in whites. It makes the point that he is not likely to be angry at whites in some blanket way.... [H]is earliest and most formative human connections were with whites. So his very family background disarms him as a challenger, and gives whites that little grace note of surprise that relaxes them.[22]

The message from Steele is that Obama puts white liberals, moderates, and even some conservatives at ease. But this type of thinking seems like an old way of thinking—these issues deserve more complexity than dualities and division.

In his autobiography, *Dreams from My Father,* Obama makes it clear that he learned early on that white Americans were much more comfortable with well-behaved black men who did not seem angry and abrasive all the time. In his speech on race in Philadelphia, Obama even mentioned his grandmother as an example of a white woman who feared black men to a certain degree. Obama quickly learned that while society admired black men who were accommodating and nonthreatening, it could not abide aggressive, angry black men. Cooper concludes that Obama's "unisex" performance "on the world's biggest stage frees up all sorts of people to perform their identities against the grain."[23]

Cooper is correct in his assertion that Obama's masculinities create new and exciting possibilities; however, the landscape and interrelation of Obama's masculinities are far more complex than the traditional binaries of good-bad and masculine-feminine. Indeed, Obama shows an awareness and thoughtfulness about his own masculinities. His gendered practices as a son, grandson, student, professor, father, husband, and politician demonstrate that Obama's masculinities are complex. As shown in the sections that follow, one way to understand the construction of Obama's masculinities is to position him in relation to others.

MEDIATED CONTRADICTIONS: OBAMA IN THE MEDIA DURING THE ELECTION

Masculinity is an active process, a public demonstration that identity is mediated by as many factors as there are men. Biology remains important in the presence of the male body as *site* (location) and *sight* (vision to others) of signification. As R. W. Connell points out, "through social institutions and processes, bodies are given meaning. Society has a range of body practices which address, sort and modify bodies." These body practices vary from "deportment and dress to sexuality, surgery, and sport."[24]

An election season becomes a social process that gives bodies meaning. Gender definitions are produced through active negotiation in the various rigors of the extended electoral setting. The various media (print, television, internet) debate the meaning(s) of these bodies on display.

While we will focus on the possible meanings of one particular body—that of Barack Obama—since masculinities always function in relation to other gender constructions, including femininities, we will include some other bodies too. We will take a look at a sample of what various figures in the media, from *New York Times* columnists to MSNBC anchors, said about Obama's masculinity during the election cycle.

Obama is part of a new breed of African American leaders drawn from the professional class. Like Deval Patrick, the governor of Massachusetts, Barack Obama can—as Richard Goldstein says—"afford to dream big."[25] Goldstein paints a picture of Obama-as-redeemer and hints at what defines Obama, calling him "a jock who doesn't have to set up a photo-op to sink a basket. He passes the buddy test."[26] Obama's masculinity is rooted in authenticity; the athletic aspects of his identity reach back to his high school basketball days in Hawaii, but have kept their authentic edge because Obama still plays in pickup games often, as he has his whole adult life. He is not simply posing for the cameras as George W. Bush might on his mountain bike, or Bill Clinton might on his jogging track. Goldstein adds, "[Obama] does this even though he isn't macho in the classic sense. All sorts of problems arise from his mellow presentation of masculinity, but it is very much in keeping with the post-hip-hop style."[27] With these details, Goldstein contrasts Obama with a traditional hegemonic masculine construction.

But, in the new Obama era, what is hegemonic and traditionally masculine any more? If Obama is now "the man," then what becomes "macho in the classic sense"? Is it a rich Wall Street broker (although nearly everyone has gone broke)? Is it the archetypal rugged cowboy, like the Marlboro Man (who was weakened by cancer in his later years)? Is it the pumped-up Arnold Schwarzenegger (whose state government is broker than the brokers)? Obama may be "mellow," as Goldstein says, but only at certain moments. When Obama needs to assert himself, he has no problem rising to the occasion. At the same time, his mellow-ness helped him during the presidential debates, when it was the older statesman, the more traditionally hegemonic senator John McCain, who appeared angry, more reactionary than Obama, and, ultimately, in need of mellowing out. At least within the black community, Goldstein defines Obama's upscale maleness as "post-hip-hop": "animated rather than alienated," "preppy rather than felonious," "butch but not bitchifying."[28] While Goldstein creates binaries with these descriptions, his work is helpful because it offers a variety of ways to look at Obama's creation of masculinity.

During the Democratic primaries, Obama's masculinities were often contrasted with Hillary Clinton's gender, a mix of femininity and female masculinity. Clinton's femininity was manifest in New Hampshire when she shed tears at a table of women while talking about the tough election process. But, taking a cue from the right wing, Clinton's toughness took on a traditional masculine bent as she declared, in a much-discussed advertisement from the campaign, that she would be the one you would call on in a crisis "at three AM." Not Barack Obama, but her. Of course, the counternarrative to that ad was the joke posted on right-wing websites that, when Hillary Clinton receives the late-night call, she yells, "Bill, it's for you." But Hillary Clinton's contrast to Obama did not work completely as planned. In the *New York Times*, Maureen Dowd opined that Obama has a "more feminine management style" and that voters, to Clinton's dismay, are now "eager to move from hard-power locker-room tactics to a soft-power sewing circle approach."[29] Obama's contradictory brand of maleness means he does not have to prove his manliness in stereotypical ways. Maureen Dowd reported that Obama "demurred at throwing a spiral because his pass might not be as good as the [University of Texas] Longhorn [quarterbacks in attendance]."[30]

Obama's contrasts sent some commentators into a spiral of their own. The bow-tied conservative of the MSNBC television network, Tucker Carlson, commented about Obama: "The guy is a lousy campaigner because he is caught up in his own rhetoric, don't you think? . . . I mean, when he gets up there, he says we're waging a war against cynicism. It has nothing to do with the concerns of ordinary people, and it is also, frankly, kind of wimpy."[31] And again, on another day, when Obama's campaign established a book club, Carlson and his guest proclaimed: "Well, everybody knows that a book club is no place for a man. . . . I don't know where to begin. Not only are you a man starting a book club, you're starting a self-serving book club." His guest, Willie Geist, responded: "It makes you wonder what he won't compromise of himself. Are we going to have manicure/pedicure parties next? You know what I mean?"[32] Along those lines, the word *squishy* was used by some in the media to describe Obama, as they tried to paint him as soft and his masculinity as weak. In contrast, in a guest editorial for the *New York Times*, Gloria Steinem suggested (a bit naively) that she supported Hillary Clinton over all the other candidates because Clinton had "no masculinity to prove."[33] But Clinton did have something to prove, and her favorite masculine counterpart, Bill, figured in this equation somewhere, for both Hillary Clinton and Barack Obama. It is clear that Obama learned how to soften his own persona by watching the former president. Obama's use of the word *hope* was straight out of Bill Clinton's election playbook, as he was born in that little place called Hope, Arkansas. And although Obama does not quite feel your pain like Bill Clinton does, he still radiates empathy in a similar way.

OBAMA IN RELATION TO BUSH

Barack Obama's masculinity can be framed in stark contrast to the shoot-'em-up cowboy masculinity of the Bush administration. Obama can still talk to the folks without being folksy, or needing to clear brush from his (newly purchased just before the election in 1999) Crawford, Texas, ranch. In September 2003, the American Enterprise Institute, a right-wing think tank and a contributor to many of the Bush administration's policies and ideas, focused its *American Enterprise Magazine* on the notion of traditional masculinity, proclaiming and essentializing real men. The cover stated in thick, bold, black letters: "Real Men: They're Back."[34] Throughout the magazine, it was suggested that, in the post–9/11 era, we are in need of manly men to protect us at all times. One article, for example, is named "The Return of Manly Leaders and the Americans Who Love Them." Other articles are titled "Political Virility," "What Men Think about Modern Manhood," "What Women Think about Modern Manhood," "Is Manliness Optional?" and "Can Art Be Manly Again?" In his article in the same issue, "Why We Need Macho Men," Steve Sailer wondered if one of the reasons Al Gore lost in 2000 was because he has a sibilant lisp, making him sound a bit gay (22). The author did not mention that, according to the popular vote, more Americans actually voted for Gore than for Bush; the general public could not have been put off that much. The magazine systematically presented "real men" as supermen, as hypermasculine constructions that we were supposed to believe described Bush and his administration—typified by the edition's cover, showcasing the silhouette of a tall, muscular man standing in the flaming wreckage of the Twin Towers, or the Baghdad Green Zone. This superhero figure stood poised to take on the world or, to the contrary and ironically—if more recent history is our guide—to leave massive destruction in his wake.

Obama's masculinity stands in contrast to that polarity. Instead of a steel-cast Superman, Richard Goldstein senses Obama as Spider Man: "[l]ess reflexive than reflective," lithe, svelte, a crooner of sorts.[35] Goldstein is convinced that, with the body of a Justin Timberlake, Obama is "bringing sexy back."[36] Alongside his sexy pensiveness, Obama stays loose and laid-back; and although Obama protests that he does not like it when people take interest in his body and how he looks on the beach, he did opt to pose for *Men's Vogue* and *GQ.* Obama's superhero persona revealed itself during the campaign when Obama told a woman in Iowa that he sought to protect the country as much as Republican candidates Mitt Romney and Rudy Giuliani did: "Don't think that I care any less . . . about making sure that my daughters don't get blown up," Obama said to her. "I live in Chicago," he continued. "It's a much more likely target than Grundy County."[37]

DOMESTICATED BUT NOT WEAKENED:
OBAMA AND MICHELLE

If we see gender in relation to other genders, then the relationship or comparison that affects Obama most completely is with Michelle Obama. Throughout the media, including in Obama's books, their marriage adds to Obama's masculinity on several levels. Again, there is a contradiction here, too. In his writings and his presentations to other media, Obama has positioned himself, sometimes comically, to appear domesticated or neutered by his family life. But the reality is that Obama's family life—including the presence of his two daughters, Sasha and Malia—makes him a more well-rounded man, bolstering his likability and authenticity. Barack Obama may not have a "normal" name like other men in the presidential arena, such as George, Bill, Dick, Al, or Jimmy, but he enacts the everyman role in his own way.

In *The Audacity of Hope,* Obama sets up the contradiction in his masculinities that is predicated on domesticity. While starting his Senate career, Obama lived by himself in Washington, D.C., while Michelle and their daughters stayed home in Chicago. Obama "tried to embrace [his]

newfound bachelorhood" by "gathering take-out menus from every restaurant in the neighborhood, watching basketball or reading late into the
night," working out late at night, or rejecting familial chores by "leaving
dishes in the sink and not making [his] bed."[38] Here, Obama positions
himself as a traditionally masculine, virile, twenty-something again—
free from the trappings of family minutiae and responsibility. Nonetheless, that positioning was undone by reality, as Obama recounts it:

> But it was no use; after thirteen years of marriage, I found myself to be fully
> domesticated, soft, and helpless. My first morning in Washington, I real-
> ized I'd forgotten to buy a shower curtain and had to scrunch up against the
> shower wall in order to avoid flooding the bathroom floor. The next night,
> watching the game and having a beer, I fell asleep at halftime, and woke up
> on the couch two hours later with a bad crick in my neck.[39]

In this anecdote, Obama literally positions his male body as weak: "soft"
and "helpless." The future president is pressed against the shower tiles,
naked, fetal, wet, and, most of all, pathetic. Then, later, his poor body
suffers, overworked and crick-necked. These are the elements of comedy, too; Obama undercuts the expected norms of a powerful politician.
Still, Obama endears himself to us with these anecdotes, boosting his
authenticity as a whole individual and nurturing the everyman image that
America expects of its president. Like his story about the T.G.I. Friday's in
southern Illinois, Obama lets us know that his masculinity is a construction. He trumps our analysis of that identity by analyzing himself first.
Obama lets us know that he is aware of the clash of masculinities in his
whole self—the contradictory gap between ideal and real.

Further on in *The Audacity of Hope,* Obama offers another example of
his contradictory masculinities, as Michelle tempers Obama's senatorial
self with a shock of domestic reality. After finishing a successful hearing
on restricting weapons proliferation, Obama called Michelle—who was
still back in Chicago—to tell her the good news about the possibility
of passing a significant bill. But the public success clashed with private
reality:

> Michelle cut me off.
> "We have ants."
> "Huh?"
> "I found ants in the kitchen. And in the bathroom upstairs."
> "Okay..."

"I need you to buy some ant traps on your way home tomorrow. I'd get
them myself, but I've got to take the girls to their doctor's appointment after
school. Can you do that for me?"

"Right. Ant traps."

Obama goes on to wonder if Ted Kennedy or even his future general election opponent, John McCain, had to worry about such small domestic
issues. But Obama's presentation of this contradictory situation positions
Michelle Obama as the keel that steadies his boat when the waters get too
choppy or rise too high. Reports of the first family moving into the White
House, where Michelle Obama has told the residential staff that Sasha
and Malia must learn to make their own beds, corroborate this steady-
ing effect. What's good for the girls is good for their daddy, and Obama's
writings attest to that.

Camille Paglia asserts that Michelle Obama helps Barack Obama
stand in contrast to the Clintons. Calling Michelle a powerhouse, Paglia
argues that the "Obamas represent the future. Not the past."[40] Indeed,
his masculinity is more textured because of his extraordinary wife. Ras
Baraka asserts that Obama becomes a "real man" when he continues "to
love his family" and "hit the fist with Michelle Obama because that's
what they do." Baraka also adds that Obama should "continue to represent his community—who he is, his ideals, or what he feels for real. And
he [should] use his power and resources to take care of the world. And
that's what men do."[41] And Esther Armah puts things further in context
when she discusses what Obama's masculinity creates in African American society and beyond: "The beauty of the presence and the emergence
of Barack Obama isn't Barack Obama, it's Michelle Obama. Because in
Michelle, for black women there was an affirmation that their strength
could find them a great guy."[42]

That Obama includes details of masculine domesticity in his book
is part of the point here. He takes the time to discuss the minutiae of his
two-parent home amid the unsuccessful marriages and the problems of
children in African American families. He makes it clear that, although
he succeeded despite not being raised with a father, he does not see his
upbringing as ideal. He convinces us of the joys and necessity of active fatherhood—Obama calls it "what it takes to be a full grown man."[43] While
Cooper proposes that Obama is the first feminized, unisex president,
many of the details in Obama's books make his identity less simple. Coo-

per never discusses Michelle, their daughters, or Obama's fatherhood, and that is a huge absence in presenting the private-made-public persona of the president. The image of Obama as father figure and domesticated husband is a fascinating and complex one. On the one hand, it defuses popular perceptions of black men as violent, hypersexualized, and irresponsible; on the other, the Obamas perform marriage and domesticity with a hint of sexuality, so that Barack Obama does not come across as emasculated by marriage, a familiar trope in white middle-class America.

POST-ELECTION THOUGHTS ON OBAMA'S MASCULINITY

Ultimately, the way we see another's gender is as subjective as gender itself. The version of Obama's identity presented in this chapter may be completely different from the reader's perception. Richard Goldstein underscores Obama's diverse capabilities when he asserts that Obama "straddles racial divides" and "straddles continents" because of his contrasting parentage and international upbringing. In a way, Barack Obama brings the female solo performer Anna Deveare Smith to mind, as she embodies many different races and genders in her performances. For instance, in *Twilight, Los Angeles, 1992,* she monologues as former Los Angeles police chief Daryl Gates, Rodney King, and a Korean shop owner, among many others. Theatre scholar Jill Dolan has called her work "monopolylogues" because of the multiplicity of perspectives coming from her one voice.[44] Proving that contradiction can also be convergence, in a similar way we can see ourselves in Obama, and we can see others in him. Since the 2008 election, that simultaneity of seeing has been everywhere in the media, in places as diverse as sports reports on CNN's website, the *Daily Telegraph,* and *New York Times* blogs, where commentators have further constructed and deconstructed aspects of Obama's masculinities. Former NBA great Reggie Miller has informed us about what Barack Obama's point-guard skills tell us about his leadership style.[45] Along with an array of men's health professionals, Terry Kirby wonders what men can learn from Obama, given that one of the busiest men in the world manages to balance work and keep a killer physique.[46] Judith Warner, a writer for the *New York Times,* blogs—in the coyly titled "Sometimes a President Is Just a President"—that she has received many letters from women telling about their sexual fantasies involving the president.[47]

Undoubtedly, by the time you read this, Obama's identity will have evolved in new, unexpected, and perhaps essentially contradictory ways. From the moment that the Bushes were helicoptered away on Inauguration Day, Obama brought a whole new character to the presidency. Now that Obama is literally "the man," there has been less media chatter concerning Obama's feminine side (conversely, more attention has been given to Michelle Obama's chiseled arms). But with two young daughters in the White House, Obama cannot help but maintain domesticity alongside the power that he has used to tackle the economy, the auto industry, and (to some extent) the health care industry. One dramatic example of Obama's transcendent identity was when he addressed the Arab world in his speech in Cairo in June 2009. As a commander in chief with a background in the Islamic faith, Obama straddled continents and changed how we view the African American/multiracial/presidential male. In turn, in that moment, many in the outside world changed the way they thought about America.

NOTES

1. Obama, *Audacity of Hope,* 75.
2. Obama, *Dreams from My Father,* 327.
3. Connell, *The Men and the Boys,* 13.
4. Ibid., 13–14.
5. Cooper, "Our First Unisex President?" 633.
6. Esther Armah, interview in Byron Hurt, *Barack & Curtis: Manhood, Power, & Respect* (2008), www.bhurt.com and www.youtube.com (accessed January 5, 2009).
7. Ibid.
8. A number of journalists and commentators have observed that Obama comes across as calm, cool, and collected without any hostility or anger.
9. Courtland Milloy, "Maybe It's Time We Redefined Manliness," *Washington Post,* September 10, 2008, B1.
10. David Remnick, "The Joshua Generation," *New Yorker,* November 17, 2008, 68.
11. Ibid.; Obama, *Audacity of Hope,* 49–50.
12. Barack Obama, "A More Perfect Union—The Race Speech," March 18, 2008, Philadelphia, Pennsylvania.
13. Qtd. in "Dreams of Obama," *Frontline,* PBS, January 20, 2009.
14. Frank Rich, "If Terrorists Rock the Vote in 2008," *New York Times,* June 29, 2008.
15. Milloy, "Maybe It's Time We Redefined Manliness," B1.
16. Cooper, "Our First Unisex President?"
17. Ibid., 644–645.
18. Barack Obama, "Barack Obama's Remarks at the Democratic Convention," *USA Today,* July 27, 2004, www.usatoday.com (accessed March 9, 2008).

19. Cooper, "Our First Unisex President?" 650.

20. Julie Bosman, "Obama Calls for More Responsibility from Black Fathers," *New York Times,* June 16, 2008, A15.

21. Steele, *A Bound Man,* 106–107.

22. Ibid., 101.

23. Cooper, "Our First Unisex President?" 660.

24. Connell, *The Men and the Boys,* 58.

25. Goldstein, "The Redeemer," 58.

26. Ibid., 52.

27. Ibid.

28. Ibid.

29. Maureen Dowd, "Quién Es Less Macho?" *New York Times,* February 24, 2008 (accessed online, www.nytimes.com, March 9, 2008).

30. Ibid.

31. Tucker Carlson, "Tucker," *MSNBC,* July 2, 2007, www.mediamatters.org/items/200707110003.

32. Ibid., July 12, 2007, www.mediamatters.org/items/200707130009.

33. Gloria Steinem, "Women Are Never Front Runners," *New York Times,* January 8, 2008 (accessed online, www.nytimes.com, March 9, 2008).

34. *American Enterprise Magazine: Politics, Business and Culture* 14, no. 6 (September 2003). All citations for this edition are given parenthetically.

35. Goldstein, "The Redeemer," 52.

36. Ibid.

37. Amy Sullivan, "Obama's Other Breakthrough: A Big-City President," *Time,* January 13, 2009.

38. Obama, *Audacity of Hope,* 72.

39. Ibid.

40. Camille Paglia, "Hillary without Tears," *Salon,* January 10, 2008, www.salon.com/opinion/paglia/2008/01/10/hillary.

41. In Hurt, *Barack & Curtis.*

42. Ibid.

43. Obama, *Audacity of Hope,* 347.

44. Dolan, *Utopia in Performance,* 83.

45. Reggie Miller, "Obama's Hoops Style and His Presidency," *CNN,* January 14, 2009, http://edition.cnn.com/2009/POLITICS/01/14/miller.obama.basketball.

46. Terry Kirby, "Barack Obama Works Out for 45 Minutes, Six Days a Week. What Can Other Men Learn from His Example?" *Daily Telegraph,* January 19, 2009, http://www.telegraph.co.uk/health/men_shealth/4271779/Barack-Obama-redefining-the-male-physique.html.

47. Judith Warner, "Sometimes a President Is Just a President," *New York Times,* February 5, 2009, http://warner.blogs.nytimes.com/2009/02/05/sometimes-a-president-is-just-a-president.

BIBLIOGRAPHY

American Enterprise Magazine: Politics, Business and Culture 14, no. 6 (September 2003).

Connell, R. W. *The Men and the Boys.* Berkeley: University of California Press, 2001.

Cooper, Frank Rudy. "Our First Unisex President? Black Masculinity and Obama's Feminine Side." *Denver University Law Review* 86 (2009): 633–661.

Dolan, Jill. *Utopia in Performance: Finding Hope at the Theater.* Lansing: University of Michigan Press, 2005.

Goldstein, Richard. "The Redeemer: Barack Obama." In *The Contenders.* New York: Seven Stories, 2008.

Obama, Barack. *The Audacity of Hope.* New York: Three Rivers, 2006.

———. *Dreams from My Father: A Story of Race and Inheritance.* New York: Three Rivers, 1995.

Steele, Shelby. *A Bound Man: Why We Are Excited about Obama and Why He Can't Win.* New York: Free Press, 2007.

SEVEN

THE MALE RAPUNZEL IN FILM: THE INTERSECTIONS OF DISABILITY, GENDER, RACE, AND SEXUALITY

JOHNSON CHEU AND CAROLYN TYJEWSKI

According to various disability studies scholars, disabled men have frequently been feminized within mainstream media, including film.[1] This argument seems to suggest that this gendered position is a disempowered one and is created mainly, if not exclusively, through the use of gendered stereotypes. Like Jimmy Stewart's character, L. B. Jefferies, in *Rear Window,* the disabled male apparently can only watch the world around him and is unable to effect change without another's help.[2] This chapter does not dispute this particular reading of mainstream media (past or present). Instead, what we will examine is another potential reading of disabled male characters within popular media, particularly film, and how this reading stems from the use of gendered, raced, and sexualized tropes to create what we are calling the *male Rapunzel.*

Theorists Michael Omi and Howard Winant in *Racial Formation in the United States: From the 1960s to the 1990s* help to buttress our notions of interplay. They contend that "race is a matter of both social structure and cultural representation."[3] Thus, race becomes a matter of not just the hierarchical social structures that exist within a given society, but also, as they call it, the various "projects" that society creates to maintain hegemony. The confluence of social structure and representation leads to connections with other forms of hegemony. They write: "Thus race, class, and gender (as well as sexual orientation) constitute 'regions' of hegemony, areas in which certain political projects can take shape. They share certain obvious attributes in that they are all 'socially constructed,' and they all consist of a field of projects whose common feature is their linkage of social structure and signification."[4] Omi and Winant's linking of structure and culture and their drawing of parallels between identity groups help to illustrate our own theory that these categories are indeed relational, and it is the confluence of these relations that creates the male Rapunzel in both *Gattaca*[5] and *Bone Collector.*[6]

The male Rapunzel is an empowered male position. While popular memory of the Rapunzel tale is the damsel in distress pining at a tower window for her Prince Charming, the Grimm brothers' fairytale was not written that way. She was an empowered woman capable of not only devising a plan of escape, but executing it when she saw fit *without* the prince.[7] Therefore, the male Rapunzel is, simply put, a male character supposedly trapped in a traditional tower who devises an escape plan and executes it whether or not the proverbial prince shows up.[8] It is true that Rapunzel as "a maiden in distress leaning from a tower window and searching the horizon for a rescuer" is "the single most pervasive image evoked in the popular mind."[9] However, as critic Ruth Bottigheimer claims, the women in the Grimm brothers' tales are often empowered. She notes, "of all the successful spells actually laid in Grimm's tales, the overwhelming majority, if not all, are usually performed by young, beautiful and usually nubile girls."[10] Such a reading of Rapunzel turns on their ear the stereotypical feminine roles and the tales that exemplify them. Roles that teach a young girl, as Madonna Kolbenschlag notes in *Kiss Sleeping Beauty Good-bye,* "to wait, forever, if necessary, for the expected *other* who will make her life meaningful and fulfilled"[11] become questioned by the invocations of past fairytale femininity (with all its active and empowered meanings).

One can see the beginnings of this articulation in *Pretty Woman.*[12] While Vivian wants "the fairytale ending," Edward is "rescued right back." Although this film still plays with the popular memory of the fairytale, it also begins to reposition the tale. Arguably, both Vivian and Edward wish for escape from their traditional towers, they each have a plan, and they execute it. While on the surface it appears that they rescue each other, ultimately they rescue themselves. Though problematic, each character's position as "weak" and "strong," "capable" and "incapable," "masculine" and "feminine" plays off the other and off gendered and sexualized tropes (i.e., "the hooker with the heart of gold" and "the unsatisfied and emotionally disconnected business person").[13] As in the fairytale Vivian wants so desperately to replicate, the gender roles are not black and white—one strictly masculine and the other strictly feminine. They are both more ambiguous, and this destabilization creates opportunities for Vivian and Edward to rescue themselves from their respective situations.

While the image of the hooker in cinema is usually negative, critiques of *Pretty Woman* have portrayed Vivian somewhat differently. As Harvey Roy Greenberg notes in his article "Rescrewed: *Pretty Woman's* Co-opted Feminism": "Her [Vivian's] harlotry is clearly provisional until some prince climbs her tower (or jumps her bones). Meanwhile, she's turned prostitution into free-spirited, street-level capitalism. Calls her own tricks, has no pimp, uses no drugs, flosses her teeth, and practices irreplaceable safe sex."[14] Clearly, she is atypical of prostitutes in film and, while she may appear to be waiting for rescue, she provides, in many ways, a self-empowered figure. While Greenberg's analysis of the film remains somewhat dour, he concludes, "a surprising number of women with feminist backgrounds or sensibility still have greatly . . . enjoyed *Pretty Woman*."[15] This implies, as does the box-office success of the film, that viewers have bought into, among other notions, the idea of Vivian as an empowered figure. But the hooker with a heart of gold remains a myth. As Jane Caputi notes in *"Sleeping with the Enemy* as *Pretty Woman*, Part II"*: "In reality, few prostitutes have been saved by capitalists with hearts of gold while the numberless women who regular play a redeemer-of-troubled-man role do so at great risk of damning themselves to a dysfunctional, if not abusive, relationship."[16] Beyond the myth, Greenberg's work is film criticism, not a study of the reception of the film by the audience. Therefore, feminists' enjoyment of *Pretty Woman* may or may not have anything to do with their understanding of the character of Vivian.

While both Vivian and Edward are, arguably, psychologically scarred and do invoke some of the aspects of the male Rapunzel, what we are discussing in this chapter are the later articulations of the male Rapunzel in Andrew Niccol's *Gattaca* and Philip Noyce's *Bone Collector*. Within these films, what occurs can be construed as the feminization of the male character with a disability.[17] In other words, the male character with a disability is constructed in such a way as to suggest, on the surface, femininity rather than masculinity, dependence rather than independence, etc. However, what is also occurring is the destabilization of this supposed feminization through the subject's agency: the plan and execution of his "escape," his interactions with the world around him, etc. This destabilization occurs through the use of raced, gendered, and sexualized tropes and the mitigation of all of these identity categories.

What we are suggesting is that disability, gender, race, and sexuality are interlinking (indeed, interlocking) categories that inform, play off, and create meaning for and about one another. To put it simply, they are relational. Siobhan Somerville shows, in *Queering the Color Line*, how race informs and is informed by gender, sex, and sexuality in film, medicine, and the popular culture of the early twentieth century.[18] In discussing concepts of race and sex in the eugenics movement at the turn of the century, for example, she writes, "The beginning of sexology, then, circulated within and perhaps depended on a perverse climate of eugenicist and antimiscegenation sentiment and legislation." In examining texts such as the works of Pauline E. Hopkins and James Weldon Johnson's *The Autobiography of an Ex-Colored Man,* she claims, "the mulatto . . . became an important, if contradictory, figure in sexologists' attempts to characterize the sexual invert."[19] Somerville shows that the mulatto figure is both a raced and sexed identity; these identities do not operate independently but rather interdependently within societal constructs and representations. The male Rapunzel, like Somerville's discussion of the mulatto figure, is an interconnected, relational figure within the films we examine.

Within each of these films, we will look at one specific disabled male character, how that figure is positioned in relation to the other main characters, and how the use of tropes, relationally, creates a reading of this male character as a Rapunzel. Within *Gattaca,* we will examine the character of Eugene, played by Jude Law, and within *Bone Collector,* we will look at Lincoln Rhyme, played by Denzel Washington.

Gattaca is set in a futuristic United States in which the genetically designed occupy the upper strata of society while the naturally conceived are discriminated against and occupy the lower rungs of society. The film centers primarily on Vincent, a naturally conceived human. Within the society of *Gattaca,* the genetically enhanced who have fallen on hard times can sell their DNA (their identity) on the black market to those naturally conceived, who then assume the identity of the genetically designed individual. Jude Law's character, Jerome Eugene Morrow, becomes paralyzed and chooses to sell his identity to Vincent Freeman, which allows Vincent to assume the identity of Eugene and take his place in the upper strata of society working as an engineer at the Gattaca space corporation.[20]

The Bone Collector's main character is Lincoln Rhyme, once a top forensics investigator until a "tragic" accident left him paralyzed and bedridden.[21] After the accident, Rhyme assists NYPD investigators in solving crimes through the use of technology and his vast knowledge of forensics. Based on the Jeffery Deaver detective novels, the driving plot of the film revolves around Rhyme assisting a young beat cop, Amelia Donaghy (Angelina Jolie), to advance her career by tracking down a serial killer.

Lincoln and Eugene possess a presumed fixity of place: Eugene, except when accompanied by Vincent, leaves his home only once, and Lincoln is, until the climax of the film, in bed in his apartment. Like L. B. Jefferies in *Rear Window,* they appear to have limited movement. Lincoln and Eugene are positioned as fixed through the use of establishing shots and fixed camera positions. In *Bone Collector,* Lincoln is first shown to be bedridden within his apartment. His sole independent movement at this point is the continual turning of his head in various conversations. When his eyes fixate on one of the apartment's windows, a bird sits on the sill while the street appears several stories below. The high-rise is his metaphorical and literal tower in which he is presumed to be trapped because of a disability. Similarly, in *Gattaca,* viewers know that Eugene and Vincent live in a futuristic high-rise by a series of establishing shots throughout the film of an isolated building that Vincent is either driving away from or to. Eugene's fixity is also established through narrative. In Vincent and Eugene's initial meeting, the camera lingers on Eugene and his wheelchair. Vincent scans the apartment and, eyeing the long spiral staircase, asks, "Who lives up there?" Eugene replies tersely, "Well, I certainly don't." In exterior shots in both films, the camera looks up at the windows of each character's apartment, implying that he is fixed in that place. Unable to move outside the realm of the private and domestic, both men are presumed to be trapped in their respective towers due to disability.

However, unlike in *Rear Window,* these two characters do plan and execute escapes from the proverbial towers within which they are imprisoned. Both men discuss suicide. In *Bone Collector,* Rhyme requests that his friend Dr. Barry Lehman help him in his "final transition." In *Gattaca,* Eugene's wish for suicide is displayed through suggestive acts of excessive smoking and alcohol abuse; statements he makes, such as "If at first you don't succeed, try, try again"; and his eventual confession to Vincent, late in the film, that he was not drunk when he stepped out in front of the car that paralyzed him. While viewers are led to believe at the beginning of both of these films that these men are trapped by their disabilities and that both desire to escape, what becomes clear as the films progress is that disability is not what traps them nor is it, arguably, what either is seeking to escape.

In *Gattaca*, Eugene's drunken confession that he wasn't drunk when he was hit by the car lets the audience know that he was suicidal prior to becoming paralyzed, and his discussion of the silver medal (that he eventually places around his neck before killing himself) provides a hint of what Eugene appears to be wishing to escape. There is a discussion of this symbol in an early scene in the film. In this scene, Vincent attempts to transform himself into Jerome Morrow, and Eugene asks him, "What makes you think you can be me at all?" He then shows Vincent a silver medal and says, "Jerome Morrow was never meant to be one step down on the podium. With all I had going for me, I was still second best." For Eugene, the silver medal represents his failure at being a success— something society had told him that he should be without question, work, or effort. Therefore, his desire to escape his life is a wish to escape not disability, but rather the socially prescribed role of the genetically perfect.

Whereas Eugene runs from perfection, Lincoln Rhyme wishes to escape his solitude. Although there are no narratives giving the background of Rhyme's life story prior to the accident, the audience is given clues about his past through shots of awards won and books written, but very little human contact with friends or family members is shown. The scene depicting his accident has him crawling through a narrow tunnel, alone; his only contact with others is through the use of the headset, a hint of his life to come. This scene, in combination with the setup shots of material objects, suggests that his life directly before his accident somewhat mirrors his life after it: he has no family with whom he interacts and no connections to others beyond his career, which becomes more solitary when he chooses to remain in his home after the accident. Like Eugene, Lincoln Rhyme wishes to escape not disability, but rather his self-imposed solitary confinement.

While both characters appear fixed within their towers and both desire escape, they also invoke changes in the world around them. For example, Eugene, through his interactions with both Vincent and Irene, helps
to make possible Vincent's rise from a stigmatized status, while Lincoln
uses his detective skills to help solve serial murders and to train Amelia
Donaghy in forensics. Indeed, through the use of Amelia's earpiece and
indicated by crosscutting shots, Lincoln is at every crime scene, talking
Amelia and the other characters through their respective assignments.
Amelia, in a sense, becomes Lincoln's legs. So, while on the surface, it
appears that these men do not move and are incapable of action, they are
very active within these films and have agency, making their presumably
feminized and fixed positions tenuous at best.

As we have previously suggested, it is the relational arrangement of
these characters that destabilizes their positions as passive, active, dependent, independent, feminine, masculine, white, black, gay, straight,
disabled, and non-disabled subjects. Eugene and Lincoln are not just gendered; they are also raced and sexualized through the use of black filmic
tropes. *Gattaca* utilizes a tragic mulatto theme, whereas *Bone Collector*
utilizes a different yet related motif of forbidden interracial relations.
Typically, within the tragic mulatto genre, the lead character is a white-
looking black female and that character's mother plays a supporting role.
In *Gattaca,* the roles are reversed in several ways. Vincent is a young man
rather than a young woman. Eugene plays the "mother" role: he is the
only "relative" who can identify Vincent as other and, therefore, must die
by the end of the film. Vincent is also marked by his surname, Freeman,
as being of African descent.[22] Yet, his family's only acknowledgment of
their past is in their request of the geneticist that their next son have "fair
skin"—to which the African American geneticist gives a knowing smile.
In *Bone Collector,* the filmic trope of forbidden interracial relationships is
more obvious to the audience, and yet the races of the main characters
are constantly flipped. The interplay, for example, makes Amelia Donaghy
into a nonwhite woman, and Lincoln's request for "my Thelma" (as he
often refers to Queen Latifah's character) is a sign of his whitening. The
play of race within these two characters makes them both overtly sexual
subjects while also sexually repressed. Because *Bone Collector* and *Gattaca*
are racially charged scripts (in terms not only of characters but also of the
play of light and dark within the films), race and sexuality flip meanings

as well. The use of these genres positions Lincoln and Eugene as female and yet male; black and yet white; disabled and yet non-disabled; and, in the case of *Gattaca*, straight and yet gay.

In both films, gender is constantly in flux. This is done through the interplay of relational positions among Eugene, Vincent, and Irene (in *Gattaca*) and between Lincoln and Amelia (in *Bone Collector*). The characters become an amalgam of contradictory markers, signs of instability, strength, and agency through this constant flipping of race and gender.

In *Gattaca*, this flipping is further emphasized by the extreme whiteness and masculinization of Irene (Uma Thurman). Irene is often shown in a simple black pantsuit with her hair pulled back. Although this attire and hairstyle may denote nothing except themselves, they may, by contrast, connote or signify other things, such as a reserved masculine air and, certainly at work, a desire to be considered "one of the boys." In fact, when thus attired, she often plays a masculine role. During the course of the film, the mission director of *Gattaca*'s next planned space flight is murdered. When Irene's boss wants her to play a more typical feminine role of helping the investigators, she protests, saying that it would put her behind in her work and potentially jeopardize her position in line for promotion; to this, her boss responds, "Your place is assured." This scene is filmed with both of them standing toe-to-toe as it were, while Vincent lingers inconspicuously in the background. Here, Irene assumes the typical man's role of prioritizing work over a more womanly role of helping others. As is often the case, Irene's masculinity is enhanced by her expressionless face, her eyes unblinking, her mouth perpetually tight, unsmiling. Likewise, when one of the cops asks if she has an alibi for the night of the murder, she claims, "I was home alone." The cop reminds Irene of her sex appeal, her femininity, saying, "I find that hard to believe," to which she offers no response. In contrast, when she plays a more feminine role, such as in the nightclub scene when she is on a date with Vincent, her masculine business attire is shed in favor of a slinky dress, and her hair is down.

This slipping between masculine and feminine, between strong and "weak" (Irene is technically disabled because of "an unacceptable likelihood of heart failure"), signifies an interplay of the characters' identity roles. When Irene is masculine, Vincent and sometimes Eugene are more feminine; in short, Vincent and Eugene play off Irene and Irene plays off them as well. In the guise of Jerome Morrow, Vincent gains entrance into the Gattaca corporation. Realizing his lifelong dream, Vincent cannot help but gaze daily up at the sky, i.e., expressing his desires and wearing his heart on his sleeve. As Vincent and Irene stand side by side, she comments dryly, "You're the only one who watches every one [ship launch]." Her hands behind her back, staring blankly, emotionless, in essence she is schooling him to be more masculine, to act more like a man, more, in fact, like her. She advises him, "If you want to pretend like you don't care, don't look up." Within this scene, Vincent's desires are exposed in a business setting. In relation to Irene's self-assured air and sarcastic comment about "not looking up," Vincent becomes feminine to Irene's masculinity. Throughout the film, all three characters (Eugene, Vincent, and Irene) become destabilized in terms of gender and sexuality.

Vincent's and Eugene's bursts of emotionality play off Irene's emotionless poise. In one such sequence, Vincent prepares himself to go out. As he comes down the stairs, Eugene inquires, "Where are you going?" When Vincent states simply, "I'm going out tonight," Eugene pries further, asking, "Who's going?" and Vincent replies blandly, "Everybody." Eugene turns into a quasi-jealous lover here, repeating rather tersely "Everybody," while lighting a cigarette and pouring himself a shot. He literally pouts here, assuming a stereotypical feminine role to Vincent's masculine one. This scene contrasts with others that align Vincent's gendered position as the emotional feminine to Irene's more masculine. The roles of all the characters are once again interconnected, and always changing. As the scene continues, Irene's position as Vincent's love interest plays off Eugene as Vincent's jealous lover. As Vincent runs back upstairs to put in his contacts (thereby erasing his "disability"), Eugene huffs contentiously and turns toward the window. When Irene arrives to pick up Vincent, Eugene spies her from above and the two exchange fleeting glances, as though Eugene and Irene were two lovers fighting over Vincent; Eugene is the lover left behind as Vincent cavorts with another.

Yet, at other times, Eugene is the masculine one to Vincent's more feminine role. Upon learning of the mission director's death and that Vincent's eyelash has been found in the subsequent combing of the premises, Vincent becomes overly emotional, worried that his real identity as someone naturally conceived will be discovered. As he wails, "They'll recognize me," Eugene counters with "*I* don't recognize you." He assumes a commanding masculine air as Vincent drinks, chastising him, "Keep your lashes on your lids where they belong. How could you be so careless?" During this scene, Eugene sits at the table, calm and rational, while Vincent sweats over his perceived demise. Ultimately, each character's position informs the other and, in the process, each is destabilized.

The same destabilization occurs in *Bone Collector*. As discussed previously, the racial identities of Lincoln and Amelia fluctuate between nonwhite and white, and their genders appear to be in relational flux as well. At the beginning of the film, the audience is introduced to Amelia in a manner that portrays her as masculine. As her lover awakes, she is staring out the window with a cup of coffee. As she dresses for work (like Irene's, Amelia's hair is pinned back), her lover offers, "I made breakfast." She replies with her back to him, "No thanks." To which he comments, "Another slam, bam, thank you ma'am." The scene continues with her lover assuming a feminine role to her masculine one. The camera shifts from a wide shot of the couple to a close-up of him imploring, "My therapist tells me I'm not getting what I need out of this relationship. . . . C'mon, I think we make a great couple." Showing no interest in his feelings, she responds flatly, "You know, I care about you. . . . I can't make a commitment." With her hair slicked back, putting on her uniform, and too consumed with work (and avoiding emotional closeness) to want anything more than sex from her lover, Amelia becomes the masculinized character both to her lover and to Lincoln's feminized role as stationary, passive, and in need of help. This scene is crosscut with scenes of Lincoln in bed, which connects the two characters (and foreshadows their relationship) while, at the same time, connecting and flipping their gendered positions.

Amelia's introductory scene is, in a sense, replicated in a scene with Lincoln after he has a flashback. During this scene, a combination of raced and gendered tropes are used to change both characters from emotionally detached and distant to more flirtatious. When Amelia awakens at Lincoln's bedside, her actions are imbued with sexual tension. Her hair is loose (rather than tied tightly back as it is throughout most of the film) while she gently plays with Lincoln's trachea scar and then strokes his finger. Her eyes close to enjoy the erotic moment, and Lincoln awakens to remind her that there are "laws against molesting the handicapped." She smiles, embarrassed. By positioning Amelia as molester/seducer, Lincoln becomes the innocent ingenue luring her into dangerous situations and attracting her through his mysteriousness. However, Amelia's loose hair, bedside manner, and blush at his sexual comment suggest femininity. Their relationship is fraught with sexual tension. Earlier in the film, Amelia brings over a piece of evidence, a strip containing an unknown odor, which she accidentally drops in his lap. As she apologetically reaches down to retrieve it, he says rather seductively, "Take your time," and grins. She then holds the strip to his nose for him to smell, and he beckons her to "hold it closer." These two scenes function as evidence of the flipping of gender roles between them. In one, she is the seducer to his femme fatale; in the other, he is the flirt beckoning her. Throughout the play of the relational positioning of Lincoln and Amelia, gender and race contribute to and are informed by the flipping of roles. Within the motif of forbidden interracial relationships, the African American male is frequently seen as the pursuer of the white female. Yet, within these scenes, Amelia becomes the aggressor as Lincoln flirts with her at the same time. Thus, Lincoln and Amelia, like Eugene, Vincent, and Irene, become an amalgam of contradictory markers, signs of instability, strength, and agency through this constant flipping of race and gender.

In the process of destabilizing racial and gender representations, representations of disability are also destabilized because of the interconnectedness of these categories. As stated previously, Eugene and Lincoln are at once disabled—seen as fixed, passive, and helpless—while, at the same time, they are active and involved in their own lives and the lives of those around them. This interplay is made possible through the destabilization of the raced and gendered tropes, which allows for the opportunity at the end of the films for these characters to escape from their respective towers.

Eugene, in crosscut sequences with Vincent, who is seen beginning his first space mission, is shown incinerating himself, fulfilling his earlier suicidal intentions to end his supposedly superior life. In configuring Eugene as a male Rapunzel, it is necessary to view him as at once both masculine and feminine, as both disabled and able, as both someone who waits and someone who acts. In order to see his flipping of roles, the others, Vincent and Irene, must slip roles too, fade in and out of their varied identities. In the end, Eugene does literally escape the physical world, his tower of genetic superiority that trapped him.

Lincoln's escape begins in the climactic scene when the killer, Marcus Andrews, is revealed and comes to Lincoln's apartment to kill him. While one might think that his disability positions Lincoln as weak and incapable, he saves himself. Marcus at first has the upper hand when he breaks Lincoln's finger and shocks him with the heart defibrillator. Indeed, the suspense mounts as Lincoln struggles to breathe. But then the tables begin to turn. Lincoln releases the bed's elevation device, crushing Marcus's hand. As Marcus pulls Lincoln from the bed to the floor, it appears that all is lost; Lincoln plays possum, suggesting that he is on his last breath. When Marcus leans in to hear what he imagines might be Lincoln's last words, Lincoln takes a chunk out of Marcus's neck. While Amelia arrives and shoots Marcus before he dies, Lincoln has already delivered the fatal blow and, in effect, decided to escape his solitary life through the creation and maintenance of relationships rather than suicide.

For both of the filmic narratives we have discussed, escape from one's positionality becomes possible through the exposure of its illusory fixity. Unfixing race, gender, and sexuality, consequently, unhinges disability in *Gattaca* and *Bone Collector*, making these aspects present and absent, multiple in meanings, and contingent upon the characters and events surrounding them. In *Queering the Color Line*, Somerville notes, "The challenge is to recognize the instability of multiple categories of difference simultaneously rather than to assume the fixity of one to establish the complexity of another."[23] Our reading suggests that the contemporary filmic figure of the male Rapunzel materializes not when looking at a single trope—race, gender, sexuality, or disability—but when examining the interlinking relationships among them.

NOTES

1. See Longmore, *Why I Burned My Book*; and Morris, *Pride against Prejudice*.
2. Hitchcock, *Rear Window*.
3. Omi and Winant, *Racial Formation in the United States*, 56.
4. Ibid., 68.
5. Niccol, dir., *Gattaca*.
6. Noyce, dir., *The Bone Collector*.
7. In the fairytale, Rapunzel is the one who comes up with the idea to use her hair as a rope. The prince and she have two children while she is still within the tower. Rapunzel then escapes the tower, leaving the prince behind in the tower with the witch,

and lives with the children for quite some time before the prince finds her. Grimm and Grimm, *Complete Fairy Tales*, 46–49.

8. The use of the word *proverbial* is to signify those instances where we are speaking metaphorically rather than literally.

9. Bottigheimer, *Grimms' Bad Girls and Bold Boys*, 101.

10. Ibid., 40.

11. Kolbenschlag, *Kiss Sleeping Beauty Good-bye*, 12.

12. *Pretty Woman*, dir. Gary Marshall (Disney/Touchstone, 1990).

13. While this is not a film we consider here in detail, we would argue that both characters (Vivian and Edward) can be read as hookers with hearts of gold and as unsatisfied and emotionally disconnected businesspeople.

14. Greenberg, "Rescrewed," 10.

15. Ibid., 13.

16. Caputi, "*Sleeping with the Enemy* as *Pretty Woman*, Part II," 7.

17. Within *Gattaca*, the three main roles are all characters with disabilities (Vincent, played by Ethan Hawke; Irene, played by Uma Thurman; and Eugene, played by Jude Law). However, we focus specifically on Eugene.

18. Somerville, *Queering the Color Line*.

19. Ibid., 31.

20. Part of what we are arguing in this chapter is that there is no Jerome Morrow; he is a fiction. Therefore, Ethan Hawke's character will be referred to as "Vincent" and Jude Law's character will be referred to as "Eugene."

21. Disability studies has questioned the presumption that the onset of a disability is a tragedy. Therefore, the use of the word *tragic* in quotation marks is a recognition of how mainstream society tends to view this event rather than what may actually occur.

22. Historically, "Freeman" was a surname taken by African Americans who were freed, that is, no longer slaves, in the colonies.

23. Somerville, *Queering the Color Line*, 5.

BIBLIOGRAPHY

Bottigheimer, Ruth. *Grimms' Bad Girls and Bold Boys: The Moral and Social Vision of the Tales*. New Haven, Conn.: Yale University Press, 1987.

Caputi, Jane. "*Sleeping with the Enemy* as *Pretty Woman*, Part II; or, What Happened after the Princess Woke Up?" *Journal of Popular Film and Television* 19, no. 1 (1991): 2–8.

Greenberg, Harvey Roy. "Rescrewed: *Pretty Woman*'s Co-opted Feminism." *Journal of Popular Film and Television* 19, no. 1 (1991): 9–13.

Grimm, Jacob, and Wilhelm Grimm. *The Complete Fairy Tales of the Brothers Grimm*, 3rd ed. Trans. Jack Zipes. New York: Bantam, 2003.

Hitchcock, Alfred, dir. *Rear Window*. Universal, 1954.

Kolbenschlag, Madonna. *Kissing Sleeping Beauty Good-bye: Breaking the Spell of Feminine Myths and Models*. Garden City, N.Y.: Doubleday, 1979.

Longmore, Paul K. *Why I Burned My Book and Other Essays on Disability*. Philadelphia: Temple University Press, 2003.

Morris, Jenny. *Pride against Prejudice: Transforming Attitudes to Disability.* London: Woman's Press, 1991.

Niccol, Andrew, dir. *Gattaca.* Sony Pictures, 1997.

Noyce, Philip, dir. *The Bone Collector.* Universal, 1999.

Omi, Michael, and Howard Winant. *Racial Formation in the United States: From the 1960s to the 1990s,* 2nd ed. New York: Routledge, 1994.

Somerville, Siobhan B. *Queering the Color Line: Race and the Invention of Homosexuality in American Culture.* Durham, N.C.: Duke University Press, 2000.

EIGHT

MASCULINITIES IN DATING RELATIONSHIPS: REALITY AND REPRESENTATION AT THE INTERSECTION OF RACE, CLASS, AND SEXUAL ORIENTATION

JIMMIE MANNING

As evidenced by the continued success of reality television programs centered upon the topic, representations of single men in search of romantic relationships continue to thrive as a part of American popular culture. Since the late 1990s, reality-oriented dating shows such as *The Bachelor, Boy Meets Boy,* and *The Flavor of Love* have kept struggling networks afloat;[1] launched new cable channels;[2] and set ratings records.[3] While critical examinations of these programs have explored the authenticity of reality television[4] and challenged the role that women play in them,[5] few have questioned how the programs interact with white masculine roles in dating rituals.[6] Additionally, I have been unable to identify any studies that explore the intersections of race, sexuality, and masculinity in conjunction with reality dating shows.

This chapter will examine the roles of men in search of romance as constructed through three reality television programs, with particular consideration of the freedoms and pleasures afforded to individuals in relation to sexual orientation and race. After a brief history of television dating shows in order to place these programs in a historical context, I will look at the importance of the relationships among television texts, audiences, and the construction of masculine identities. Next, I will offer an overview of the three texts analyzed in this study: ABC's *The Bachelor* (a program featuring white heterosexual men in search of future wives), the Bravo reality series *Boy Meets Boy* (where a white gay man seeks a "mate"), and the trendsetting VH1 series *The Flavor of Love* (featuring rapper Flavor Flav, a black heterosexual man, looking for a partner). Finally, I will analyze the three programs in consideration of their similarities and differences, focusing upon each program's construction of masculine dating identity, and the cultural implications of these portrayals, especially their patriarchal, homophobic, and racist discourses.

A BRIEF (CRITICAL) HISTORY OF TELEVISION
DATING GAMES IN THE UNITED STATES

Even though unscripted television programming featuring romantic pairings may seem like a relatively new phenomenon, romance-based game shows have been around in various forms for more than forty-five years. Probably the best known of the earlier incarnations is *The Dating Game*, a program that began in 1965 on ABC.[7] The program featured men or women who would ask opposite-sexed singles questions in order to determine whom they most likely would want to date. The winner of the game, or the person who answered the questions with the most approval, won an actual date with the single conducting the interview. Unlike the three shows analyzed in this chapter, *The Dating Game* did not feature representations of candid, naturalistic scenes where the participants interacted outside of the studio. In fact, the participants in *The Dating Game* were not allowed to see each other until after the winner was selected; all decisions about whom the contestants would end up with were based on the interviews, which were conducted through a divider. The couples featured were decidedly mainstream pairings: interracial couples were never portrayed and most of the participants involved were white. Almost immediately after the original's run came to an end in 1986, it was revived for a short time as *The All-New Dating Game* (with the same old premise) and again in 1997 (reverting back to its original title, *The Dating Game*).

Appearing later and also quite popular was *Love Connection*, a syndicated dating show that aired from 1983 to 1999.[8] Hosted by Chuck Woolery, the show featured single men and women viewing prerecorded videos of potential dating partners. After viewing the videos, they would choose one of the candidates, go on a date, and then return to the studio with the dating partner to share their experiences. The studio audience would then vote on whom they believed the single man or woman should have initially chosen from the three original dating videos, and if the audience choice matched the single's choice, then the date would be paid for by the show. *Love Connection*, while still largely white and completely heteronormative, did engage nonwhite races more than *The Dating Game* did (although not by a large margin) and would occasionally offer opportunities for interracial couplings in the 1990s, even if the participants seldom selected these dating partners.

In 1991, a hybrid of *Love Connection* and *The Dating Game,* a late-night dating show called *Studs,* premiered via syndication and notoriously bombed despite being planted firmly on the popular culture radar.[9] That show featured single females, usually white, asking bachelors risqué questions ripe with sexual innuendo. The program was unique in that, while sensationalistic, it allowed the women sexual agency and addressed sexuality in relationships. The program sent two women out on separate dates with the same three men. After the dates, each of the women individually video recorded statements about the successes and failures of the dates, and the men would have to guess which of them was being talked about in the clip as it was played on the program. The stud with the most correct guesses became the one the show would pay for one of the women to date again, but only if she listed that man as her favorite dating partner. Consequently, and given the nature of the program, this often played into the idea of the male contestants fulfilling their manly duties by paying for dates, exhibiting suave behaviors, and proving to have talent or promise in terms of sexual ability. A failure to carry through on these criteria would result in the male dating partners not being labeled as studs, being mocked on national television, and ultimately losing the game.

A similar risqué style was employed for *Singled Out,* an MTV program where a single man or woman was given a pool of fifty single individuals who were willing to go on a date.[10] The single man or woman would be given a series of questions, often colorful phrases filled with sexual innuendo, that aimed at determining their preferences in a dating partner. For instance, a woman may have been asked if she liked a man who was "Sticking up high" or a "Down there guy." If the contestant selected "Sticking up high," then all of the "Down there guys," or guys who were shorter than 5'10", would be eliminated. Of course, this allowed men to assert their masculinity and select petite women with large breasts; and women often voiced their preference for tall muscular guys with athletic skills and sexual prowess. The eventual last person standing in the dating pool became the winner of an all-expenses-paid date with the contestant. As juvenile as *Singled Out* was in terms of how it treated dating and sexual situations, the show was also quite progressive in that it featured participants from a range of races and ethnicities (both as contestants and in the dating pool) and same-sex and mixed-sex dating pools were assembled as appropriate for the occasional gay, lesbian, or bisexual contestant. This tradition continued through other MTV dating shows, such as *Dismissed* or *Next,* where racial and sexual diversity were common even if dating relationships in general were minimized or exploited. Remarkably, many of the gay men appearing on *Dismissed* were somewhat feminine, a marked progression from the butch gay men appearing on *Singled Out.*

Moving closer to the format presented in the shows analyzed for this study was the rash of syndicated dating shows that emerged around the new millennium, such as *Blind Date* (1999), *Shipwrecked* (2000), and *The Fifth Wheel* (2001).[11] In these contests, people's dates were documented on camera as dating partners awkwardly or abruptly addressed dating faux pas, engaged in sexual situations, and (in some of the programs) resolved interpersonal turmoil since an individual would go on a date with more than one person and these partners would compete. These shows were frequently marked with flashy animated graphics that were added during the editing process to highlight the comedy of a dating situation, even if that comedy would not necessarily have been there without the manipulation of the graphics. The comedic nature of the shows was often constructed through overtly sexual women who displayed gratuitous eroticism during the course of a date, catty women who competed for the affections of a man, or skinny white boys who had little to no coolness factor but who tried to pretend they did. Viewers of these programs often called in to question the reality of these shows, especially given the outlandish situations and behavior exhibited by the participants. For example, it was not uncommon for the participants to strip naked and get into a hot tub on their first date; nor for elaborate public outcries to occur in restaurants because meals were not prepared correctly. Despite the classist and racist stereotypes present in the programs, they found success on late-night television.

Noticing these shows' success in syndication, UPN tried to mimic their candid style with *Chains of Love* (2001), a reality dating show featuring dating partners chained to each other.[12] This show quickly failed and brought embarrassment to the network as critics frequently used it as an example of what was wrong with contemporary television.[13] Despite the critical and cultural mocking of *Chains of Love*, the idea of making reality dating shows work was an appealing one, especially given the monster success CBS was experiencing with its reality game show *Survivor*. The potential for profits with reality programming were high, given the low costs of production and the immediate popularity of the seemingly new genre.[14]

As can be seen from this brief history of television dating games in the United States, public interest in other people's' pursuit of dating relationships is not a new phenomenon, and the form and content of dating programs continue to evolve. This is particularly true in how newer versions of these programs allow for larger views into the personal lives of individuals and, consequently, deeper understandings of what is and is not ideal in terms of dating partners or activities or behaviors in dating relationships. It is important to consider how portrayals of dating relationships have the potential to affect individual viewers' personal standpoints regarding dating beliefs and practices, especially given that the genre in which many dating shows now appear is called *reality*. The reality genre employs a production style that emphasizes the notion of real people doing real things, advancing the marriage between (or, rather, a blurring of the boundaries of) a production of consent and a reflection of consensus.[15] That is, reality television seems to intensify the already-present notion that television can allow individuals to learn some realities about the world, even if those realities are based upon representations featuring artificial, contrived, or even inaccurate scenarios. Additionally, the alleged reality being set forth by these shows demonstrates a limited understanding of what a dating relationship can be.[16] With understandings of racial and sexual diversity continuing to evolve in social cultures, it becomes important to question how these concepts evolve in visual cultures and how the representations of these texts interact with the social world.

It would appear from the more than forty-five-year history of dating programs that the notions of who can date whom, and how, have become more open, progressive, and even public since the inception of the romantic game show (even if they are still quite problematic). Of course, gender considerations are often a key component of dating relationships.[17] It stands to reason, then, that changes in gendered representations (and responses to those representations) also allow insight into evolving and potentially emerging notions of dating in culture, especially when a given text is geared toward representations of dating rituals and practices. Before turning to the gender implications of the dating texts examined for this chapter, it is also important to reflect upon how audiences tend to engage texts regarding romantic issues in general. This both allows a fuller understanding of how individuals can relate both *to* and *through* texts such as *The Bachelor, Boy Meets Boy,* and *The Flavor of Love* and allows insight into how the texts add to larger discourses regarding masculinity, dating rituals, and the rhetoric of relationships.

AUDIENCES ENGAGING DATING TEXTS

The relationship between an audience and a television text is typically a complex one. Social scientists continue to develop understandings of how individuals relate *to* a text—that is, how they interact with a text and give it a life of its own—and how they relate *through* a text, or how they see their lives in regard to textual narratives.[18] As regards the former concept, it is evident that audiences relate quite well to the texts selected for this examination. Success for *The Bachelor* soon resulted in a hit spin-off, *The Bachelorette*.[19] While neither is still a Top 20 primetime television show, they continue to get high ratings in the eighteen-to-forty-nine age demographic that networks strive to accommodate and to draw a large number of women viewers.[20] *Boy Meets Boy* also proved to be a ratings success despite controversy about the setup of the show, and it and *Queer Eye for the Straight Guy* are credited with putting fledgling cable network Bravo on the map.[21] Finally, *The Flavor of Love* gave VH1 its highest ratings ever; it appealed to both men and women[22] and led to three spin-off series (*I Love New York, Charm School,* and *Rock of Love*).[23] That the texts have been largely engaged and continue to be discussed certainly speak to their ability to add to the larger discourse surrounding dating relationships.

Discourse, as defined by Fiske, is "both a topic and a coded set of signs through which that topic is organized, understood, and made expressible."[24] In many ways, the discourse surrounding a text establishes "both the production of the programs and the production of meaning from them."[25] In other words, the discourses surrounding a text provide an understanding of how people make sense of their social experiences. To this end, a text must present some semblance of the structure of an individual's social world—either as they believe it to be, how they hope it will be, or how they allow it to occur. The exploration of texts depicting what are supposed to be real dating practices by real people allows the men and women engaging these texts to compare, contrast, and possibly adjust their own behaviors. Simply put, the men watching the bachelors in *The Bachelor, Boy Meets Boy,* and *The Flavor of Love* gain a rhetorical understanding of how they might behave in a dating circumstance, especially if they identify with the bachelors in those shows, and women come to understand their potential roles in dating relationships as well.

RITUALS AND CEREMONIES: THE BACHELOR

The critical textual analysis for this study begins with an overview of *The Bachelor.* The first show of its kind,[26] *The Bachelor* in many ways set the standard for the contemporary dating show paradigm. While other dating contests came before it, the format of *The Bachelor* was one that was wholly unique, if somewhat off-putting to many: to help one lucky bachelor find his true love, the show gathered twenty-five eligible women (defined by one of the show's producers as "single and between the ages of 21 and 35," "adventurous, ready for marriage," "intelligent," and "ambitious")[27] and temporarily moved them to luxurious living quarters as they attended socials, went on group dates, and, as the competition continued, engaged in one-on-one dating experiences. When the show began as a midseason replacement in March 2002, it provided something the then-floundering ABC television network needed at the time: a hit. Airing in the same time slot that had made the romance-themed contest *Temptation Island* a widely watched reality show for Fox, *The Bachelor* became ABC's first new Top 20 series since *Who Wants to Be a Millionaire?* collapsed and left the network mired with ratings problems. Unlike *Temptation Island,* however, *The Bachelor* carried a different approach and tone. While *Temptation Island* offered a scandalous and often dramatic approach toward dating by splitting up preexisting couples and tempting them with attractive others, *The Bachelor* instead placed romance upon a pedestal, advancing the notion that true love is waiting for everyone—we just need a way to find it.

As the program continued, the bachelor had to make choices about whom he was interested in pursuing and whom he was not. To illustrate these choices and to keep the selection process moving, each episode of *The Bachelor* ended with a rose ceremony, an event where the bachelor individually invited each woman who was to remain to accept a single red rose. The rose ceremony also allowed the women some agency in the process, as each of them had the opportunity to refuse a rose, although few women actually declined an invitation to stay in all of the seasons of the program. With a limited number of roses available, each ceremony found some women leaving the show, and they had to pack their belongings and deliver a final, often tear-filled, confessional monologue to the camera. The remaining women would then engage in a toast with the bachelor as they looked forward to the next step in the process. Ultimately, the process yielded two final contenders, and the bachelor had to choose the woman with whom he wanted to spend the rest of his life. The series ideally culminated with a marriage proposal; after this intense six-week process, he was supposed to be confident that he had discovered his life partner.

From this brief description, it is almost easy to forget just how artificial and rushed the dating process devised by *The Bachelor* was, largely because the description—much like the show itself—seems to keep a constant focus on the romance of the situation. Despite the artificiality of one man dating twenty-five women, all of them living in the same house, and only having known each other for a brief period, each of the bachelors (with the possible exception of Bob Guiney) was nothing if not intent on showing his utmost appreciation of the women by greeting them with gentle phrases, elegantly kissing their hands, offering gentle bows, and always opening doors and demonstrating traditional gentlemanly respect in every way. The women seemed to buy into this masculine performance quickly, as even in the earliest rose ceremonies women sobbed to the cameras after they were rejected. Of course, it makes sense that the crying may not have been so much for the loss of the bachelor but also because they had been dumped in front of a national audience (and, given the dubious nature of the reality in reality television, may have been an act in and of itself). Still, the program played as if all of the concerns these women had was about their lost opportunities to "connect" (a favorite word on the series) with a man they were often represented as believing to be their "soulmate." If viewers tuned in to *The Bachelor* hoping to catch women who threw hissy fits, attacked other women, or made grand shrieking exits as they left the show, then they came to the wrong program. After all, this was the show that ushered in the feel-good era of ABC reality, and tearjerker shows like *Extreme Makeover: Home Edition* and *Supernanny* soon followed.[28]

Interestingly, the women in the program were often positioned in terms of how they could fulfill what the various bachelors needed. To this end (and as can be expected from the title), the women really were not the focus of *The Bachelor*. As each of the individual bachelors kissed and canoodled with the remaining women as the episodes progressed, the focus centered almost exclusively on how his needs could be fulfilled. What did he want? What did he need? How would he ever make the right decision and find his true love? Based on the monologues the bachelors provided directly to the camera (likely the result of responding to questions posed by an interviewer), it becomes evident that the purpose of these displays was to establish what they, as the prized men, needed from a dating relationship and, to this end, also offered constant evaluations of the various women as if the women were a product being evaluated before a purchase. The relish that many of these men exhibited as they considered the pros and cons of the various women almost mirrored the stereotypical discourse of a man weighing his options in regard to purchasing a new vehicle. Playing into this patriarchal fantasy of woman shopping (where the women have been prescreened to ensure the highest quality), the answers the women provided in interviews often asserted why they thought they were right for the bachelor and how they could fulfill his relationship needs. Many women even commented on how they could improve their demeanors (read: change personalities) if that was what it would take to win the love of the bachelor. Regardless of who was talking directly into the camera and sharing feelings, it was almost exclusively about the needs of the bachelor and how these women could fill those needs. Seldom were the tables turned and it was considered if a given bachelor was right for one of the women. The bachelor was constructed as the ideal man for a relationship, not through direct statements but in the very nature and structure of the show, where he was automatically assumed to be the prize. In order to demonstrate how deserving they were of this ideal masculine specimen, the women had to prove their ability to fulfill a traditional man-pleasing femininity.

While the bachelors were initially only good-looking single men in their thirties, as the novelty of the program dissipated a variety of special bachelors were selected for some of the seasons. These bachelors were still single men in their thirties, but each of them also had an additional quality, such as being a millionaire (Andrew Firestone of season 3), a football player (Jesse Palmer of season 5), and an authentic crown prince (Prince Lorenzo Borghese of season 9).[29] Bob Guiney was selected after he became a fan favorite from the spin-off program *The Bachelorette*. His evolution from rejected prospect on *The Bachelorette* to full-fledged bachelor doing the selecting provided insight into the physical expectations of a bachelor on the program as well as the entitlement one might feel when assuming the role, especially after being placed into the feminine pleasure-offering role via *The Bachelorette* (where the patriarchal system was flipped and a dream woman—sometimes a woman rejected in a previous edition of *The Bachelor*—chose from a pool of eligible men). On *The Bachelorette*, Bob was the quintessential nice guy: a little pudgy, always cracking jokes and making the bachelorette smile, and ultimately rejected for buffer, more traditionally masculine men. When he moved to the titular role on *The Bachelor*, however, Bob had lost a lot of weight, was sporting a new haircut, and appeared to be a new man. His transformation changed beyond his appearance, too, as he also became quite interpersonally physical, constantly pawing the women, and, at least on camera, making out with more of the women than past bachelors had. It was almost as if he were taking advantage of his new status and enjoying the dominant masculinity he had been denied in his nice-guy role on the other program; at the same time, in order to play this new role, he had effected a change in his physical appearance to match the masculine expectations associated with being the bachelor.

In terms of how *The Bachelor* positioned dating, beyond the masculine expression of the male dating partner, it is apparent that in many ways the program was also suggesting that dating should be largely about rituals. The bachelor was always introduced to the women in a formal social setting, greeting each woman as she arrived in a fancy car. They made pleasant conversation over wine at the social as he instantly began to assess the women and decide who offered immediate chemistry. Through the social, the show created an artificial setting that encouraged the fantasy of meeting a lover at an elegant party. Again, at the center of this fantasy was the tall, dark, and handsome stranger; but in the case of the program, only one stranger was available and there was an artificial sense of competition. After the social, the dating rituals continued with individual and group outings filled with picnics, candlelight dinners, and walks along beaches. Each season, the bachelor also visited the parents of the finalists, discussing his intentions for the daughter who might one day be his wife (and again calling forth patriarchal notions of the man being a true gentleman and discussing with the father his intentions for the daughter). The final rose ceremony was dedicated to the bachelor proposing to his final choice for a life partner. Perhaps this was the one area where rushed ritual and artificial tradition could not be created within the context of the show: seldom did the bachelors actually propose to their prospects. This began with the first season's Alex Michel, who defied expectations by not proposing to his bachelorette, opting instead to pledging to get to know her better before making such a serious decision.

HOW SWEET IT IS: BOY MEETS BOY

Similar to the concept of *The Bachelor*, the program *Boy Meets Boy* presented a dating game where a single man seeking a life mate quickly went through an artificial dating process—only in this case, the bachelor was seeking another bachelor from a pool of men, referred to as "mates" in this program. While this sounds like a progressive approach to the development of a television series, a twist inserted into the series by the producers elicited considerable criticism from queer activist groups and disgruntled fans who thought it was cruel: while half of the mates from which featured bachelor James Getzlaff was choosing were actually gay, the other half were straight men who were pretending to be gay. Bravo sold this twist as opening "avenues of heated on-air discussions and debates that [would] challenge socially pre-conceived notions of what is considered gay and straight behavior," but the twist was derided by many due to the $25,000 prize promised to the straight mates if one of them could successfully fool James and be chosen for the final round. In that case, James would win nothing and potentially appear a fool. Additionally, the promised "heated on-air discussions" never occurred, with most of the assertions regarding queer appearance coming from the announcer, who had to remind the audience how groundbreaking this concept allegedly was.

It would appear that, on a dating show, being a straight man posing as a gay man could lead to problems in terms of physical affection, but since James was expressly not allowed to be physically intimate with any of the contestants, the straight men were, in a sense, protected from an awkward intimate encounter. This did not protect James, however, from becoming emotionally attached to the straight men who were posing as gay. In order to maintain the façade of an open and honest gay dating pool and to facilitate the dramatic tension in the program, the producers ensured that all of the straight men could not be removed early in the game by dividing the men into groups. James had to choose one member from each group for elimination, thus ensuring that straight men would remain in the game since he could never choose all straight men to eliminate. Along to help James in the dating process was his best friend, Andra. Andra networked with the potential mates and offered James her advice on whom he should keep and whom he should get rid of in the process. She also provided a memorable outburst (later mocked on the Fox sketch comedy show *MadTV*) when the producers of the show revealed the twist to James; she shrieked, yelled, and protested that the producers had deceived her. James, surprisingly, did not seem too upset about the twist once it was revealed (although later, via a behind-the-scenes DVD extra, he and Andra openly talked about their disappointment in being duped by the producers). Though James was certainly an attractive bachelor, his personality was low-key as he gently went from date to date (often framed as "one-on-one time" in the show) and quietly engaged in superficial and polite conversation.

With so much of the show dedicated to the twist, a lot of time was spent explaining, reexplaining, and justifying the twist for the audience and soliciting thoughts and opinions about the twist from the various contestants, particularly the straight men, who talked about their perspective of being inside the straight closet and having to hide their sexual orientation. The show seemed to focus less on James's dating at times and more on presenting straight men enacting gay stereotypes followed by the announcer praising the show for breaking down stereotypes and showing how the line between gay and straight was being blurred. In examining the show, one has to wonder how audiences did not figure out who was gay and who was straight sooner (the viewing audience did not learn this information until James eliminated a participant). In hindsight, it appears that the straight men were the ones acting the most stereotypically gay while the gay men exhibited little to no personality. Perhaps the most interesting element of the show was not James's mate selection but instead the masculine bonding that seemed to occur among all of the men during the various activities (which included mountain biking, going dancing, and picnics) and while the mates intermingled and learned more about each other at the ranch. In the framing of gay dating identity through the show, the dating experience of the gay man was one where little physical interaction occurred, a female friend was in attendance, and maintaining a sweet politeness was key. Moreover, it was largely white and non-eventful.

NO LONGER A PUBLIC ENEMY: *THE FLAVOR OF LOVE*

The history of *The Flavor of Love*,[30] another program that borrowed the general format of *The Bachelor*, actually begins with *The Surreal Life*, a program that borrowed its format from the popular MTV reality show *The Real World*. Like *The Real World*, *The Surreal Life* placed a number of people in a house and filmed what happened as they interacted. Unlike the MTV show, *The Surreal Life* only featured celebrities (usually lower-status celebrities whose careers had already peaked). After two successful seasons on the WB network in 2003 and 2004, the program moved to VH1. During its first season there, two of the house guests were Brigitte Nielsen, a film actress probably best known for her brief marriage to Sylvester Stallone, and Flavor Flav, a member of the groundbreaking and critically acclaimed rap group Public Enemy. The two formed a strong bond and became intimately involved, although the terms of the relationship were often blurred as Nielsen refused to commit to a monogamous relationship with Flav and both seemed indifferent to the relationship at times. After a strong audience reaction to the relationship between the two, a spin-off called *Strange Love* chronicled Flav's attempts to stop Nielsen from marrying her fiancé. When Flav's efforts to stop the marriage were unsuccessful, yet another spin-off, *The Flavor of Love*, emerged. This show explored the world of Flavor Flav as he, like the men in *The Bachelor* and *Boy Meets Boy*, narrowed down a pool of candidates until he found the person with whom he would spend the rest of his life.

While the series of programs leading up to *The Flavor of Love* probably introduced Flavor Flav to many, it also reintroduced him (in a new light) to others who remembered his involvement with Public Enemy.

Formed in 1982, Public Enemy was part of the emerging rap and hip-hop scene in the 1980s.[31] Their music was widely praised by critics, with the prestigious *Village Voice* Pazz and Jop critics poll naming the album *It Takes a Nation of Millions to Hold Us Back* the best of 1988—a first for a rap album.[32] Public Enemy's lyrics often focused on racism with a particular emphasis on black misrepresentations in a hegemonic media system and political injustice in terms of social services and institutions. Flavor Flav (real name: William Drayton Jr.) served as the group's hype man, and he soon become known as one of the best in the business.

The politics for Flavor Flav's music were left behind for this program with only the stereotypical patriarchal benefits of being a male music star indicating anything about his career. Along these lines, the women who appeared on *The Flavor of Love* looked more like groupies than like women engaging in a dating process—at least in light of how women engaging in a dating process typically look in television texts. Like in the other two programs explored in this chapter, all of the dating partners lived under one roof with Flav—in this case, in his lavish mansion. In both editions of the program (a second season emerged when things did not work out with Flav and the woman he selected during the first season), Flav was introduced to the women through an elaborate ceremony where he presented himself and the women began to cheer. Almost instantly, the picture cut to individual confessional scenes where Flav described his admiration of the women (usually in terms of beauty) and where the women admired Flav (usually in terms of status). Almost immediately, the viewer was also introduced to the women's opinions of the other women—usually through talking trash and explanations of how they were more deserving of "what Flav has to offer" than the other "ho's" and "insincere bitches" in the house.

Racial matching seemed to be in play in *The Flavor of Love*, as most of the women, like Flav, were African American, but other racial categories were represented, too. This did not appear to be posturing or tokenism, as many of the non-black women continued into later rounds of the game, with a white woman advancing to the top three in the first season. Decisions were made about who would remain in the dating pool and who would be asked to leave through the clock ceremony, a process similar to (perhaps mocking?) the rose ceremonies seen on *The Bachelor* but using clock necklaces, Flavor Flav's trademark since his Public Enemy days. To help Flav keep track of the women, he assigned each a nickname at the beginning of the series, and this name was used by Flav and the others involved with the game until the woman was not offered a clock in the ceremony; only then would her real name be revealed to the audience. The nicknames seemingly blended street credibility and a critique of each woman's looks, personality, and sexuality. Examples include Hoopz, Hottie, Buck Wild, and the most popular contestant, New York. Tiffany "New York" Patterson appeared in the original edition of the program—where she made it into the final two before being rejected by Flav—and then returned for the second, where she was invited to offer Flav her perspective on the new batch of women and, after assessing that none of them were good enough, was invited back into the dating pool. Much to her dismay, she was again rejected during the final ceremony after making it to the final two.

New York plays a large part in understanding *The Flavor of Love*, in that she served as the extreme example of what most of the women on the show appeared to be while, at the same time, defying their subservient role toward Flav. Based on comments from Flav, her personality intrigued him in that she seemed truly dedicated and ready to be faithful, yet she raised fear in him in that she demanded her needs be met in the relationship, too—primarily in terms of monogamy, the value Flav had requested earlier in his relationship with Brigitte Nielsen but was denied by her. When New York channeled her aggression toward other women, Flav seemed to watch with pleasure as he understood that her anger was being stoked by her desire for him. Nowhere was this more important than in the second-to-last clock ceremony in the first season, when New York was selected to receive a clock over her chief rival, Pumkin. Infuriated by New York's boasting during the ceremony, Pumkin spat upon New York. In reaction, New York slapped Pumkin in a ferocious manner, knocking her into a camera as both women spouted profanity-laced insults and tried to continue the fight. Following the incident, Pumkin was escorted out of the room and Flav consoled New York, listening to her explanation of how she did not mean to disrespect him by fighting with Pumkin. She only desired to stand by her man.

While New York was probably the most flamboyant in behavior, she was surely not the exception in that her actions, like the actions of many of the other women on the program, would be rejected by many as uncivil.

During the run of the series, she verbally threatened the other women, she pulled a steak knife on one, and when parents came to meet Flav in one of the final rounds she joined her mother in bullying both her father and another contestant's family. It was not until Flav noticed the extreme behavior of New York's mother (who immediately expressed her dislike of Flav) that he seemed to reconsider his relationship with New York. New York's mother, in addition to trying to micromanage the behavior of her daughter, also yelled at and berated New York's father during their visit to the mansion. This aroused Flav's concerns, especially since New York was being demanding about what activities she wanted to pursue for her and Flav's final date.

Interestingly, these representations of bad behavior did not seem out of place. While New York brought about a reign of terror during the program in a variety of ways (and earned her own *Bachelorette*-like spin-off in the process, *I Love New York*), the other women Flav pursued were busy trashing each other's rooms and drinking so much they became sick, and in one case a woman defecated on the floor. While these things concerned Flav on some level, they were not always deal breakers. Reasons for dismissal often centered upon sexual history (one woman was revealed as a sex film star, another had a cold sore that was framed in the program as an STD), genuine allegiance to Flav (wannabe actresses and singers were not always looked at kindly by the co-contestants or by Flav), or authentic personality traits (a woman was ridiculed at a clock ceremony for not having a genuine "ghetto" accent). Dating relationships, as framed by *The Flavor of Love*, are filled with gratuitous behavior by women as they backstab each other and use sex as a way to hold 'a man's attention, and in many ways women are instantly expendable as the slightest of (what the man considers to be) flaws are revealed.

EMERGENT MASCULINITIES: COMPARING THE TEXTS

It is evident that the cultures of the three shows are quite different. Exploring these cultures as they are set out for each of the dating masculinities privileged (white heterosexual, white gay, and black heterosexual) allows the different dating masculinities to emerge, especially in comparison to the femininity that characterizes the dating partners and the legitimacy of what the man needs in order to fulfill his identity. From the descriptions of the texts alone, it can be seen that these dating relationships are quite different. While all three explicitly claim elements of romance via the announcers, the dating partners and the bachelors themselves make it evident that different kinds of romantic notions are in play for each of the three programs. Moreover, these romantic notions are quite stereotypical and somewhat heteronormative in both the patriarchal and queer senses, even in the case of James where no women are a part of the dating pool. To understand this, we need to acknowledge how each of the three bachelors is given the ultimate power to determine who stays and goes in his situation. This is not as true for James who, because of the twist in his program, must choose from groupings of dating partners instead of the whole pool of partners; but in each show the men (more so than their dating partners) have the ultimate say as to who is allowed to continue being part of the process. In Flav's case, he even changes the rules (as presented to the dating partners) by bringing a new dating partner into the mix during the second season. His ability to change the system stands in stark contrast to James, who not only does not have this authority but who is told that the system presented to him is a hoax—he must play by rules that are different than he expected. So, while all three have agency to determine who stays and goes, in two ways James has less choice. Additionally, James's system involves him consulting with his best friend, Andra. While her suggestions are only suggestions, the only time the bachelors or Flav consult others for their dating decisions are when they choose to consult others. The bachelors consult their friends, or Flav invites family members or others in to offer advice. James, while raising no objection in the program, is forced by the system to consult with a heterosexual woman—reinforcing the stereotype of the female best friend (colloquially known as the *fag hag*), speaking to James's seeming inability to make a dating decision on his own, and propagating the stereotypical notion that dating a gay man also means dating his female best friend. In a sense, the gay man is emasculated in comparison to the other two bachelors in that his agency is limited; and, moreover, in its own subtle way the show's culture privileges heterosexuality by allowing a woman to take part in choosing his mate.

While the notion of structure speaks largely to a lack of equality based upon sexuality, examining the dating rituals and activities represented in the programs speaks both to sexuality and race. While all three programs certainly portray stereotypically romantic dating situations, such as candlelight dinners, picnics, and long walks across beautiful landscapes, the intimate behaviors in those situations vary greatly based on the program being examined. In *The Bachelor* and *Boy Meets Boy*, highly elaborate romantic dating scenarios are portrayed as the only types of dating experiences. This is not the case in *The Flavor of Love*, where the dates are often blended with contests where the women must prove they are fit to be paired with Flav. For instance, one date took place at a chicken restaurant where the women were forced to not only cook the food but to clean overly filthy kitchens and restrooms. As the women grimaced and completed the disgusting tasks, Flav watched from a vehicle outside of the restaurant where he laughed at what the women were going through (although later he told them, in a sincere voice, that it really meant a lot to him that they cared enough to do those tasks). In another episode, he required the women to do strip dances for him as he literally groped portions of their bodies. While the groping was consensual, at the same time it appeared demeaning. Both the toilet cleaning and the stripping excursion, in addition to the many other activities portrayed in the program, demonstrate the careless misogyny both the producers and Flav engage and—as demonstrated by Flav's smiles, leers, and laughter—are met with pleasure. To be masculine in the world of *The Flavor of Love* is to demean women, placing them in disgusting activities, watching them fight with each other, and in most cases using them almost solely for sexual pleasure.

Flav, in marked contrast to the men of *The Bachelor*, seems to flaunt his sexual activity with the women and hops from one bed to another in a display of the hypersexual stereotype often unfairly imposed upon African American men. This construction of sexual identity reveals masculine fragility, however, as Flav is allowed pleasure and status from sexually conquering women, but any sexual experience on the part of the women in the dating pool presents those women as a threat, usually leading to mockery and punishment by elimination. The two winners of the show each represented a noticeably nonsexual persona, with Hoopz having an almost masculine demeanor of relaxation while Deelishis displayed more of a motherly vibe. A similar nonsexual vibe plays out in *The Bachelor*, but in a much different context. The men of *The Bachelor* are seldom represented on-screen as going further sexually than kissing the women, and even this seems to happen later in the relationships for most of the men. *The Bachelor* demonstrates a controlled sexuality, again tying into the construction of gentlemanly masculinity. This sexuality is so controlled, in fact, that many times it almost appears as if the men of *The Bachelor* are asexual. This is in part due to the nature of group dates, but sitting in the hot tub on *The Bachelor* seems a bit naughty, at best, while sitting in the hot tub in *The Flavor of Love* is filled with sexual exploration and exploitation. In many ways, it seems that the dating masculinity in *The Bachelor* calls for a restraint of sexual longing even though most masculinities are cultivated with the understanding that men enjoy sex. To this end, it seems fair to question the limited sexual exploration in *The Bachelor* but especially in *Boy Meets Boy:* with sex being such an integral part of relationship satisfaction, it would make sense that the sexual side of a potential relationship be explored in some manner.

James is not allowed any agency in this exploration as he is told that he can have no physical intimacy with any of the mates on the program—not even kissing. This is problematic in two ways: (1) it seems to be a mechanism for protecting the straight masculinity of the confederates who are only pretending to be gay; and (2) it impinges upon the stereotype that gay men cannot control their sexuality, and so a rule must be put into place that does this for them. The twist of adding straight men to the dating pool already speaks to the novelty of a gay sexuality in that the producers are asserting that gay sexuality is something they can manipulate for the purposes of entertainment. One can only imagine an edition of *The Bachelor* where lesbians or drag queens are thrown into the mix of eligible women and told they will be rewarded for fooling the titular character. That scenario appears ridiculous and unfathomable, yet duplicity almost seems natural (if repugnant) for *Boy Meets Boy.* Beyond this, and almost paradoxically, the show joins the representational prototypes of the gay man who remains sexless. This representational quandary distinguishes gay masculinity from straight masculinity in that the gay man is not rewarded for acquiring sexual partners but is instead placed into the female sexual domain of slut; and in that the gay masculinity is a problematic one where control must be asserted, and so representations assert this control by avoiding the notion of sexual partners altogether. By the producers' assertion of this control in the program, whether for the reasons listed here or otherwise, James is being denied both a source of pleasure and a basic interaction mechanism inherent to dating. Moreover, James is consenting to a homophobic system where he is being used as a lab rat of sorts while straight men are encouraged to mimic gay men in stereotypical ways.

In many ways, the rules put forth for James also make him into a representation of someone he is not, even if he is consenting to the production of the representation. A similar representational crisis emerges in considering Flavor Flav in *The Flavor of Love,* as he, too, appears complicit in promoting a system that seemingly works against his preestablished identity. *The Flavor of Love* is in many ways the type of anti-black media text he critiqued as a part of Public Enemy. This is apparent in the first show in the first season where, when meeting the women, he makes a grand entrance in a pink suit with exaggerated accessories and while performing a diminutive dance. Rather than the comedic and thought-provoking political rap pioneer filled with racial pride and a sense of social urgency one might have expected, it was almost as if an imposter had taken the stage to mock Flav's legacy. This is in stark contrast to the proud black masculinity he exuded with Public Enemy, an identity that was intellectually and politically aware as opposed to simplified and completely hedonistic. In exploring *The Flavor of Love,* it is difficult not to feel the racist construction of the text and its implications. The women's behavior, as documented above, is explicitly labeled "ghetto" (which is often read as *black* in a racist system of discourse)—and while non-black women are included in the cast, many of them mimic the language patterns and use the accents typically associated with African American street culture. This is even brought to the forefront as one of the women is criticized for not really having a "black accent" but using one for the purposes of the show. Unfortunately, it seems as if the behavior exhibited in the whole program is being labeled as black; and this blackness is filled with negative racial stereotypes, misogyny, and problematic understandings of dating in black culture.

Similarly, *Boy Meets Boy* highlights gay individuals participating in a system that belittles and diminishes both gay pride and queer diversity. In many ways, the show (except for the prohibition of intimate behavior) mirrors *The Bachelor* almost exactly in tone and style. People are polite, white James largely responds to other white males, and the dates, while clearly romantic, reflect a heterocentric approach. This is not to suggest that queer and straight worlds do not overlap; and many dating considerations coincide in both cultures. The problem with the representation is that none of the space outside of this overlap is portrayed: queerness is demonstrated in a way that strips it of its queerness, at least in terms of dating relationships. Oddly, and as I pointed out earlier, the queerest interpersonal element of the show is the straight men who are pretending to be gay. The diversity portrayed by these men, however, is based completely in superficial stereotypes. If the assertion that the producers openly express in the show were true—if the line between gay men and straight men is blurring—then they would not need the straight participants to act gay. They would simply be themselves. Moreover, there would (again) be no need to place rules or limitations upon James in terms of how he could interact with the other men. The blurring of the masculine lines would allow for a space where both could exist without altering their behavior.

MASCULINITY AND MEDIATED DATING
RELATIONSHIPS: A TEMPORARY CONCLUSION

Television programs making a game of the dating process have a rich history of problematic representations, often portraying racist dating practices, a lack of sexual diversity, superficial dating practices, and a sensationalistic view toward dating. With the new line of dating programs modeled after and instigated by *The Bachelor,* these problematic representations continue in profound ways, given how much of the intimate nature of the dating process is revealed (and what that reveals) and how the structures of these programs create a rhetoric of who may date and how. In the case of *The Bachelor,* a dating pattern typical of a wealthy white class highlights a gentlemanly masculinity, in which the man pampers the woman, offering, in a patriarchal economy, respect in exchange for gratitude. The woman, in a complementary move, wishes to please the man and demonstrate her worthiness to be his life partner. The man is always at the center of concern, which supports his masculine dominance despite his seemingly nondominant nature.

The producers of *Boy Meets Boy* appropriated *The Bachelor's* system, filling the pool with white participants and creating an unequal balance where only James's needs are considered and the other men participate in a mock-patriarchal contest to please him. Additionally, *Boy Meets Boy* intensifies this already problematic formula by failing to exercise sensitivity regarding sexuality and in the process emasculates and desexualizes James. This occurs through pairing James with a female friend who will help him to make his dating decisions, prohibiting James from engaging in intimate contact with the other men in the contest, and through a twist in the game where straight men are placed in the dating pool in an attempt to trick James.

Just as *Boy Meets Boy* offers a homophobic spin on *The Bachelor* formula, *The Flavor of Love* offers a racist spin. The intelligent and politically savvy rapper Flavor Flav is transformed by the program into an unintelligent and misogynistic racial stereotype who appears to derive pleasure from the women who engage in lewd and violent behavior in order to win his affections. The program also ghettoizes black culture and identity, even through the non-black participants; supports the negative stereotype of black hypersexuality; and largely constructs the masculinity of Flav through his sexual dominance as he engages in sexual activity with several of the women in the program. This masculinity is a fragile one, as Flav rejects women who appear to be sexually active despite his own portrayed promiscuity.

These representations of masculinity are unfortunate, and they also play into a larger construction of dating identity. If these programs are collectively considered as part of the larger discourse regarding relationships, it is evident that a rhetoric of relationships is being enacted where people understand that a patriarchal dating balance almost certainly has to exist; sexual diversity is something that must be modified before being presented and is also something that can be toyed with; and racial diversity in dating relationships seldom exists outside of whites imitating the black other, and even then these relationships are filled with a demeaning misogyny and quasi-promiscuous sexual practices. Unfortunately, such representations often politicize relational understandings by mocking and making less important the potential relational experiences of an othered category of people.[33] As analysis of the three programs explored in this chapter clarifies, many of the problematic notions are traceable to the patriarchal and privileged representations displayed in *The Bachelor*. Exploring audience ethnographic accounts of relationships and comparing them to televised representations of relationships—not only in reality dating shows, but in fictive accounts of romance and dating and in considerations of masculinity—could be a positive next step in understanding how audiences see others and themselves in such programs.[34] Only then can the blurred lines between a production of consent and a reflection of consensus be fully realized. Only then can the rhetoric of relationships aimed at building male masculinity (and female femininity) be fully illuminated and sexist, homophobic, and racist discourses be stifled.

NOTES

1. Brophy-Baermann, "True Love on TV," 11.
2. Kooijman, "They're Here, They're Queer."
3. Ryan, "A Deelishis Ratings Hit."
4. Morrow, "Reality for *The Hills*."
5. National Organization for Women, "Watch Out, Listen Up!"
6. Dubrofsky, "*The Bachelor*."
7. Schwartz, Ryan, and Rostbrock, *Encyclopedia of TV Game Shows*, 55.
8. Ibid., 110.
9. Ibid.
10. Ibid., 112.
11. Ryan and Rostbrock, *Ultimate TV Game Show Book*, 118.
12. Brooks and Marsh, *Complete Directory to Prime Time*, 147.
13. Ibid.
14. Ibid., 148.
15. For a discussion of the production of consent and the reflection of consensus, see Gramsci, *Selections from the Prison Notebooks*.
16. Dubrofsky, "*The Bachelor*," 41.
17. For a discussion regarding gender and dating processes, see Wood and Dindia, "What's the Difference?" 19–38.
18. Shrum, "Media Consumption and Perceptions," 69.
19. Futon Critic, "Showatch."
20. Ibid.
21. Kooijman, "They're Here, They're Queer," 106.
22. Ryan, "A Deelishis Ratings Hit."
23. VH1, "*Flavor Flav*."
24. Fiske, "Popularity and Ideology," 14.
25. Ibid.
26. Brooks and Marsh, *Complete Directory to Prime Time*, 29.
27. Fleiss, "*The Bachelor Revealed*."
28. Brooks and Marsh, *Complete Directory to Prime Time*, 29.
29. "*The Bachelor*," ABC.
30. Brooks and Marsh, *Complete Directory to Prime Time*, 66.
31. McQuillar and Brother J, *When Rap Music Had a Conscience*, 20.

32. Christgau, "Dancing on a Logjam."
33. Manning, "Because the Personal Is the Political," 7.
34. Manning, "'I Never Would Have Slept with George!'" 131.

BIBLIOGRAPHY

The Bachelor. ABC. http://abc.go.com/primetime/bachelor/index.

Brooks, Tim, and Earl F. Marsh. *The Complete Directory to Prime Time Network and Cable TV Shows, 1946–Present,* 8th ed. New York: Ballantine, 2003.

Brophy-Baermann, Michelle. "True Love on TV: A Gendered Analysis of Reality-Romance Television." *Poroi* 11 (2005): 11–14.

Christgau, Robert. "Dancing on a Logjam: Singles Rool in a World Up for Grabs." *Dean of American Rock Critics.* http://www.robertchristgau.com/xg/pnj/pj88.php.

Dubrofsky, Rachel E. "*The Bachelor:* Whiteness in the Harem." *Critical Studies in Media Communication* 23 (2006): 39–56.

Fiske, John. "Popularity and Ideology: A Structuralist Reading of *Dr. Who.*" In *Interpreting Television: Current Research Perspectives,* ed. William D. Watkins and Bruce Rowland, 167–184. Beverly Hills, Calif.: Sage, 1984.

———. *Television Culture.* London: Methuen, 1987.

Fleiss, Mike. *The Bachelor Revealed.* ABC, September 25, 2002.

Futon Critic. "Showatch." *The Futon Critic.* http://www.thefutoncritic.com/showatch .aspx?id=bachelor.

Gramsci, Antonio. *Selections from the Prison Notebooks of Antonio Gramsci.* Ed. and trans. Quintin Hoare and Geoffrey Nowell Smith. New York: International, 1971.

Kooijman, Jaap. "They're Here, They're Queer, and Straight America Loves It." *GLQ: A Journal of Lesbian and Gay Studies* 11, no. 1 (2005): 106–109.

Manning, Jimmie. "Because the Personal Is the Political: Politics and the Unpacking of (Queer) Relationships." In *Queer Identities/Political Realities,* ed. Bruce Dreshel and Kathleen German, 1–8. Cambridge: Cambridge University Press, 2009.

———. "'I Never Would Have Slept with George!' Symbolic Boasting and *Grey's Anatomy.*" In *Grace under Pressure: Grey's Anatomy Uncovered,* ed. Cynthia Burkhead and Hillary Robson, 130–145. Cambridge: Cambridge University Press, 2008.

McQuillar, Tayannah Lee, and Brother J of the X-Clan. *When Rap Music Had a Conscience: The Artists, Organizations, and Historic Events That Inspired and Influenced the "Golden Age" of Hip-Hop from 1987 to 1996.* New York: Thunder's Mouth, 2007.

Morrow, Terry. "Reality for *The Hills* Comes Heavily Scripted." Scripps Howard News Service. http://www.shns.com/shns/g_index2.cfm?action=detail&pk =THEHILLS-TV-05-26-06.

National Organization for Women. "Watch Out, Listen Up! 2002 Feminist Primetime Report." *National Organization for Women.* http://www.nowfoundation.org/ issues/communications/watchout3.

Ryan, Joal. "A Deelishis Ratings Hit." *E! Entertainment Television.* http://www.eonline .com/news/article/index.jsp?uuid=745288fc-1913-40ef-b6d7-d7eb665d2cc8&entry =index.

Ryan, Steve, and Fred Rostbrock. *The Ultimate TV Game Show Book.* Los Angeles: Volt, 2006.

Schwartz, David, Steve Ryan, and Fred Rostbrock. *The Encyclopedia of TV Game Shows.* New York: Checkmark, 1999.

Shrum, L. J. "Media Consumption and Perceptions of Social Reality: Effects and Underlying Processes." In *Media Effects: Advances in Theory and Research,* ed. Jennings Bryant and Dolf Zillmann. Mahwah, N.J.: Erlbaum, 2002.

VH1. *Flavor Flav.* http://www.vh1.com/artists/az/Flavor_Flav/motv.jhtml.

Wood, Julia T., and Kathryn Dindia. "What's the Difference? A Dialogue about Differences and Similarities between Women and Men." In *Sex Differences and Similarities in Communication,* ed. Daniel Canary and Kathryn Dindia. Mahwah, N.J.: Erlbaum, 1988.

NINE

"DO YOU HAVE WHAT IT TAKES TO BE A REAL MAN?": FEMALE-TO-MALE TRANSGENDER EMBODIMENT AND THE POLITICS OF THE "REAL" IN *A BOY NAMED SUE* AND *BODY ALCHEMY*

MICHEL J. BOUCHER

In a scene which helps to both open and close Julie Wyman's documentary film *A Boy Named Sue* (2000), Theo, a female-to-male transsexual whose transition the film follows, crosses a street and walks toward the camera.[1] Based on visual images alone, Theo appears to be a biologically born male. He has a short goatee and wears a baseball cap, a blue button-down shirt, jeans, and sneakers. As cars sit at the traffic light behind him and other pedestrians walk in the background, Theo walks toward the camera and says, "You know one thing that's been tripping me out lately is just being out in the world. People are so ruled by what they see, you know, they take in something visual and let it stop there. I don't expect people to really go much further than that, but it's just a trip, you know, I just think, God, you know, you have *no idea* who I am at all."

With this comment, Theo addresses the complex relationships in our culture among sex, gender, and visibility, as well as the ways in which our assumptions about sex and gender inform our social practices and everyday interactions. He calls attention to the difficulty of attaining visibility and recognition as a female-to-male trans man (FTM). As men who were labeled female and raised as girls, FTMs challenge the definitions of what it means to be a man in our culture. As an FTM, Theo relies for recognition upon the ways in which our culture takes gendered signs as both direct significations and the "natural" effects of a particular bodily sex that is either male or female. Yet, he also recognizes the limitations and ambiguity inherent in visual images of gender, particularly as they are used to signify a binary system of sex/gender where female is conflated with "woman" and male is conflated with "man." As he walks toward the camera, Theo confronts the viewers with their own assumptions about the meaning of gender signification and the ways in which, in his words, we may be taking in the visual and letting it stop there. The emphasis on Theo's body in *A Boy Named Sue* not only represents the bodily transition of a female-to-male trans person, but also documents the instability and malleability of "sex" as it is manifested in and articulated through the body and other visual gender signs.

Loren Cameron, a contemporary photographer, also uses his work to create visibility and representation for trans men. His goal is to produce social change by creating images that encourage people to see and comprehend a form of gender that is conceptually impossible within the boundaries of dominant ideologies of sex and gender that locate biological sex as the determining factor of gender identity: "What was initially a crude documentation of my own personal journey gradually evolved into an impassioned mission. Impulsively, I began to photograph other transsexuals that I knew, feeling compelled to make images of their emotional and physical triumphs. I was fueled by my need to be validated, and wanted, in turn, to validate them. I wanted the world to see us, I mean, really see us."[2] With this comment, Cameron describes the parallel emergence and inseparability of his development as a photographer, his gender transition, and his desire to produce FTM cultural visibility. The language Cameron uses in this quote is significant. That he wants the world to "really see" trans men and describes a "need to be validated" and "to validate" others suggest the misrecognition and/or invisibility that trans men experience. At the same time, this language captures his desire to create conditions that might lead to a psychic sense of "realness" and legitimacy for trans men that is born out of seeing oneself accurately reflected back through the eyes of others in a nonpathological way. When one is "validated," one is perceived, recognized, and affirmed as worthy and legitimate; one becomes "real."

Similar to the way that Theo highlights the limited gaze of his viewers, Cameron uses his photographs to confront viewers with the power and limitations of their own gaze. "Distortions" is a section of Cameron's book that contains three black-and-white self-portraits. Each photo portrays Cameron naked from the chest up and framed by comments and questions aimed at him as a transsexual man. The questions and comments that surround Cameron's torso emphasize the various and contradictory ways in which his body is framed by others. Starting at the lower left corner of the final photo and making its way up the left side is the statement "You must be some kind of freak." Starting at the opposite, upper right corner of the same photo and going down the right side is the question "Do you have what it takes to be a real man?" These two lines, both framing Cameron's body and mirroring each other, visually capture one of the core dilemmas for transsexual people: the social and legal demand to prove one's gender as real within a culture that consistently uses the trans body—whether or not it is surgically and/ or hormonally altered—to assert that the person is not a "real" man or a "real" woman.

The comment that Cameron "must be some kind of freak" is an emphatic assertion that Cameron's gender and his embodiment of it stand clearly outside of what can be comprehended as "normal," or even as "real," within our dominant sex/gender system. It at once conveys sentiments of disturbance and surety. Because Cameron so disrupts what the speaker sees as "natural," the speaker, with the word *must,* emphatically and forcefully stabilizes Cameron's status as freak. The speaker must keep Cameron outside of normative discourse if the speaker is to keep his or her conceptual framework of sex/gender intact. On the other hand, mirroring this assertion is "Do you have what it takes to be a real man?" This question implies that Cameron does not, in fact, have that which would qualify him as a "real man," and yet, as a question rather than an assertion, it also opens up the possibility that Cameron could prove otherwise. If Cameron can somehow represent his identity in a way that makes sense to the speaker, if he can frame his body and identity in a way that allows the speaker to understand them within a more familiar conceptual framework, one that resonates with some aspects of the viewer's concept of the real, then perhaps Cameron can move out of the realm of freak and into the realm of the real. Cameron's photos and their narrative accompaniments are an attempt to facilitate this transition while also reconstructing the boundaries of what is considered real so that trans men might be included. As a result, he reconfigures the dominant definitions of manhood and relies upon them for recognition at the same time.

What exactly does it mean when the word *real* is used to modify and describe gender? In *Webster's Online Dictionary, real* is described as "having verified existence; not illusory."[3] Similarly, in the *Oxford English Dictionary*, *real* is described as "actually existing or occurring in fact," as "not imagined or supposed."[4] Interestingly, in the *OED*, the fourth definition is listed as "rightly called; proper: *a real man*" (emphasis in original) as if using *real* as an adjective for *man* makes them both self-evident.[5] Most often, realness as it relates to gender is understood through the culturally constructed concept that one's biological sex is the natural determining factor of one's real gender. In other words, the concept of "realness" as it relates to gender most often implies that there is an inherent linearity between one's biological sex and one's gender identity: if a baby is born male, he automatically grows up to define himself as a man, and if a baby is born female, she automatically grows up to define herself as a woman. Similarly, with regard to legal matters, it is the body, most often one's birth body, that is called upon to determine whether one's gender identity has "verified existence" and is "not illusory." Unless one has a letter from a therapist which can be used to "verify" one's gender as other than one's birth sex, and a surgeon who can verify having changed the physical sex of one's body, it is one's birth body that determines one's sex on legal documents, in marital and parental status, and in other legal classifications. This process maintains and polices the discursive link between biological sex and gender identity by requiring significant physical changes to the body, an erasure of signs of one's birth sex, before one can be legally recognized as the gender with which one identifies. It also makes gendered realness only available to those who want to make such changes to their body, who feel comfortable doing so, and who can afford the medical procedures that enable the process.

Legal sex designation, though, is only one element that operates in the politics of the real. Realness is also conferred through nonlegal, discursively produced social definitions of gender, their interrelatedness with race and class discourses, and the ways in which these discourses shape social interactions and opportunities. Discursive constructs of so-called "real" women and real men have also always been a means through which the privileges of whiteness, maleness, and heterosexuality could be preserved. For instance, even though a person's legal birth sex might be designated as "male," in some contexts a non-trans man might be regarded or described as not a real man if he is gay or has characteristics which our culture defines as feminine or outside of masculinity. From as early as Sojourner Truth's famous speech, "Ain't I a Woman?" black women activists have highlighted the ways in which the socially constructed category of the ideal woman has been asserted through whiteness; its associations with sexual purity, staying out of the paid workforce, passivity, and delicateness have historically been contrasted with constructs of black womanhood that have been associated with sexual aggressiveness and availability, working outside of the home, and physical stamina.[6] In the dominant U.S. culture, white masculinity is most often associated with controlled rationality, hard work, being a breadwinner, and the ability to assert authority, protection, and control, while black men are often associated with criminality, sexual aggression, the need to be controlled, and being lazy.

Given this context, trans people are in a peculiar predicament when they come up against the demand to establish their "realness" in relation to gender. If this idea of an essential, natural, sexed body is understood as existing prior to the discourse that is used to confer and define the "realness" of a person's gender, in what ways can trans bodies be brought into the realm of the "real" and given representational form? If gender "realness" is figured through race, how do racial discourses shape the possibilities and impossibilities of gendered "realness" in dominant culture for trans men? In what ways are some discourses of "realness" sometimes evoked in order to override the failure of another? Does this practice ultimately secure the very boundaries of "realness" that trans people might be trying to subvert and/or reorganize? Can it be avoided?

Wyman's *A Boy Named Sue* and Cameron's *Body Alchemy* raise interesting questions about and contribute to contemporary academic discussions concerning the relationships among subjectivity, discourse, the body, and the cultural production of gender "realness." These texts represent the dilemmas and limitations of trans representation, as well as the possibilities for the profound transformation of reality that might emerge from the acceptance of trans identities and gendered embodiments. They encourage us to think critically about the ways in which reality and readability are constructed, so that ultimately we might be able to imagine new ways of signifying the body which could multiply rather than limit the possibilities for its legibility.

DISCURSIVE FRAMINGS OF THE FTM BODY

From the late nineteenth century, when sexologists first began categorizing, seeking the causes of, and constructing identity categories based upon cross-gender practices, trans bodies have been concentrated sites for discursive production and contested power relations. Originally conceived as symptoms of "homosexuality," cross-gender presentation and behavior were wrenched by turn-of-the-century sexologists from the arena of religious sin and moved into the category of "sexual deviance."[7] As a result, cross-gender behavior became one of the cornerstones of a sexually deviant personality. In this context, the body was seen as a legible text, a reflective key to determining and naming sexual difference. As Siobhan Somerville points out in *Queering the Color Line: Race and the Invention of Homosexuality in American Culture,* nineteenth-century sexology drew its data from the racist methodologies of comparative anatomy, a move which encouraged sexologists and race "scientists" to discover and catalog differences in the body as signs of "deviance."[8] Importantly, Somerville argues, racial discourses and sexological discourses were shaped through each other so that to discuss them as separate, or even parallel, occurrences would not be accurate. Distinguishing factors of race were often determined through "differences" in the sexed bodies of African Americans, for instance, and methodologies used to establish racial differences were applied to the categorization of sexual deviants.[9] In *Queering the Color Line,* Somerville lays the groundwork for thinking about the ways in which gender, sexual, and racial ideologies emerge through one another to produce our "natural" understandings of the body, an idea to which I will return later in this chapter.

Moving away from and defining themselves in contrast to the medical models of gender and sexual deviance which emerged out of sexology and entered the fields of psychology and medicine, some feminist theorists, particularly radical feminists, have understood transsexuality, and in particular the medical diagnosis and treatment of transsexuality and body modification, as an effect of patriarchal oppression. This construction of transsexuality initially emerged from Janice Raymond's controversial book *The Transsexual Empire: The Making of the She-Male.* Although it has been challenged by many trans and non-trans theorists, particularly because of its inflammatory language, echoes of Raymond's arguments remain within some more civil feminist discussions about transsexuality, so it is important to continue to address some of the premises of her work.[10] Raymond's central argument is that trans people are effects of patriarchal oppression. She argues that trans people are produced by what she refers to as a patriarchal medical "empire," a collection of social and medical institutions which work to maintain and reproduce gender stereotypes and assert control over women's bodies and spaces. Raymond's brief consideration of FTMs in *The Transsexual Empire* posits:

> [T]he female-to-constructed-male transsexual is the token that saves face for the male "transsexual empire." She [*sic*] is the buffer zone who can be used to promote the universalist argument that transsexualism is a supposed "human" problem, not uniquely restricted to men. . . . women have been assimilated into the transsexual world, institutions, and roles, that is, on men's terms, and thus as tokens.[11]

Raymond quotes Judith Long to explain further why Raymond uses the term *token* in her own work: "Tokenism may be analyzed as an institution, a form of patterned activity generated by a social system as a means of adaptation to a particular kind of pressure."[12]

The concept of FTMs as tokens of a medical empire is rarely supported in the twenty-first century by even radical feminist thinking, perhaps because of the increased visibility of FTMs and of those willing to claim such an identity. However, the ideas implied in tokenism, that FTMs are "really women" who have internalized the effects of a misogynist culture and that FTMs transition in order to gain privilege in a patriarchal system, still exist in some contemporary discussions about FTM trans people.[13] Despite the various sexual identities of FTM people, FTMs are often understood as "really" lesbian women, who succumb to social and economic pressure by choosing to "pass" as men rather than live as gender-deviant women and challenge patriarchal norms.[14] From this perspective, the agency of trans men can be located only in a passive decision to accommodate misogynist gender norms. This perspective forecloses the possibility that trans men can challenge social definitions of manhood and prescriptions about who can be a man and how men should behave. It eclipses the variety of gender/sexual identities within trans communities as well as the political activism and progressive cultural and theoretical work that emerges from a trans social location.[15]

In *The Transsexual Empire*, Raymond draws from both essentialist and social constructionist theories of gender to make her argument that FTMs are not real men and that MTFs (male-to-female transsexuals) are not "real" women. Referring to trans women as "male-to-constructed-females," she argues that they cannot be "real women" because they were not "born and located in this culture as women" and therefore do not have a history of having been raised female.[16] Raymond argues that it is primarily chromosomes and "the subsequent history that attends being chromosomal female or male" that determine a person's sex, and she disputes the idea that one's assigned sex can be changed.[17] Although Raymond maintains that gender norms are socially constructed, particularly the socially prescribed gender roles and the social expectation that women are "feminine" and men are "masculine," she preserves a "natural" and unalterable link between one's biological sex (male, female, intersex) and one's real gender designation (man or woman). Raymond asserts that "transsexualism urges us to collude in the falsification of reality—that men can be real women," and, referring to transsexuals, she laments that "our suspension of disbelief in their synthetic nature is required as a moral imperative."[18]

In these statements, Raymond critiques "the falsification of reality" which, in her opinion, is actively produced by trans people and their medical practitioners and repeatedly emphasizes the "synthetic" nature of transsexual people. Her language and the cultural and legal battles over who can be considered a real man or a real woman reflect the stakes of a debate which, at its core, is about how reality is constructed and which versions of the real will ultimately receive social, cultural, and legal affirmation. Underlying Raymond's statement about the supposed synthetic nature of trans bodies and the "falsification of reality" that trans people and their medical practitioners create is an assertion which assumes the existence of natural, prediscursive bodies and a fundamental reality that is not governed and constituted by cultural ideologies about gender and the body, which have come to be seen as natural.

Rooted in poststructuralist thought, queer theorists generally take a very different stance toward trans people and the sexed body. Most queer theorists have not been particularly interested in the etymology of transgender identities or in ways to "treat" transsexuality. Instead, queer theory often looks at transgender expression as proof of the constructedness and fluidity of gender and sex, and at times even idealizes trans "performances" as subverting the sex/gender system. Queer accounts of transgender identities often draw from Judith Butler's theory of gender performativity, a theory which has put trans people on the map of academic discussions and has done an amazing job of disarticulating what had been thought of as a natural link between biological sex and gender identification.[19] Asserting a poststructuralist analysis of sex, Butler argues that sex itself is a product of discourse rather than a prediscursive state of nature:

> Gender ought not to be conceived merely as the cultural inscription of meaning on a pregiven sex (a juridical conception); gender must also designate the very apparatus of production whereby the sexes themselves are established. As a result, gender is not to culture as sex is to nature; gender is also the discursive/cultural means by which "sexed nature" or "a natural sex" is produced and established as "prediscursive," prior to culture, a politically neutral surface on which culture acts.[20]

In this way, Butler collapses the distinction between gender and sex, arguing that, if the "immutable character of sex is contested, perhaps this construct called 'sex' is as culturally constructed as gender; indeed, perhaps it was always already gender, with the consequence that the distinction between sex and gender turns out to be no distinction at all."[21]

Butler's theoretical work is crucial to understanding trans gender as, like all gender, both "real" and constructed. Butler's gender theory, particularly the tension between the discursive production and psychic incorporation of gender that is present throughout her work, can help us to understand gender as inextricably caught up with the body in ways that might be determined by discourse, but are nonetheless vulnerable to resignification. Though Butler argues that gender is a performative effect rather than an expression of an internal gender core, she also argues that there are limits imposed by the unconscious that circumscribe and organize this performativity and produce gender identification. Butler argues that it is the prohibition of homosexual desire that gets incorporated on the body as gender identity, that forms the bedrock of gender identification, so that a female who is forbidden to desire her mother instead identifies with her, and vice versa for males. Butler displaces the centrality of heterosexuality within Freudian and Lacanian theory, and instead shows heterosexuality to be an effect of homosexual desire. Butler argues that the body comes to bear a sex through psychic incorporation, which takes place on the body "such that the body must itself be understood as incorporated space."[22] It is in the tension between Butler's understanding of gender as both a discursive production and a psychic "melancholic incorporation" that we can understand the transsexual claim that biological sex does not determine gender and yet, at the same time, the frequent transsexual desire to embody the so-called opposite sex. For if bodies become "sexed" in the realm of the culturally determined symbolic, as Butler argues, and if this process takes place through psychic identifications which congeal through their incorporation into the body but which are not necessarily determined by the body, then it becomes possible for gender to both construct and signify sex. Gender constructs sex by discursively determining the limits, forms, and signs of sex. However, through an identificatory process between the individual and the symbolic, gender identifications become psychically inscribed upon the body *as* sex, and in this way gender signifies a sex that is real. If sex is psychically incorporated through symbolic identifications and is not an experience that derives from the body, then it is possible for a male-bodied person to psychically incorporate a female body image and for female-bodied people to psychically incorporate a male body image. However, since they are culturally constructed and historically contingent, gender discourse and, ultimately, the possibilities for gender identities are open to resignification, subversion, and reform.

Trans theorists Viviane Namaste and Jay Prosser point out that, in queer theory, a body of work which emphasizes anti-normativity in its political goals and often draws from Butler's theory of gender performativity, the legitimacy of trans identities tends to rest upon the degree to which they are judged to be subversive rather than reinscriptive of gender norms, creating a false discursive split between transgender ("subversive") and transsexual ("reinscriptive") people.[23] Namaste and Prosser also critique a tendency in queer theory to discuss trans identities metaphorically, a practice which glosses over and even erases the materiality of trans bodies and the actual lives of trans people. Namaste argues that trans people are too often discussed as examples of the social construction of gender rather than being recognized as embodied individuals attempting to negotiate an institutional world that violently erases the possibilities of their existence.

In her more recent work, particularly *Undoing Gender* (2004), Butler seems to directly respond to critiques such as Namaste's and Prosser's.[24] In this book, Butler pays particular attention to the material effects on those whose gendered bodies do not reside within a culturally configured grid of intelligibility, and the ways in which institutions produce and police the boundaries of who can be considered human. She looks, for instance, at the dilemma produced for trans people by the diagnosis of "gender identity disorder," a diagnosis which simultaneously pathologizes trans people and enables them to access social and political legitimacy and the resources that such legitimacy might afford. Moreover, in *Undoing Gender*, Butler works to highlight the material and social stakes involved in living within or outside of gender intelligibility. If Butler's earlier work is sometimes accused of not paying enough attention to the materiality of the body, in *Undoing Gender*, the body—how it is implicated in our social worlds and how social worlds can be transformed through it—is centralized.

There are several insights in *Undoing Gender* that are central to my analysis of Cameron's and Wyman's texts. First, Butler is fundamentally concerned with the power of norms to confer reality and in particular to determine the "intelligible field of subjects," those who will be recognizable as human within a given culture.[25] She writes that "transgendered lives have a potential and actual impact on political life at its most fundamental level, that is, who counts as a human, and what norms govern the appearance of 'real' humanness."[26] At times, she seems almost to be directly addressing critics like Raymond, who mark trans people as not real and describe trans lives as "the falsification of reality." Referring to trans people, Butler writes:

> The genders I have in mind have been in existence for a long time, but they have not been admitted into the terms that govern reality. So it is a question of developing within law, psychiatry, social, and literary theory a new legitimating lexicon for the gender complexity that we have been living for a long time. Because the norms governing reality have not admitted these forms to be real, we will, of necessity, call them "new."[27]

As in most of her work, in *Undoing Gender*, Butler grapples with the role of agency in relation to gender discourse and with the possibilities for social transformation within gender discourses that are determining and constraining but nonetheless vulnerable to subversion and subject to transformation. According to Butler, norms not only act as a discursive grid through which a subject becomes recognizable to others as human, but they also function as that through which the "I" can assert itself and come into being:

> To say that the desire to persist in one's own being depends on norms of recognition is to say that the basis of one's autonomy, one's persistence as an "I" through time, depends fundamentally on a social norm that exceeds that "I," that positions that "I" ecstatically, outside of itself in a world of complex and historically changing norms. In effect, our lives, our very persistence, depend upon such norms or, at least, on the possibility that we will be able to negotiate within them, derive our agency from the field of their operation.[28]

In Butler's work, the gendered "I" (and to Butler there can be no such thing as an ungendered I) can only emerge through the constraints imposed by a relationship between discourse and psychic identification, both of which are hopelessly caught up with the materiality of the body but not necessarily in any inherent configuration. Unlike traditional Lacanian psychoanalysts, who conceive the symbolic as an unalterable grid through which the psyche is formed, Butler holds out a belief in the possibilities of changing both symbolic structures and the discourses that produce, circulate, and uphold regulatory gender norms. At the crux of her work is the question of how an individual and/or community can assert agency within this matrix of constraint in such a way as to effect a transformation of the symbolic and the discursive structures which produce the possibilities for gendered realness.

Finally, the discursive process of transformation that Butler imagines and calls for is thoroughly political and inescapably caught up with embodiment. According to Butler, embodiment is the means through which social norms are given life. "The norm has no independent ontological status, yet it cannot be easily reduced to its instantiations; it is itself (re) produced through its embodiment, through the acts that strive to approximate it, through the idealizations reproduced in and by those acts."[29] However, according to Butler, it is also through embodiment that these same norms might be rearticulated. "To the extent that gender norms are reproduced, they are invoked and cited by bodily practices that also have the capacity to alter norms in the course of their citation."[30] If gender norms are (re)produced and enacted through the body, then it makes sense to say that the body is the materiality out of which gender transformation can and must emerge.

In *Body Alchemy* and *A Boy Named Sue,* Loren Cameron and Theo use their bodies to engage with discourse, evoking and embodying gender and racial norms as well as sometimes subverting and reconfiguring them. In this way, they are much like the dancers whom Ann Cooper Albright describes in her book *Choreographing Difference: The Body and Identity in Contemporary Dance.*[31] Albright studies contemporary dance in order to understand how people use their bodies to resist and reconfigure discourse. According to Albright, "the embodied experience of dancing can provide a counter (and resistant) discourse to representations of the body *even while* creating those representations."[32] While, as a feminist and a woman, she claims she is ever aware of the fact that "a network of social ideologies imbues the body in Western culture with ablist [*sic*], racist, classist, sexist, and often just downright repressive ideals," her life as a dancer and dance critic has convinced her that bodies "are rarely passive receptacles" of these structures. "Lived bodies strain at the seams of a culture's ideological fabric," argues Albright. "Simultaneously registering, creating, and subverting cultural conventions, embodied experience is necessarily complex and messy."[33]

Through an interconnected relationship between content and form, Wyman and Cameron use the mediums of film and photography to construct a visible cultural space for female-to-male transsexual people. In this space, the FTM trans body is not a passive product of discourse nor of gynophobic and homophobic medical institutions. Neither does this body stand outside of discourse altogether in some natural, unchangeable state or as the essential determinant of real gender. Instead, the FTM trans bodies in these texts both rely upon and call into question hegemonic ideas about the relationship between sex and gender. In their conscious construction of masculine and male-gendered bodies which contradict their culturally assigned gender, Theo and Cameron simultaneously elicit and trouble dominant ideas about the nature of maleness and its connection to masculinity. With these texts, Wyman and Cameron highlight the ways in which all bodies are entangled with discourse and perhaps, as Butler argues, unknowable outside of it. Yet, with their emphasis on the constructedness of bodies and gender, as well as film and photography, these artists remind us that, as Butler argues, even if "our very persistence" relies upon norms, we can also "derive agency from the field of their operation."[34]

REFRAMING THE BODY: MEDIATED MASCULINITIES

Coinciding with the theoretical work of Namaste, Prosser, and Butler, who call upon those who draw from poststructuralist theories of gender to account for the centrality of embodiment for transsexual people, the visual representations of trans identities in *A Boy Named Sue* and *Body Alchemy* force the viewer to experience transsexuality as, above all else, an experience of the body. There is no way of viewing Wyman's and Cameron's texts without experiencing trans identities as centrally located in the body. In *Body Alchemy*, Cameron gives us close-up shots of the results of various chest and genital reconstruction surgeries. His book includes several naked self-portraits, one of which is on the cover, and photos of trans men as they appeared before and after their gender transition. In *A Boy Named Sue*, Wyman films Theo's body over the course of six years, documenting his physical changes with her camera and presenting them to the viewer. We observe Theo get his first injection of testosterone, hear Theo's voice change over time, and watch as his facial skin toughens and his beard appears. Wyman even brings her camera into the operating room and films parts of Theo's chest reconstruction surgery. We see Theo's surgeon, Dr. Michael Brownstein, mark cutting lines on Theo's breasts before surgery. We witness Theo unconscious and laid out on the operating table, and in one crude scene, we get a close-up view of the surgeon lifting a large section of breast tissue with what appears to be a regular dinner fork. In these texts, the bodily manifestation of transsexuality is far from an abstraction. It is the primary vehicle through which the subject's identity is constructed, asserted, and made manifest in the social world.

As much as the materiality of the body is highlighted in these texts, so are the power and inescapability of discourse and its entanglement with the body as the means through which the body is seen, interpreted, and represented. The trans bodies in these texts are constantly subject to various interpretive frameworks imposed upon them by others, and both Theo and Cameron are ever aware of the limitations of the dominant sex/gender system through which they are seen and must make themselves readable as real. In *A Boy Named Sue,* the multiple framings through which Theo's body is seen and understood by others are conveyed through interviews with his friends and lovers. The sentiments of his friends when they hear Theo is going to physically transition range from panic to supportive, with most friends seeming to feel that they will support Theo even though they disagree with what he is doing, cannot understand it, or simply do not believe Theo will ever be a real man. At one point, his friend Charles says, in a tone of urgency and fear, "Sue is leaving. No, Sue is leaving. . . . She's chosen what I really conceive of as a controlled suicide." Another friend exclaims, "Theo is not going to be a real man, that's . . ." and then she stops herself and looks as if she has spoken out loud that which has been forbidden. "The more he focuses on the subtle changes [of his body], the more he seems like a woman to me [laughter]," another friend says in reference to the attention Theo pays to his changing body. Interestingly, Theo's partner, Lisi, understands Theo's fascination with the changes in his body as signifying a self-centeredness which she associates with maleness and which she finds undesirable. "She is redesigning her chemistry," Charles explains, with concern that Theo is going to be left alone in the world as a result. The idea that Theo is "redesigning" a natural body in a way that is "unnatural" and substantially different from the variety of ways we all mediate and shape our bodies so that they are seen in particular ways is a theme that is conveyed throughout *A Boy Named Sue.* Wyman often represents Theo's body and his physical transition as strange, freaky, and politically controversial. Fragmented images of Theo's body appear throughout the film and interrupt its narrative progression. These images are often out of sync with and set apart from the rest of the film. While most of the film is in color, these images are often shot in black and white and presented with eerie, discordant music or garbled, indecipherable conversation in the background. They interrupt the scenes of easy, naturally flowing conversations between Wyman and Theo and/or his friends that structure most of the film and that take place in everyday spaces, such as kitchens, bedrooms, and living rooms. Together, these effects create a *Frankenstein*-like background for the representation of Theo's body, situating his body and transition as a distorted, unnatural experiment of science in contrast to the unquestionably natural bodies that his friends occupy.

In the "Distortions" section of *Body Alchemy*, Cameron captures the representational difficulty that trans men face in a culture that is architecturally, institutionally, and discursively defined by a male/man and female/woman binary. As previously discussed, this section of Cameron's book is a series of three black-and-white self-portraits which picture Cameron from the waist up and literally framed by the various ways that others read and interpret his body. In two of the three photos, Cameron's arms are cut off at the elbows, signaling a sense of powerlessness and undermining the theme of self-creation that is present in other parts of the book. In the first photo, Cameron's face is half-shadowed as he looks timidly downward as if he wishes to disappear. Around the border are three layers of statements that alternately question his motivations for transitioning and deny the realness of his identity. For example, some of them read, "Are you misogynist?" "Why can't you just be a butch dyke?" "Maybe you're just homophobic"; "You still look female to me"; "Your voice doesn't sound very masculine." The second and third photos are constructed in similar ways, with the second photo emphasizing the way trans people are frequently exoticized and with the final one addressing the fact that trans people are often excluded from male and female spaces as well as from the categories "man" and "woman" as we culturally define them. Some of the quotes which surround the last picture include: "This is womyn-only space"; "Sorry, but I don't like men"; "You're not a man: you'll never shoot sperm"; "I can't be with you: I'm not a lesbian." In this photo, Cameron has a confused look on his face, which is again half-shadowed, and there is a shadow running down his sternum and covering his belly. This shadowing of Cameron's face and core perhaps signal that he cannot be fully represented in the binary gender paradigms that people use to understand, place, and exclude him. As Theo does when he walks toward the camera in *A Boy Named Sue* and comments on the fact that he is not being seen by the viewer, in these photos, Cameron confronts viewers with their own gaze. Quite literally, Cameron appropriates the subject positioning from which these comments emerge and highlights the viewers' gaze and the ideological structures of gender through which they look as that which, rather than Cameron himself, problematically reproduces the trans body within a hegemonic framework.

Film and photography, as representational mediums, are particularly well suited as means through which one can reconfigure the visual and cognitive field that constructs our interpretations of gender. Through documentary film and photography, the limits of time, of a particular moment, can be transcended and contrasted with those of another time. Spoken or written narrative can work with visual imagery to complicate what is seen and to open the visual to new dimensions. For example, the opening of *A Boy Named Sue* presents back-to-back images of Theo before and after transition. It begins with Theo looking at himself in the mirror as he shaves his face. In this scene, Theo has not yet begun taking hormones and has not had chest surgery. The camera zooms in on his smooth face in the mirror, the side of one of his breasts, and then back to his face again. As if to emphasize the similarities between gender and other "artistic" representations, the scene then flashes to Theo's girlfriend, Lisi, who is using pastels to create a portrait, and then back again to Theo shaving. A couple of scenes later, Theo enters his apartment and begins feeding his cat. In contrast to the shaving scene, here Theo is pictured post–physical transition. He has a goatee, a flat chest, and a deepened voice.

Two female friends enter, hug Theo, and say hello to Julie Wyman, who is filming them. One of the women asks, "So when are we going to see it?" "See what?" Wyman asks. "The video!" the friend answers. Then, we watch Theo and his two friends enter the living room, take seats on a couch, and begin watching on the TV screen Wyman's *A Boy Named Sue*, the same film we, too, are viewing. "This is a before shot," Wyman explains from behind the camera as she films the three on the couch watching *A Boy Named Sue*. Along with them, we watch Theo, before he has physically transitioned from female to male, take off his shirt and expose his female chest. Then, the film flashes back to the viewers on the couch, zooms in on Theo post-transition stroking his goatee, and then shoots back to Theo lifting his shirt and standing bare-chested before us.

In *Body Alchemy*, Loren Cameron also presents us with a series of side-by-side photographic shots of trans men before physical transition and after physical transition. As Wyman does with Theo, these back-to-back shots construct a visible trans positioning which usually cannot be captured in real time and everyday interactions. By foregrounding and contrasting before and after shots of trans men, Wyman and Cameron create visual cultural representations for trans men who have histories as females. These contrasting images force the viewer to see the trans men as whole people who happen to have resided on both sides of the female-male binary.

In *Body Alchemy* and *A Boy Named Sue,* transsexual men use narrative in relationship to bodily images as a way to construct FTM trans visibility. In *Body Alchemy,* Cameron photographs naked trans bodies, including close-ups of FTM genitals, highlighting their differences from those which are deemed "normal" by our culture. Yet, these photographs are sandwiched between collections that emphasize the sameness of trans bodies, their ability to blend into our sex/gender system without notice. "We are everywhere, and you can't tell by looking at us," these photos seem to proclaim. There are photos of trans men who are police officers, ministers, and construction workers. There are trans men pictured in association with different religions and races. They are everyday people, who do everyday things. Yet, the narrations that accompany the photographs, like the photos that mark trans bodies as different, often construct the subjects as also different from men labeled male at birth. In one photo, Erik is pictured sitting casually on a mountain bike. He has long, straight, brown hair and a light mustache and goatee. "I'm basically the same person, except before, I looked like a female," explains Erik. "I've heard how women talk about men, and I don't ever want to be that fool." With his comments, Erik differentiates himself from men who were labeled male at birth and raised as male even as he is pictured as someone who looks like one of them. When he explains that he has "heard how women talk about men," he emphasizes his liminal positioning as one who has lived on both sides of the conceptual border between men and women and therefore has been privy to sex-segregated discussions.

In *A Boy Named Sue,* some of Theo's narrative operates in a similar way to the narratives that reinterpret gender categories in *Body Alchemy.* At one point, importantly at a time when Theo has physically transitioned, he remarks, "I'll never be a typical guy," noting that there are gestures and codes within male communities that he has not been socialized to understand. With this comment, Theo marks a distinction between himself and men who were labeled male at birth, but nonetheless does not see himself as outside of the social category "man." Instead, his positioning inside of it widens what this category can mean and therefore destabilizes our social understanding of it. It is through the combination of narratives and bodily images that an FTM trans visibility is constructed in Wyman's and

Cameron's texts. This technique, along with the side-by-side contrasting images of different time periods, allows them to call into question the stability of both the photographic image and gender representation, or at least the way in which dominant culture understands gender signs as significations and effects of a particular, stable, and natural bodily sex.

Both video production and photography are important representational genres for marginalized people because they are accessible to those without formal training in Hollywood film production or advanced academic training in the sciences or humanities. Even if the narrative of a trans person is mediated by a filmmaker, as in *A Boy Named Sue,* there are often opportunities for the speaker to "talk back" to the dominant discourses which situate them as sick, perverted, mentally ill, or social freaks. In *Body Alchemy,* Cameron is both the photographer and sometimes the object being photographed, so that he has full control over the images that he creates of himself. In sharp contrast to the self-portraits in "Distortions," which emphasize the interpretive framework imposed upon Cameron by others, the self-portraits in the "God's Will" section portray Cameron as an empowered agent who actively constructs and represents his own identity. Whereas in "Distortions," Cameron's arms are sometimes cut off at the elbows and his face is half-shadowed, in "God's Will" Cameron's entire body is posed in full light and positioned in body-building poses that emphasize his role in its creation. If, in "Distortions," references to Cameron's body are used to posit him as not a real man ("You piss like a woman"; "You're not a man: you'll never shoot sperm"), in the "God's Will" section, Cameron uses his own body to disrupt the biological parameters that define a real man. As a representational medium, photography proves to be key to accomplishing this task.

Significantly, *Body Alchemy's* cover photo comes from the "God's Will" section. This photo is an impressive, black-and-white, naked self-portrait. Cameron stands sideways with his left leg forward, so that his thick thigh just barely blocks our view of his genital area. His trunk is turned toward the camera, baring a muscular male chest, and his neck and head turn sideways, showing a bearded profile. Across his chest and along his forearms and the fronts of his legs are black, flame-like tattoos. Cameron's well-defined arms, with gently flexed muscles, move out from his body at the elbows, forming a circular shape that begins at his head and moves down his two arms, breaking only where his two fists become separated by the pelvic region of his body. In one hand, Cameron clutches a photographic shutter release and shoots this photograph; in the other, he shoots himself in the buttocks with a syringe of testosterone. Located in a parallel position within Cameron's cover photo, the shot of testosterone that he is giving to himself mirrors the photographic shutter release with which he shoots his image. The mirrored position of the syringe and the shutter release draws an analogous relationship between the construct-edness of gender as it is communicated on and through the body and the constructedness of a photograph. The parallel positioning of the shutter release and the syringe also emphasizes the merging of Cameron's desires to bring into visible, material form both his artistic vision as a photogra-pher and his personal vision of his gender. It highlights Cameron's com-bined use of photography and his own trans body as mediums through which he can construct a new and differently gendered "real." Far from be-ing a "token" of the patriarchal "medical empire," as Raymond describes FTMs, here Cameron is pictured as the epitome of the self-made man.

Through photography, Cameron is able to portray the duality of his sexed body and contrast it to dichotomous, visually based assumptions about the naturalized connection between bodily sex and gender identity. In Body Alchemy's cover photo, the positioning of Cameron's hands on either side of his genital area, which is covered by his thigh just enough to keep the viewer from using it to determine his sex, calls attention to the significance of genitalia in the dominant constructions of sex, as well as their vulnerability and instability as a gender sign. In the "God's Will" section, Cameron seizes the instability of this signifier of sex as a means through which he can create FTM representations. Cameron's pose, particularly the shielded genitalia, draws from that aspect of maleness which derives phallic power from representations that hide and protect the inherent vulnerability of the naked male body. This common repre-sentational strategy creates images where one assumes but rarely sees the penis, thereby maintaining an image of invulnerability and fortification that constructs the dominant definitions of white manhood and partially underpins their social power. Cameron both draws from and plays with the representational power of this male pose in order to construct gen-dered "realness" for trans men. When one sees Cameron's body as it is represented on the cover of his book, there are no signs that he was not born male other than the syringe of testosterone that he is shooting into his buttocks. The full view of his muscular torso, his reconstructed chest, and the thin beard that lines his jaw creates an image of what one assumes to be a non-trans male. In other words, his positioning constructs an image of gendered "realness" that appeals to the ideology that the body is the factor that determines whether or not a trans person's gender can be considered "real." In this way, the concealment of the genital area takes on a double significance; it calls upon dominant images of "realness" to at once construct "realness" for trans men and then to undercut the biological "realness" that these visual images represent by unveiling the assumptions embedded in them. This second step becomes obvious when one looks at the cover photo in conjunction with the rest of the photos in the "God's Will" section.

When placed within the context of the other photos in its section, the cover photo engages in a different form of representational play than it does when it stands alone on the cover. Looked at in relation to the other two photos from this section, the cover photo is clearly one of a series of three. Inside the book, Cameron undercuts the connection between body and gender, as well as the phallic power and its relation to the assumed penis that his cover photo draws upon, by including photos of his body where the genital area is fully or partially exposed; in one photo, it is actually emphasized. Inside the book, the cover photo (the third in the series) faces the second in the series so that they can be contrasted simultaneously. In the second photo, Cameron turns his naked, muscular body toward the camera in a full frontal pose. His legs are apart and his hips are thrust forward, exposing and even emphasizing the genital area. Cameron's left hand, positioned beside his genital area and clutching the photographic shutter release, calls attention to his female-originated male body, as do his frontal positioning and his forward-thrust hips. His right hand holds a hand weight and his arm curls up so that his bicep is emphasized. In this photo, Cameron looks directly at the viewer in a way that both dares and invites the viewer to look back. Cameron's expression conveys a refusal to be shamed, marginalized, or made to back down. Here, he poses the literal duality of his trans body (represented in the frontally posed photo) against the visually based dichotomy of the dominant gender ideology (represented in the cover photo). By opposing the cover photo, within which Cameron looks completely male based upon his shielded genitalia, against the frontally posed second photo where

his genital area is exposed, Cameron effectively undermines the visually based notion of gender and biological sex as dichotomous and inherently linked and destabilizes the idea that people's biological sex can be
read by their gender presentation. In the cover photo, he draws from this
dominant ideology to construct and convey his identity as a "real" man.
Inside the book, he uses these photos in conjunction with each other to
destabilize the image of gender "realness" that he has created in the cover
photo. The irony in Cameron's overall representational dilemma is that
he must rely upon the dominant assumption of gender "realness" that is
established through the body in order to represent its contingency and
instability.

In Cameron's work, as in Butler's theoretical work, "constructed" and
"real" are not inherently contradictory. Cameron forces us to think about
the ways in which gendered bodies are constructed in numerous ways by
both trans and non-trans people. By including the photo where he holds
a hand weight, Cameron contextualizes the changes he has made to his
body through testosterone and surgery within the larger cultural practice
of weight lifting as a form of bodily transformation, one which Cameron
also practices. In this way, Cameron's bodily transformation through
surgery and hormones become an extension of other cultural practices
which are normalized in our culture and even exalted as hypermasculine.
By including the photographic shutter release in his work and mirroring it
with the tools of his bodily creation, and through his self-conscious and
constructed poses of himself and his photographic subjects, Cameron
reminds us that representation in general and photographic and gender
representation in particular are visual constructions. Yet, as a construction, gender is not merely representational play. In both *Body Alchemy*
and *A Boy Named Sue,* there is an urgency that drives the men to make
such significant changes to their bodies so that they can be seen and recognized by others. The constructedness of gender images does not make
that which is signified by these images any less real.

Although both Wyman and Cameron use their work to create visibility for FTM trans bodies within a culture that structurally erases
trans men, these two artists ultimately seem to have different purposes
for their texts, which affect their strategies of representation and the
ways they frame the trans bodies in their work. The purpose of Cameron's photographs is to create positive images of trans men as engaged

participants in society and to assert pride in FTM identities and bodies. This goal is clear and unapologetic in his work. Wyman's representation of Theo's FTM transition and identity is more ambivalent. Her goal seems to be to explore the politics and social and interpersonal effects of Theo's transition. Wyman never really takes an affirmative stance toward Theo's identity. Instead, she documents the various problems and sentiments that his decision to transition evokes in others and gives these sometimes critical and negative reactions equal weight with Theo's narrative. Her text asks questions about the ethics of physical transition for FTM people, while Cameron's main goal is to affirm FTM identity and embodiment.

As previously noted, there is an underlying sentiment in Wyman's film which presents Theo's bodily changes as risky, unnatural, and ultimately somewhat freaky. At the end of *A Boy Named Sue,* Theo's identity and body remain located outside of intelligible discursive space. Some of this may be due to the fact that Theo himself seems somewhat resigned to the idea that his identity is ultimately unrepresentable in our visual social world. Undoubtedly, though, the denormalization of Theo's body and identity in this film is also related to the fact that, unlike in Cameron's autobiographical work, Theo's narrative and the representations of his body are both completely mediated by Wyman's position as filmmaker. The end of the film harks back to the beginning when Theo was walking through traffic and telling the viewer that people have *"no idea* who I am at all" because they "take in something visual and let it stop there." Dressed in the same clothes as in the opening scene, in the final scene Theo is standing outside of a building and smoking a cigarette. He explains that one difference between himself and his former romantic partner, Lisi, is that Lisi needs people to look at her and clearly see that she is a "dyke." "People make all kinds of assumptions when they look at me, and I don't really care. They're not gonna get it right. I'm a big ol' bi trans guy with a pussy. Bet you wouldn't have figured that out by looking at me," Theo explains. Despite the fact that Theo's body and identity remain positioned as outside of discourse in Wyman's film, his own narrative does assert a clear identity, which might become more representable if he were constructing the text himself. In the final conversation between Wyman and Theo, Wyman asks, "What kind of man are you going to be?" Turning the question back on Wyman and asserting the validity and "realness" of his identity in the present, rather than as something he wants to attain in the future, Theo answers, "I don't know. You tell me. What kind of man am I? What kind of man have I always been?" In this way, Theo asserts the "realness" of his clear and constant identity as a man, even if the dominant constructs of manhood place him outside of its defining boundaries. Theo knows what kind of a man he is. He asserts it very clearly when he says, "I'm a big ol' bi trans guy with a pussy," and then highlights the limitations of the dominant gender discourse and the framework through which he is being seen, not his own identity, as the source of his representational dilemma and outsider status when he says, "Bet you wouldn't have figured that out by looking at me." By turning the question back on Wyman, Theo emphasizes that Wyman's question is her concern, not his, and he escapes the defensive position into which trans men are so often placed.

If, in Wyman's film, Theo remains stuck outside of discourse, Cameron successfully addresses some of the difficulties of representation for trans men, while also creating a way out, a means of representation and possibility for trans men that will allow them to be seen and recognized in dominant culture. He manages to signify trans men as "real" men without erasing their particular histories of having been labeled female at birth. Because of the discursive construction of "realness" and its function as an operation of power, however, Cameron's approach creates problems of its own. How can Cameron create "realness" and recognition for trans men without simultaneously and implicitly producing the realm of the "not-real" within which others will have to reside? What are the possibilities for representation that are open to trans men in U.S. culture as they construct bodily, cultural, and relational masculinities that represent and communicate their identities as trans men? Do trans men need to draw from the masculinities produced by non-trans men in order to be seen and validated as "real" men in our culture, or are there opportunities to use FTM experiences and transitions in a way that reconstructs the ideologies of "real" masculinity so as to subvert some of the power relations that are caught up with them?

When Cameron highlights his agency in constructing both his gender and his photographic representations, an opportunity emerges for an exploration of masculinities, definitions of manhood, FTM identities, and their relationships to each other. Cameron does, in some ways, seize

this opportunity to reconstruct manhood by highlighting the constructedness of what is usually assumed to be a natural and immutable connection between gender and biological sex. In other ways, however, Cameron
relies upon and reproduces certain assumptions about the meaning of
masculinity and some of the ways in which the "realness" of masculinity
in U.S. culture, and its widespread cultural appeal, is mediated through
the dominant structures of patriarchy, whiteness, heterosexuality, and
normative national identity.

In *Second Skins,* Jay Prosser points to the importance of narrative in
constructing trans subjectivity and visibility. He highlights the stories we
tell about transsexuality as the factor which actually enables the possibilities for trans embodiment and recognition in our culture. Prosser argues
that in "transsexual autobiography the trajectories of transsexuality and
autobiography are entwined in complex ways, narrative and bodily form
conducting each other."[35] Reflecting the title of his book, Prosser likens
transsexual autobiography to a "second skin." Narrative, argues Prosser,
is "a kind of second skin: the story the transsexual must weave around
the body in order that this body may be 'read.'"[36] Yet, Prosser does not
grapple with the fact that, like sex, skin in our culture is never a neutral
signifier. We need to ask: what are the structural components to this story
which confer readability? Can any skin in our American culture confer
meaning that is not always also racialized? And if this racialization is not
accounted for in a theory of transsexual embodiment, then in what ways
is the recognizability of some trans bodies dependent upon the erasure
of others?

In order to establish cultural familiarity for his trans masculinity
which might otherwise remain unreadable and unintelligible, Cameron
evokes the American ideologies of the self-made man and the journey
west. The self-made man image is of one who, in the face of seemingly
insurmountable obstacles, succeeds in self-determination through independence and will power, and it is often evoked as a way to construct the
idea of class mobility and self-recreation in the United States. It is also,
however, an American mythology that erases the realities and effects of
the institutional and discursive barriers in the United States, which make
class mobility and professional achievement more difficult for people of
color, immigrants, white women, and trans people. Historically, this mythology and its ties to the idea of the journey west as a sign of opportunity

and self-recreation have operated as means through which whiteness, masculinity, and national identity could be woven together. Under the auspices of manifest destiny, the symbolism of the journey west justified extreme violence, deception, and the forced removal of indigenous peoples from their lands all in the name of possibility and economic success. Framing transsexual transition in these terms links transsexuality to the dominant national narratives and, since they are reflected through each other, shores up both transsexuality and national identity as white. When Cameron draws from these mythologies as the narrative "second skins" that make his gender readable, the possibilities for producing trans representation that might emerge from his work become unnecessarily circumscribed and exclusionary.

Unlike the narratives in some sections of his book, which work in tension with their accompanying photos, Cameron's narrative construction of masculinity supports and complements rather than critically engages with his photographs. As I have discussed, Cameron's self-portraits in the "God's Will" section emphasize his personal agency, autonomy, and disciplined self-will as the means through which his identity becomes manifest in the world. With a body-building routine, a scalpel, and access to testosterone, all of which he makes visible in the photographs in this section, Cameron constructs himself physically and photographically. Referencing himself as the self-made man, Cameron explains that he has no formal training in photography, but slowly has taught himself the techniques he employs in his work. Cameron wants us to think of him as having learned from his father that men are people who pull themselves up by the bootstraps and overcome obstacles in order to succeed. Beside one of his self-portraits, where he squats in work boots and Carhartt overalls in front of a pallet of large bags of cat food, he writes, "I learned a lot about hard work from my father. He taught me how to mend fences and haul hat, and sometimes we worked right into the night if rain was coming. . . . My Dad believed everybody should pull himself up by his own bootstraps, and even though I was his daughter, he raised me to have the same masculine work ethic."[37] Drawing from the dominant American ideology of the journey west as one of opportunity and promise, Cameron notes that he moved to California "with only a duffel bag and a hundred bucks in my pocket," and, as implied elsewhere in the book, with the dream that his "fame and fortune were to be found in a city by the ocean."[38] Right after he found out from two lesbians that San Francisco might be a home for him, he explains, "I purchased my last bus ticket, grabbed my duffel bag and went out West."[39] Defining his gender transition through this ideology of the self-made man and the promise of self-recreation through the journey west, Cameron writes, "Taking testosterone as hormone therapy and developing a body-building regimen, I ever so slowly and painfully began to reinvent myself."[40]

While Cameron's very presence within this American ideology of white masculinity in some ways destabilizes it, his visibility as a trans man is constructed through his ability to rest both within and outside of this American imagery, to elicit it and stretch its boundaries. Unlike the contrasts and tensions Cameron builds between narrative and photo in order to destabilize the discursive relationship between bodily sex and gender identity and to make his transsexuality visible, Cameron's written narrative underwrites, supports, and reinforces his visual representations of himself as a self-made man. The rifts and vulnerabilities embedded in the dominant definitions of masculinity and their entanglement with whiteness and national identity are, strangely, not exposed and exploited in Cameron's work.

In his discussion of transsexual narratives in *Second Skins*, Prosser highlights "mirror scenes" as important moments in transsexual autobiographies. Through these scenes, Prosser analyzes the issue of visibility in trans culture, the desire to see one's felt self reflected back at oneself. Mirror scenes, argues Prosser, are "a convention of transsexual autobiography," which "recur across texts in strikingly similar fashion."[41] Through mirror scenes, argues Prosser, autobiographers represent in their selves a split between their internal body images and the images reflected back. "The difference between gender and sex is conveyed in the difference between body image (projected self) and image of the body (reflected self). . . . at an angle to Lacan's mirror phase, the look in the mirror enables the transsexual only disidentification, not a jubilant integration of body but an anguishing shattering of the felt already formed imaginary body—that sensory body of the body 'image.'"[42] This reflected split, according to Prosser, initializes the transsexual plot, one which Prosser understands as being propelled by surgical reconstruction "in order that the subject may be corporally integrated."[43] The written autobiography works on the psychological level in the way that surgery works on the somatic level:

to cohere the divided self. "I was a woman, I write as a man. How to join this split? How to create a coherent subject? Precisely through narrative. Over the course of recounting, the narrative continuity, the trajectory of autobiography (tracing the story of a single self), promises, like the transsexual transition itself, to rejoin this split into a single, connected 'life.'"[44]

Presumably, this mirror image is not just about the actual bodily reflection that comes back at oneself, but also, perhaps even more significantly, the reflection one sees as one is looked at by others, for written autobiography, as sex transition, is a public act. It is because Prosser is reading gender as the central axis of the formation of subjectivity that he is able to argue that, working through each other, the trajectory of both autobiography and sex reconstruction lead to a coherent subject, "a single, connected 'life.'"[45] For, in the autobiographies that Prosser reads, the main source of "difference," or of the way in which one's self-identity fails to be accurately reflected back to oneself, is solely related to gender, an experience that centralizes whiteness, particularly white people of upper- or middle-class status. Similarly, in "Distortions," Cameron represents the invisibility and misrecognition that are experienced by trans men as singularly rooted in ideologies of gender/sex. The comments and questions that surround Cameron's photos in this section and that represent Cameron's misrecognition all reference Cameron's gender/sex as the single characteristic through which he is unable to be seen. Cameron's work does not address the ways in which race sometimes enables and sometimes prevents an experience of "realness."

The co-producing relationship between gender and race and its effects on FTM visibility and recognition are more apparent in a study of trans men of color conducted by Brandin Dear. In this study, Dear interviews eleven trans men who self-identify as African American, black, or multiracial in order to understand their "relational experiences in the areas of race, gender, and racism."[46] His work describes a different configuration of "distortions" than that addressed by Cameron. These men discuss, among other things such as the importance of mentorship, the ways in which their transition has forced them to negotiate a host of different perceptions from dominant society that distort the ways in which they are seen. On the one hand, they experience a hypervisibility that is driven by a distorted dominant view of African American men and that increases the surveillance of them. As one participant explains, "I got pulled over 200% [more] in my first six months of transition than I had in the previous 23 years of driving. Even as a black butch woman I did not have the same kind of stuff, where I felt people were just, law enforcement especially were just really focused on my movement and what I was doing."[47] Another man also discusses the increase in his contact with law enforcement: "Since I transitioned I think I have been stopped by the police maybe ten times, been arrested three, for things that were eventually thrown out of court. Before that, I never had any involvement with the police."[48]

On the other hand, this same hypervisibility produces an increased invisibility. The participants in Dear's study describe the ways in which distorted stereotypes about men of color in dominant society repeatedly shroud and shadow their ability to be seen as respectable human beings, particularly by white people. Dear's study "revealed [that] the presence of African American males often evoked fear and caution in others. More than half of the participants described situations in which people seemed more fearful and cautious around them when perceived as African American men."[49] As one participant explains, "People expect worse from you. You still get the thing where people expect you to be stupid or violent. You've got people locking car doors and clutching purses when you walk by car doors and stuff like that."[50] Another participant said: "From the Caucasian world there is far more fear, far more trepidation. People are very leery of you. When you come into a place people rush to find out what you want there."[51]

As a result of these experiences, the men in Dear's study understand the effects of gender/racial discourses as central to their experience of transitioning from female to male. In offering advice to other African American trans men, one interviewee says, "I would say, be prepared. Allow yourself to go there, realize that you are becoming what unfortunately a lot of people fear. *That is part of the transition,* that is why you need support."[52] The context of hypervisibility and misrecognition that these men describe inevitably affects the experiences of FTM transsexuality. Whereas transition for many white trans men makes them less noticeable and vulnerable as they move through the world, trans men of color become more susceptible to institutional and interpersonal surveillance and discrimination and continue to experience a sense of misrecognition due to the ways in which gender is formulated through and blended with racial stereotypes in our culture.

When gender and race are understood as always defining one another, whiteness, too, becomes more visible as a core component of transition and a means through which gender is experienced. For instance, the fear, caution, and hypervisibility that the men in Dear's study describe vary quite a bit from that described by prominent white trans activist Jamison Green, one of the men pictured in Cameron's book. In Green's autobiography, *Becoming a Visible Man*, he argues that, in general, he experiences people as being friendlier to him than when he was perceived as a woman. "Strangers spoke to me more often," Green explains. "[I]n line for anything in a public space, people seemed perfectly willing to turn and speak to me—something that would rarely happen before. People didn't notice me as much either; they didn't stare at me or lean away from me as they had done when they couldn't tell what sex I was. I had to learn to be at ease with the interactions of strangers."[53] Green does describe the ways in which women feared him more after he physically transitioned, but in general he describes an increased ease in social situations that is facilitated by both his gender and his race. After physical transition, others assumed Green's respectability as a white man, and he came under much less public scrutiny rather than more, as the men of color describe. As a result, unlike the men in Dear's study, Green's transition gave him more of a feeling of belonging, safety, respect, and acceptance than he felt prior to transition, particularly when his gender was not readable.

This is not to say that Jamison Green, as a white trans person, now has unlimited access to white male privilege. He does not now have access to all of the privileges and legal advantages that come with being a non-trans white man (for example, he is vulnerable to discrimination and possible violence if his trans identity is revealed, his parental rights and his ability to be recognized as a "real" man in legal cases are not guaranteed, and if he gets married, the legality of the marriage could be challenged), but the structures of visibility he navigates as a white trans man are very different from those navigated by the men of color in Dear's study. For Green, racial structures help to facilitate an experience of gender recognition, whereas for the men in Dear's study, gender and racial stereotypes continue to distort their experience of being seen and recognized, even, or perhaps especially, when their bodies are read as male.

The images of powerful self-will that Cameron uses in his self-portraits and personal narrative to give representational form to his transsexual identity are also enabled and gain meaning through his white body. Since gender is always read and produced through race, some of the same characteristics that might provide social approval for Cameron's body would signify differently for men of color, particularly African American men. Cameron's sculpted and artistically posed muscular body in his series of photos evokes an image of self-discipline, a triumph of spirit over matter, and a strong, controlled, channeled, and uninhibited self-will. On display for viewing purposes, his body and his gender are portrayed as works of art and self-creation. In his discussion of visual representations of "the white man's muscles" in films such as *Rocky* and *The Terminator,* Richard Dyer argues that "the built body is an achieved body, worked at, planned, suffered for. A massive, sculpted physique requires forethought and long-term organisation; regimes of graduated exercise, diet and scheduled rest need to be worked out and strictly adhered to; in short, building bodies is the most literal triumph of mind over matter, imagination over flesh."[54] In the context of this description of bodybuilding as a representation of "mind over matter, imagination over flesh," using bodybuilding as a metaphor for Cameron's gender transition seems particularly apt in that it is his psychic vision of himself that needs to trump the social categorization of his body as "female." But Dyer's point is that the white built body in our dominant representational schema is used to construct and evoke the concept of an indomitable and superior spirit within white men, which is used to uphold their dominance.

But since black men's masculinity and power have been historically constructed as fearful and in need of constraint by the dominant white culture, muscularity and masculinity signify differently on the bodies of trans men of color. Although undoubtedly unintentional, Cameron's self-portraits in the "God's Will" section, which convey disciplined, willful, and contained self-construction, contrast with the one photo of a black bodybuilder in his book. Although this photograph is not the only one of a trans man of color, when compared to Cameron's portraits of himself as a body-builder, it represents the ways in which muscularity and masculinity are signified differently through race. This photograph of a man named Chase portrays a hypermasculinity that appears barely under control. As is typical in Cameron's work, the narrative works in tension with the photograph. While the written description describes Chase as a "self-employed fitness trainer" and a "disciplined, competitive athlete" who is "pursuing a degree," the photo contrasts sharply with the Greek-style artistic display of Cameron's body. Chase is in a seated position. His arms hang at his sides with his hands out of sight. The rest of his body looks as if he is lifting heavy weights in each hand, but we can't be sure because the tools of active self-construction are not pictured here as they are in Cameron's self-portraits. Overall, Chase is portrayed as containing a force that is straining against his tensed body. His head is tilted back in a way that emphasizes his neck muscles, which are bulging. His eyes are shut tight and his lips are parted. He seems to be clenching his teeth. His closed eyes and head tilted back and facing upward imply pain, strain, or perhaps yearning. In any case, his gritted teeth, strained neck, bulging muscles, and tightly shut eyes convey a sense of barely contained self-restraint, an energy that seems to be bursting out of or at least pushing at the edges of his physical body, a portrayal that is very different from Cameron's posed, sculpted, self-controlled, artistic display of his own body.

To portray himself as a "real" man who is also trans, Cameron surrounds his genital area with dominant signs of masculinity, in particular an emphasis on his muscularity. He resignifies his "female" genitalia, not by hiding or erasing its significance, but by literally incorporating it into a magnified masculinity symbolized by his flexed and posed muscular body and stern, self-determined looks. In his photos of other trans men, too, he creates and relies upon images of trans men who all embody very traditional forms of masculinity. The occupations of the men he photographs are all traditionally associated with men. None of the men smile, and all of the men pictured seem to "pass" unproblematically as non-trans men.

It is through these traditional images of masculinity that Cameron establishes cultural familiarity for trans masculinity which might otherwise be unreadable, unintelligible, or categorized as "freaky." In this way, Cameron's assertion of his "realness" is a bit different from Theo's. Since Cameron's aim is to produce gendered "realness" for trans men, he must, in some way, rely upon and stabilize dominant images of "real men" in order to fit trans men within this definition and so ultimately to expand its boundaries. In an interesting self-reflection on his own desire for muscularity as a means of defining his masculinity and establishing a feeling of safety and security, Cameron writes:

> So much about my coming to manhood has been about a quest for size. I
> mean, I really need to be a big man. All of the men I've looked to as role
> models have been body-builders and athletes. . . . They look so virile and in-
> vincible. . . . I know deeply that being a man and having strength isn't at all
> about my maximum bench press, but it doesn't seem to matter. All I can say
> is that, as my muscles grow, being five foot three doesn't feel quite so small.
> Sometimes I wonder if I'll ever feel big enough. I wonder if I'll ever feel safe
> in this body.[55]

In this quote, Cameron's feeling of vulnerability as a female-to-male trans
person comes through; his desire to look invincible, by his own admission, is connected to feeling small. Cameron is critically aware of the
limitations of this dominant discourse of masculinity. Yet, despite his
rational thought which tells him otherwise, Cameron turns to muscularity and its connection with might as a means of producing a sense of safety
and security. Undoubtedly, Cameron is safer when he can walk through
the world perceived as a white man. Yet his wonder about whether he
will ever feel truly safe, connected in his parallel sentences with being
big enough, also shows that more is needed to secure the safety of trans
people in the world, even the safety of white, middle-class trans men, who
have so much more privilege than most trans people. Indeed, at the center
of dominant masculinity in our culture is its vulnerability and therefore
the constant need to defend one's masculinity and to appear ever more
masculine. However, his muscularity, and the definition of masculinity
which is caught up with it, will never bring the type of safety and security
for which Cameron yearns.

   In the above quote, Cameron describes being stuck within a representational framework that, despite his own discomfort with it, collapses
muscularity and masculinity, and links security and strength to physical
invincibility. Yet, Cameron's reflection also represents a consciousness
about masculinity, a critical distance that can be used as a starting place
for reconfiguring dominant ideologies of masculinity and race in ways
similar to Cameron's visual reconfiguration of sex. Cameron does not
actually get to this point in *Body Alchemy*, but his work sets the founda-
tion for it and takes the initial steps. Cameron's work shows that part of
how realness functions as an operation of power is through its ability to
set up a binary between "real" and "freak." In order to not be a freak, one
must prove one is real. Yet, any claim one might make to realness auto-

matically forces one to reassert the exclusionary boundaries of realness and to reinforce the exact legitimizing power and structures of exclusion that one is trying to escape. Realness is a requirement or a demand which trans people are constantly called upon to meet, but realness is also the means through which the fulfillment of that requirement is consistently denied. It seems, then, that the only way out of this dilemma is to multiply the possibilities for realness. Rather than expanding the boundaries of realness to include marginalized people, perhaps we need to consistently challenge the ways in which power operates through realness as an organizing concept.

Trans people are not the first to face these kinds of questions and dilemmas. Like Cameron, bell hooks, an African American feminist theorist and cultural critic, explores the concept of self-recreation as it relates to resistance struggles and to the important process of moving oneself from the position of object to that of subject:

> How do we create an oppositional worldview, a consciousness, an identity, a standpoint that exists not only as that struggle which opposes dehumanization but as that movement which enables creative, expansive self-actualization? Opposition is not enough. In that vacant space after one has resisted there is still the necessity to become—to make oneself anew. . . . It is different then to talk about becoming subjects. That process emerges as one comes to understand how structures of domination work in one's own life, as one develops critical thinking and critical consciousness, as one invents new, alternative habits of being, and resists from that marginal space of difference inwardly defined.[56]

Like Cameron, hooks is interested in both resisting dominant structures and creating new possibilities for our relational and representational structures, and, like Cameron, she sees cultural texts as "a meeting place where new and radical happenings can occur."[57]

Unlike the mythology of the self-made man that Cameron embraces, which emphasizes economic success and individual self-will as that which marks self-recreation in U.S. culture, hooks understands self-recreation as tied to what she refers to as a "decolonization of the mind," a constant critical engagement with culture that works in tandem with a constant recreation.[58] Both of these elements can be seen in the above quote, where she describes the development of "critical consciousness" as well as the invention of "new, alternative habits of being." For hooks, becoming a subject is intimately tied to claiming one's marginal position as not a place "one wishes to lose—to give up or surrender as part of moving into the center—but rather . . . a site one stays in, clings to even, because it nourishes one's capacity to resist. It offers to one the possibility of radical perspective from which to see and create, to imagine alternatives, new worlds."[59]

Cameron uses his marginality to redefine the dominant definition of manhood as that which can only be occupied by people with "male" genitalia. He does this through a critical engagement with the aspect of gender realness that connects biological sex to gender identity. Yet, in order to answer in the affirmative the question posed to him, "Do you have what it takes to be a real man?" Cameron relies on rather than critically engages gender realness as it relates to dominant masculinity. Meanwhile, hooks's concept of marginality might offer trans men an avenue through which to disrupt the binary between freak and real that is produced by the operations of realness. She does not argue that one must literally stay in a marginalized social place as a means of resistance. In her case, she does not argue that she needs to physically stay in her home community in rural Kentucky or in the economic poverty that came with it. Neither does she need to romanticize this place. Rather, hooks argues that she needs to cling to the perspective that grew out of having lived on the "margin" and utilize it to "imagine alternatives, new worlds." Similarly, accessing the critical knowledge that can come from being a man who was labeled female at birth does not require one to remain female-bodied nor to keep oneself in a constant state of visible "gender trouble." It should not prevent one from being a body-builder or from using hormones and surgery to change one's body, but it might enable one to resist defining one's manhood through such practices and instead to "invent new, alternative habits of being" that could work to proliferate the possibilities of realness. The critical distance that Cameron conveys through his photography and his stated desire for muscularity could be the base from which the definitions of masculinity could be multiplied. From this critical distance, trans men might be able to highlight realness as an operation of power and to create new possibilities for what it means to be a real self-made man.

Like Butler's theoretical work, Loren Cameron's *Body Alchemy* and Julie Wyman's *A Boy Named Sue* are texts that centralize the body and its inseparable entanglements with discourse and subjectivity. Through a self-reflexivity that calls attention to the constructedness of their images, Wyman and Cameron use their visual media to highlight the ways that power and perception work together to create a contested visual field that constrains the possibilities for subject formation and self-representation, but that nevertheless is vulnerable to contestation and reconfiguration. They explore the various ways that trans bodies are framed, the effects and power of looking, and the possibilities for self-construction within a visual discursive field that most often either eradicates or marginalizes trans people.

Wyman's and Cameron's texts show that a simple binary which measures transgender lives as either subverting gender norms or reinscribing them is not adequate for representing the complicated relationships among the body, discourse, and subjectivity. In any discussion of trans politics, representation, and embodiment, it is essential to recognize "realness" as an operation of power which drives social interactions, economic realities, and the terms of psychic and physical survival. However, since power, as Michel Foucault has argued, always contains the possibilities for resistance, the real also can be a construct from which social transformation emerges. As Butler explains:

> To intervene in the name of transformation means precisely to disrupt what has become settled knowledge and knowable reality, and to use, as it were, one's unreality to make an otherwise impossible or illegible claim. I think that when the unreal lays claim to reality, or enters into its domain, something other than a simple assimilation into prevailing norms can and does take place. The norms themselves can become rattled, display their instability, and become open to resignification.[60]

By analyzing the structures of A Boy Named Sue and Body Alchemy, I have shown some of the ways that documentary film and photography can be used to give representational form to trans men by centralizing and making visible FTM trans bodies. Along with discourses of gender, the structures of visibility that frame these texts engage discourses of race, class, and American identity, discourses which sometimes enable and at other times foreclose the creation of intelligible cultural space for transsexual men. Simultaneously challenging and drawing from contemporary ideas about masculinity, race, and what it means to be a man in America, the gender and sexual shifts that Cameron and Theo embody represent what Butler refers to as attempts to create "livable lives." Understanding realness as a discursive operation of power can allow trans and non-trans people to think critically about the narratives used to signify gender as "real" so that ultimately we can produce multiple possibilities of legitimacy that can "permit people to breathe, to desire, to love, and to live."[61] Wyman's and Cameron's groundbreaking texts give us a starting place to think about the means through which bodies, and the cultural representations of them, can intercede in the dominant discourse, not only in relation to the "natural" connection between sex and gender identity, but in the very structures that create and sustain real masculinity.

NOTES

1. Wyman, dir., *A Boy Named Sue.*

2. Cameron, *Body Alchemy*, 11.

3. See http://www.websters-online-dictionary.org/definition/real.

4. See http://www.askoxford.com/concise_oed/orexxal_1?view=uk.

5. Ibid.

6. Patricia Hill Collins, *Black Feminist Thought: Knowledge, Consciousness, and the Politics of Empowerment* (New York: Routledge, 2000).

7. For a detailed discussion of twentieth-century discourses of transsexuality, see Meyerowitz, *How Sex Changed.*

8. Somerville, *Queering the Color Line*, 17.

9. Ibid.

10. For challenges to Raymond's work, see Califia, *Sex Changes*; Prosser, *Second Skins*; Meyerowitz, *How Sex Changed*; Namaste, *Invisible Lives*. For an example of the ways in which Raymond's theory continues to be employed, see www.questioning transgender.com.

11. Raymond, *The Transsexual Empire*, 27.

12. Ibid.

13. See www.questioningtransgender.com; *Gendercator*; *Boy I Am.*

14. When trans people are understood as "really men" or "really women" based upon their birth bodies, sex and its multilayered cultural and psychic constitution become oversimplified and one-dimensional. From this perspective, trans people cannot be recognized as women or men who, like most non-trans women and men, have particular embodied relationships to gender. The social histories which mark the experiences of gender and gender identity as rooted in difference more than commonality are glossed over. Instead, there is an assumption of a common experience among all non-trans women or all non-trans men that transcends other differences within each category. These so-called common experiences are perceived as so fundamental to gender that trans men cannot possibly be understood as men labeled female at birth and trans women cannot be understood as women labeled male at birth. Importantly, as we see in Raymond's assertion about the primacy of chromosomes for determining one's gender, birth bodies remain as *the* determining factor of the boundaries of "man" and

"woman," rather than as one element within a constellation of differences (including race, nationality, class, sexual orientation) that shape our experiences of gender, the ways our bodies are read and understood by others, and our own complex gender identities.

15. For example, some trans men are sexually attracted to other men and identify as gay. Others identify as bisexual or queer; others identify as heterosexual.

16. Raymond, *The Transsexual Empire*, 114.

17. Ibid., 11.

18. Ibid., xxiii.

19. Drawing from poststructuralist theories of subjectivity as discursively produced, Butler contends that gender differences do not originate in our biological or psychic makeups. Instead, Butler argues, although we may experience our selves, including our gender and sex, as substantive, these experiences are actually produced through repetitive enactments of social norms. Butler uses drag performances as an illustration of the ways in which gender, as a repeated performance, constitutes the appearance of a prediscursive subject, arguing that this subject is actually discursively produced.

20. Butler, *Gender Trouble*, 7.

21. Ibid.

22. Ibid., 67.

23. Prosser, *Second Skins*, 15; Namaste, *Invisible Lives*, 14. Prosser and Namaste both quote Butler's analysis of the documentary film *Paris Is Burning*, in particular her reading of one of the trans women, Venus Extravaganza, to show how transsexual people are often positioned as marking the limits of what Butler refers to as "gender trouble." Tragically, Venus, a transsexual prostitute, is murdered by a customer before the film ends. Butler uses this murder to exemplify the ways in which a simultaneous appropriation and subversion of hegemonic norms can easily cross over into a "fatally unsubversive appropriation" (Butler, *Bodies That Matter*, 128). According to Butler, Venus engages in a "tragic misreading of the social map of power" when she imagines that her ability to become a "complete woman" through sex-reassignment surgery will allow her to escape oppression and marginalization. Instead, argues Butler, when she "passes" as a woman, "Venus is treated by the symbolic in precisely the ways in which women of color are treated" (ibid., 131). According to Prosser and Namaste, Butler's analysis of Venus's murder erases the specificity and consequences of Venus's transsexual embodiment and occupation as a prostitute. Namaste writes that "since Butler has reduced Extravaganza's transsexuality to allegory, she cannot conceptualize the specificity of violence with which transsexuals, especially transsexual prostitutes, are faced" (Namaste, *Invisible Lives*, 13). Prosser argues, "Butler's essay locates transgressive value in that which makes the subject's real life most unsafe" (Prosser, *Second Skins*, 49).

24. Butler, *Undoing Gender*.

25. Ibid., 48.

26. Ibid., 28.

27. Ibid., 31.

28. Ibid., 32.

29. Ibid., 48.

30. Ibid., 52.

31. Albright, *Choreographing Difference*.

32. Ibid., 3.

33. Ibid., 5.

34. Butler, *Undoing Gender,* 32.
35. Prosser, *Second Skins,* 101.
36. Ibid.
37. Cameron, *Body Alchemy,* 42.
38. Ibid., 10.
39. Ibid.
40. Ibid.
41. Prosser, *Second Skins,* 100.
42. Ibid.
43. Ibid.
44. Ibid., 102.
45. Ibid.
46. Dear, "African American Transgendered Men," 1.
47. Ibid., 36.
48. Ibid.
49. Ibid., 37.
50. Ibid.
51. Ibid., 38.
52. Ibid., 36.
53. Green, *Becoming a Visible Man,* 35.
54. Richard Dyer, *White* (London: Routledge, 1997), 153.
55. Cameron, *Body Alchemy,* 85.
56. hooks, *Yearning,* 15.
57. Ibid., 31.
58. Ibid., 8.
59. Ibid. 150–151.
60. Butler, *Undoing Gender,* 28.
61. Ibid., 8.

BIBLIOGRAPHY

Albright, Ann Cooper. *Choreographing Difference: The Body and Identity in Contemporary Dance.* Hanover, N.H.: University Press of New England, 1997.
Butler, Judith. *Bodies That Matter: On the Discursive Limits of "Sex."* New York: Routledge, 1993.
———. *Gender Trouble: Feminism and the Subversion of Identity.* New York: Routledge, 1990.
———. *Undoing Gender.* New York: Routledge, 2004.
Califia, Pat. *Sex Changes: The Politics of Transgenderism.* San Francisco, Calif.: Cleis, 1997.
Cameron, Loren. *Body Alchemy: Transsexual Portraits.* San Francisco, Calif.: Cleis, 1996.
Cromwell, Jason. *Transmen and FTMs: Identities, Bodies, Genders and Sexualities.* Urbana: University of Illinois Press, 1999.
Dear, Brandin G. "African American Transgendered Men and Their Experiences with Racism in the United States Pre and Post Transition." Master's thesis, Smith College, 2006.

Gamson, Joshua. *Freaks Talk Back: Tabloid Talk Shows and Sexual Nonconformity*. Chicago: University of Chicago Press, 1998.

Green, Jamison. *Becoming a Visible Man*. Nashville, Tenn.: Vanderbilt University Press, 2004.

hooks, bell. *Yearning: Race, Gender, and Cultural Politics*. Boston: South End, 1990.

Meyerowitz, Joanne. *How Sex Changed: A History of Transsexuality in the United States*. Cambridge, Mass.: Harvard University Press, 2002.

Namaste, Viviane. *Invisible Lives: The Erasure of Transsexual and Transgendered People*. Chicago: University of Chicago Press, 2000.

Prosser, Jay. *Second Skins: The Body Narratives of Transsexuality*. New York: Columbia University Press, 1998.

Raymond, Janice. *The Transsexual Empire: The Making of the She-Male*. 1979. Rpt., New York: Teachers College Press, 1994.

Somerville, Siobhan. *Queering the Color Line: Race and the Invention of Homosexuality in American Culture*. Durham, N.C.: Duke University Press, 2000.

Wyman, Julie, dir. *A Boy Named Sue*. Women Make Movies, 2000.

MICHEL J. BOUCHER is an assistant professor in the Department of English at the University of Massachusetts at Amherst.

BRENDA BOUDREAU is an associate professor of gender studies and chair of the Department of Humanities at McKendree University.

C. WESLEY BUERKLE is an assistant professor in the Department of Communication Studies at East Tennessee State University.

JOHNSON CHEU is an assistant professor in the Department of Writing, Rhetoric, and American Cultures at Michigan State University.

MARGARET C. ERVIN is an associate professor in the Department of English at West Chester University.

LATHAM HUNTER is an assistant professor in the Department of Film Studies at McMaster University.

JOHN KILLE is a former assistant professor in the Department of Writing, Rhetoric, and American Cultures at Michigan State University. He is currently a senior researcher for a consulting firm in the Midwest.

JIMMIE MANNING is an assistant professor in the Department of Communication at Northern Kentucky University.

MARC E. SHAW is an assistant professor of theatre arts at Hartwick College.

CAROLYN TYJEWSKI is a doctoral candidate in the Department of Cultural Studies at the University of California at Davis.

ELWOOD WATSON is a full professor of history, African American studies, and gender studies at East Tennessee State University.

256784LV00004B/2/P

LVOW102331281111
Printed in the USA
CPSIA information can be obtained at www.ICGtesting.com